HTML5
Digital Classroom

D1340271

HTML5
Digital Classroom

Jeremy Osborn and the AGI Creative Team

WILEY

John Wiley & Sons, Inc.

HTML5 Digital Classroom

Published by
John Wiley & Sons, Inc.
10475 Crosspoint Boulevard
Indianapolis, IN 46256

Copyright © 2011 by John Wiley & Sons, Inc., Indianapolis, Indiana
Published by John Wiley & Sons, Inc., Indianapolis, Indiana
Published simultaneously in Canada
ISBN: 978-1-118-01618-3
Manufactured in the United States of America
10 9 8 7 6 5 4 3 2 1

For general information on our other products and services or to obtain technical support, please contact our Customer Care Department within the U.S. at (800) 762-2974, outside the U.S. at (317) 572-3993 or fax (317) 572-4002.

Please report any errors by sending a message to errata@agitraining.com

Library of Congress Control Number: 2011922791

About the Authors

Jeremy Osborn is the Content Director at American Graphics Institute. He has more than 15 years of experience in web, graphic design, filmmaking, writing, and publication development for both print and digital media. He is the author of the *Web Design with HTML and CSS Digital Classroom* and *Dreamweaver CS5 Digital Classroom* books and has contributed to many of the titles in the Digital Classroom book series. Jeremy holds a MS in Management from the Marlboro College Graduate Center and a BFA in Film/TV from the Tisch School of the Arts at NYU.

The AGI Creative Team is composed of web design experts and instructors from American Graphics Institute (AGI). They work with many of the world's most prominent companies, helping them adopt web and interactive technologies, working with design, development, creative, and marketing teams around the world, delivering consulting, private customized training programs, and teach regularly scheduled classes at AGI's locations. The Digital Classroom authors are available for professional development sessions at companies, schools and universities. More information is available at *agitraining.com* and *digitalclassroom.com*.

Acknowledgments

Thanks to Kristin Osborn for support and encouragement, and also to Isaiah and the team at AGI. Thanks to the instructors at AGI for input, assistance and reviews. Thanks to iStockphoto.com for some of the images used in the book.

Credits

Writing
Jeremy Osborn, Adam Kinney, Todd Sellon,
Greg Ryan

President, American Graphics Institute and Digital Classroom Series Publisher
Christopher Smith

Executive Editor
Jody Lefevere

Acquisitions Editor
Aaron Black

Technical Editors
Kelly Babik, Greg Heald, Todd Sellon

Editors
Karla Melendez

Editorial Director
Robyn Siesky

Business Manager
Amy Knies

Senior Marketing Manager
Sandy Smith

Vice President and Executive Group Publisher
Richard Swadley

Vice President and Executive Publisher
Barry Pruett

Senior Project Coordinator
Lynsey Stanford

Project Manager
Cheri White

Graphics and Production Specialist
Jason Miranda, Spoke & Wheel

Media Development Project Supervisor
Chris Leavey

Proofreading
Nick Simione

Indexing
Michael Ferreira

Stock Photography
iStockPhoto.com

Contents

Lesson 2: Fundamentals of HTML, XHTML, and CSS

Lesson 3: Formatting Text with CSS

Lesson 4: Introduction to CSS Layout

Lesson 5: Advanced CSS Layout

SECTION TWO: HTML5 with CSS3 and JavaScript

Lesson 6: Using HTML5 Markup

Lesson 7: Creating HTML5 Forms

Lesson 8: Introduction to JavaScript and jQuery

Lesson 9: Working with Video and Audio Elements

Lesson 10: Working with Canvas

Lesson 11: Styling with CSS3

Lesson 12: CSS3 Media Queries and the Future of CSS3

Lesson 13: Offline Storage in HTML5

Lesson 14: HTML5 Geolocation

Lesson 15: HTML5 Drag and Drop

Appendix: HTML5 Elements and Attributes

Starting Up

Using this book

This book will get you up-and-running fast with HTML5 and CSS3. The *HTML5 Digital Classroom* is divided into two sections. The first section covers the fundamentals of HTML5 along with the essentials of styling text and creating page layouts using XHTML/HTML and CSS. If you are new to web page development, or are updating your skills from using HTML tables for layout, or simply want a refresher in CSS and HTML fundamentals, start with section one. Even if you consider yourself a skilled web pro, start with lesson one before jumping ahead to the second section where you'll dive into HTML5. The second section makes up the bulk of this book. Feel free to jump ahead to this. If you are an experienced web designer or developer, and already have a solid grasp of the fundamentals involved with coding HTML and CSS.

Some of the foundational material contained in the first five lessons of this book was originally published in the *Web Design with HTML and CSS Digital Classroom*, and it has been updated for use in this book.

About HTML5 Digital Classroom

The *HTML5 Digital Classroom* provides you with the information you need to explore and understand the rapidly evolving landscape of web technologies. You may already have some experience building web pages and websites and may even be experienced with design tools like Dreamweaver or Expression Web. While HTML5 and related technologies such as CSS3 and JavaScript are still undergoing revision, this book helps you understand the underlying concepts for organizing, creating, and delivering web content effectively using best practices.

The *HTML5 Digital Classroom* helps you to get up-and-running quickly with HTML5. While you can work through the lessons in this book in any sequence, we recommend that you start in at the first lesson and progress through the book in the sequence in which they are presented. If you are an experienced web developer, you may decide to start in lesson one, then glance over lessons two through five and resume your learning with lessons six through 15. Each lesson is designed to be stand-alone, so if you need to focus on a particular part of HTML5, feel free to jump right to that section. Each lesson includes detailed, step-by-step instructions, background information, companion video tutorials that relate directly to the lesson in the book, and lesson files for you to follow along with the concepts being presented.

The *HTML5 Digital Classroom* is like having your own expert instructor guiding you through each lesson while you work at your own pace. This book includes 15 self-paced lessons that let you discover essential skills, explore web design, and learn HTML5, CSS3 and JavaScript techniques that will save you time and allow you to more easily create effective HTML5 websites. You'll become productive right away with real-world exercises and simple explanations. Each lesson includes step-by-step instructions, lesson files, and video tutorials, all of which are available on the included DVD. The *HTML5 Digital Classroom* lessons are developed by the same team of instructors and experts who have created many of the official training titles for companies such as Adobe Systems and Microsoft. Now you can benefit from the clear and detailed instructions provided by the expert instructors that are part of the Digital Classroom team.

Prerequisites

This book relies heavily on adding code by hand, but does not require a specific text editor when working with the HTML and CSS code. The exact text editor you use is not important, but you should choose and install a text editor before you start with the exercises in this book so that you can easily open and work with the lesson files presented in this book. You may currently have your own preferences, but we've listed some options below.

Some Mac OS text editors include BBedit and TextWrangler, both of which are available at *http://www.barebones.com*. Or you can use TextMate which is available for download at *http://macromates.com*. Another Mac OS text editor is Coda which can be found at *http://www.panic.com/coda/*.

If you work on a Windows computer, you may wish to use E Text Editor which is available at *http://www.e-texteditor.com* or Microsoft Visual Web Developer Express which can be found at *http://www.microsoft.com/expression/web*.

If you already have a visual web design tool like Adobe Dreamweaver or Microsoft Expression Web installed on your computer, you can use the coding tools integrated with these software packages instead of installing a dedicated text editor. Although both Adobe and Microsoft offer free trial versions of these software tools, if you don't have either one installed, we recommend skipping them for now and instead using any one of the text editors listed above while working with this book. By using a text editor, you can focus on the design and underlying code rather than learning the user interface and functions of a specific software package.

System requirements

Before starting the lessons in the *HTML5 Digital Classroom*, make sure that your computer is equipped for creating and managing static websites. Because you will be using a variety of software tools, there is no formal minimum requirement for your computer, however we suggest that your computer meet or exceed the following guidelines:

Windows OS
- Intel® Pentium® 4, AMD Athlon® 64, or Multicore Intel® processor; Microsoft® Windows® XP with Service Pack 2; Windows Vista® Home Premium, Business, Ultimate, or Enterprise with Service Pack 1; or Windows 7
- 1GB recommended RAM
- 1GB of available hard-disk space for working with files
- 1280 × 800 display with 16-bit video card
- Broadband Internet connection

Macintosh OS
- Multicore Intel® processor
- Mac OS X v10.4 or greater
- 1 GB of RAM 1 GB of available hard-disk space for working with lesson files.
- 1280 × 800 display with 16-bit video card
- Broadband Internet connection

Using web browsers that support HTML5 tags

HTML5 is a new and evolving technology and the browser you use to preview your web pages may provide dramatic differences. We make every possible effort to point out these differences in the exercises used in this book. To ensure the best results you need to use the most current version of your browser. Throughout the book you may see references to "modern browsers." These are the browsers we used throughout:

Mozilla Firefox 4.0+ (*http://www.getfirefox.com*)

Google Chrome 11.0+ (*http://www.google.com/chrome/*)

Apple Safari 5.0+ (*http://www.apple.com/safari/download/*)

Internet Explorer 9.0+ (*http://windows.microsoft.com/en-US/internet-explorer/products/ie/home*)

Opera 11.0+ (*http://www.opera.com/browser/download/*)

You should consider downloading two or more browsers and have these available on your system. For designers and developers, it is common to have access to multiple browsers and this is important as you test HTML5 pages.

Understanding menus and commands

Menus and commands within the software tools discussed in this book are identified by using the greater-than symbol (>). For example, the command to print a document might appear as File > Print, representing that you click the File menu, then choose the Print command.

Understanding how to read HTML and CSS code changes

Many of the step-by-step instructions in the book involve typing one line (or more) of HTML, CSS or JavaScript code to a previously existing block of code. In these cases, the new code for you to add is highlighted in red to help you quickly identify the text to be added to your lesson file.

For example, this code represents a line already present in your lesson file:

```
<h1> News </h1>
```

The code highlighted here in red is what you would need to add:

```
<h1 class="frontpage"> News </h1>
```

Loading lesson files

The *HTML5 Digital Classroom* DVD includes files that accompany the exercises for each of the lessons. You may copy the entire lessons folder from the supplied DVD to your hard drive, or copy only the lesson folders for the individual lessons you wish to complete.

For each lesson in the book, the files are referenced by the file name of each file. The exact location of each file on your computer is not used, as you may have placed the files in a unique location on your hard drive. We suggest placing the lesson files in the My Documents folder or on the Desktop so you can easily access them.

Downloading and copying the lesson files to your hard drive

1 Insert the HTML5 Digital Classroom DVD supplied with this book.

2 On your computer, navigate to the DVD and locate the folder named HTML5lessons.

3 You can install all the files, or just specific lesson files. Do one of the following:

- Install all lesson files by dragging the HTML5lessons folder to your hard drive.

- Install only some of the files by creating a new folder on your hard drive named HTML5lessons. Open the HTML5lessons folder on the supplied DVD, select the lesson you wish to complete, and drag the folder(s) to the HTML5lessons folder you created on your hard drive.

Unlocking lesson files on Mac OS computers

Macintosh users may need to unlock the files after they are copied from the accompanying disc. This only applies to Mac OS computers and is because the Mac OS may view files that are copied from a DVD or CD as being locked for writing.

If you are a Mac OS user and have difficulty saving over the existing files in this book, you can use these instructions so that you can update the lesson files as you work on them and also add new files to the lessons folder

Note that you only need to follow these instructions if you are unable to save over the existing lesson files, or if you are unable to save files into the lesson folder.

1 After copying the files to your computer, click once to select the HTML5lessons folder, then choose File > Get Info from within the Finder.

2 In the HTML5lessons info window, click the triangle to the left of Sharing and Permissions to reveal the details of this section.

3 In the Sharing and Permissions section, click the lock icon, if necessary, in the lower right corner so that you can make changes to the permissions.

4 Click to select a specific user or select everyone, then change the Privileges section to Read & Write.

5 Click the lock icon to prevent further changes, and then close the window.

Working with the video tutorials

Your *HTML5 Digital Classroom* DVD includes video tutorials developed by the authors to help you understand the concepts explored in each lesson. Each tutorial is approximately five minutes long and demonstrates and explains the concepts covered in the lesson.

The videos are designed to supplement your understanding of the material in the chapter. We have selected exercises and examples that we feel will be most useful to you. You may want to view the entire video for each lesson before you begin that lesson in the book. Additionally, at certain points in a lesson, you will encounter the DVD icon. The icon, with appropriate lesson number, indicates that an overview of the exercise being described can be found in the accompanying video.

DVD video icon.

Setting up for viewing the video tutorials

The DVD included with this book includes video tutorials for each lesson. Although you can view the lessons on your computer directly from the DVD, we recommend copying the folder labeled *Videos* from the *HTML5 Digital Classroom* DVD to your hard drive.

Copying the video tutorials to your hard drive

1   Insert the *HTML5 Digital Classroom* DVD supplied with this book.

2   On your computer desktop, navigate to the DVD and locate the folder named Videos.

3   Drag the Videos folder to a location onto your hard drive.

Viewing the video tutorials

The videos on the *HTML5 Digital Classroom* DVD are saved in the Flash projector format. A Flash projector file wraps the Digital Classroom video player and the Adobe Flash Player in an executable file (.exe for Windows or .app for Mac OS). The file extension may not always be visible depending upon settings on your computer. Projector files allow the Flash content to be deployed on your system without the need for a browser or prior standalone player installation.

Playing the video tutorials

1 On your computer, navigate to the Videos folder you copied to your hard drive from the DVD. Playing the videos directly from the DVD may result in poor quality playback.

2 Open the Videos folder and double-click the HTML5videos_PC.exe (Windows) or HTML5videos_Mac.app (Mac OS) to view the video tutorial.

3 Press the Play button to view the videos.

The Flash Player has a simple user interface that allows you to control the viewing experience, including stopping, pausing, playing, and restarting the video. You can also rewind or fast-forward, and adjust the playback volume.

Lesson 06: Creating a Good Image

A. Go to beginning. B. Play/Pause. C. Fast-forward/rewind. D. Stop. E. Volume Off/On. F. Volume control.

Playback volume is also affected by the settings in your operating system. Be certain to adjust the sound volume for your computer, in addition to the sound controls in the Player window.

Additional resources

The Digital Classroom series of books can be read in print or using an e-reader. You can also continue your learning online with the training videos, or at seminars, conferences, and in-person training events led by the authors.

DigitalClassroomBooks.com

You can contact the authors, discover any errors, omissions, or clarifications that have been identified since the time of printing, and read excerpts from the other Digital Classroom books in the Digital Classroom series at *digitalclassroombooks.com*.

Seminars, conferences, and training

The authors of the Digital Classroom seminar series frequently conduct in-person seminars and speak at conferences, including the annual CRE8 Conference. Learn more about their upcoming speaking engagements and training classes at *agitraining.com*.

Resources for educators

If you are an educator, contact your Wiley education representative to access resources for this book designed just for you, including instructors' guides for incorporating the HTML5 Digital Classroom into your curriculum. If you don't know who your educational representative is, you may contact the Digital Classroom books team using the form at *DigitalClassroomBooks.com*.

Section One: Essentials of HTML, HTML5, and CSS

This book is divided into two sections. The first section covers the fundamentals of HTML5 along with the essentials of styling text and creating page layouts using XHTML/HTML and CSS.

Even if you consider yourself a skilled web professional, start with Lesson 1 in this section before jumping ahead to the second section, which starts with Lesson 6, where you'll dive into HTML5. New web designers and developers, and those updating their skills from table-based HTML development, will want to complete Lessons 1 through 5 before moving on to Section Two in this book.

Lesson 1

What you'll learn in this lesson:

- Needs fulfilled by HTML5
- The scope of HTML5
- An overview of HTML5 Syntax
- An overview of HTML5 APIs and supporting technologies

Defining HTML5

In this lesson, you will discover the features and capabilities that are part of the HTML5 specification and related web technologies. You will also understand the benefits HTML5 provides to web designers, developers and end-users.

Starting up

You will not need any files for this lesson.

This lesson provides a general overview of HTML5. The additional lessons include step-by-step exercises, while this lesson provides an overview and road map of what you will be discovering in the future lessons.

See Lesson 1 in action!

Use the accompanying video to gain a better understanding of how to use some of the capabilities shown in this lesson. The video tutorial for this lesson can be found on the included DVD.

Defining HTML5

HTML5 is a combination of new HTML markup tags, CSS3 properties, JavaScript, and several supporting technologies related to, but technically separate from, the HTML5 specification. For this reason, we make a distinction between the HTML5 specification and the HTML5 family.

You can define the HTML5 specification as new markup elements, or syntax, used by designers to build web pages in conjunction with the tags that are currently used. Many of these new elements are familiar to designers who work with traditional HTML tags, such as <p>, <ul>, and <div>. These new tags provide better tools for developers and designers, and translate to better experiences for users.

The HTML5 family includes the new tags and technologies such as CSS3, Geolocation, Web storage, Web Workers, and Web Sockets. These technologies provide a more powerful upgrade to the toolset, and result in more useful and sophisticated web pages.

New browsers add features based on consumer expectation and as part of the natural evolution of technology. As web applications become more responsive, speedy, and able to work with complex tasks such as image editing, mapping, spreadsheets, and video, users expect this level of performance from all web applications. There are limitations with the capabilities of current languages and the ease of implementing and adding these features. HTML5 provides new tools and features to help make websites more useful and exciting.

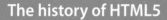

The history of HTML5

HTML4, which was nearing completion in 1998, is the markup language that forms the basis for much of the underlying framework of web pages today. Web designers and developers have been using the specification HTML 4.01 for years quite successfully, in combination with CSS to define style and JavaScript to add interactivity.

After HTML 4.0.1 was finalized, the W3C continued the evolution of the Web by ending the development of HTML 4.0.1 and starting a language called XHTML 1.0. There is little difference between HTML 4.0.1 and XHTML 1.0 (XHTML is a more strict language; for example, all tags need to be lowercase). One of the goals of XHTML 1.0 was to create a markup language that would expand and meet the demands of future technology, such as mobile devices. Many websites have been built using XHTML 1.0 as a framework, and many designers and developers appreciated the more strict rules of syntax.

As XHTML 1.0 was adopted and used, the development of another language, XHTML 2.0, began. XHTML 2.0 added several new powerful features to web pages and borrowed heavily from XML. However, there were several technical issues with the new language, and it didn't reflect the actual needs of web developers.

In 2004, a group of representatives from browser manufacturers, such as Opera, Mozilla and Apple, and a group of working web developers formed an independent group called the WHATWG (Web Hypertext Application Technology Working Group). Their mission was to create a better HTML markup specification, designed to build the new type of web application without breaking backwards compatibility with existing browsers.

The result was the Web Applications 1.0 specification, which identified the features that existing browsers shared, and proposed new features, such as the APIs that form the web family. As a result, the development of XHTML 2.0 ceased and HTML 4.0 was recreated as HTML5. However, remembering that HTML5 started as Web Applications 1.0 helps to understand what HTML5 is designed to do.

For more information about the WHATWG, visit www.whatwg.org.

HTML5 expands the definition of what a web page can do

Currently, HTML cannot play multimedia such as audio and video without a browser plugin like Flash or QuickTime. HTML also has no capability to store data on a user's computer; this is currently done with a scripting language or another technology. There is no native drawing format in HTML: graphics and animations are currently supplied as image files or through browser plugins such as Flash, Java, or Silverlight. In general, as more and more people rely on the Web and web applications, the expectations of what a web page can efficiently do is constantly growing. This user demand for higher performance and more fully featured websites is limited by the current HTML language.

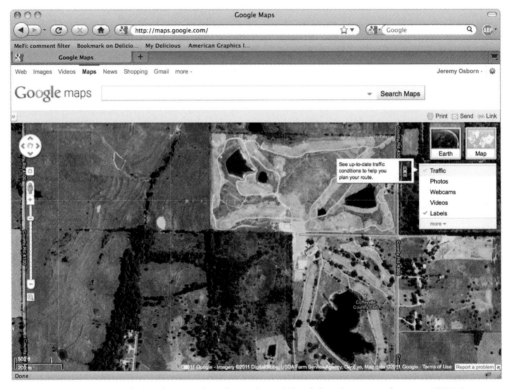

A site such as Google Maps is a high-performance web application that could benefit from the upcoming features in HTML5.

The following sections provide a brief explanation of some of the most important aspects of HTML5.

HTML5 markup

HTML5 markup introduces several new tags designed to make the structure of a web page more logical and functional. Before HTML5, the page structure relied heavily on the `<div>` tag, often paired with a CSS class or ID. For example, the code that defines the header of a web page would appear as follows:

```
<div id="header" > This is my header </div>
```

In this example, the code highlighted in red refers to the CSS ID that defines the width and height of the header, as well as background color. In the CSS code, this would appear as follows:

```
#header {
    width:960px;
    height:100px;
    background-color:gray;
}
```

The ID name `header` is arbitrary. Some designers might use the name `masthead`, `topsection,` or `box`. In the HTML5 specification, there is a unique tag called `<header>`, so the syntax is much more logical and consistent:

```
<header> This is my header </header>
```

In this example, you can directly add style properties (width, height, background color, and more) to the header rule in CSS:

```
header {
    width:960px;
    height:100px;
    background-color:gray;
}
```

The difference between the two code examples above may be difficult to understand if you aren't familiar with CSS. The first example uses a selector (#header) that is referring to a CSS ID attribute. The second example uses a selector (header) that is new to HTML5 and allows you to style the element directly. HTML5 has a number of other new elements such as <footer>, <nav>, <section>, <aside>, and <article>. These names are based on the most common ones used for layout sections in today's web pages (div id="footer", div id="nav", and so on). The goal of the new HTML5 elements is to reduce the current reliance on <div> tags and replace them with a more consistent and readable page structure. Note that HTML5 doesn't *replace* any HTML syntax; it *adds* new vocabulary to the existing list. In other words, you can still use the <div> tag, but it no longer supports the entire load of a page layout.

The structure of a website with HTML5 elements.
A. Header. B. Nav. C. Section. D. Article. E. Aside. F. Footer.

A tour of the key HTML5 elements

This book explains many of the new HTML5 elements in depth, beginning with Lesson 6. But first, Lesson 1 will provide an overview of the key additions to the HTML5 syntax.

The <video>, <audio>, and <canvas> elements

The HTML5 specification includes tags that let you incorporate multimedia without browser plugins. The <video> and <audio> tags let you embed video and audio into your pages as you currently do with images using the <img> tag. The <canvas> tag supplies HTML with a native drawing and animation format. This tag could also provide an alternative platform for the type of graphics and animation found in Flash movies. However, there are significant issues that need to be addressed.

The `<video>` and `<audio>` elements embed media files into your pages

The structure for embedding video and audio is simple, as the following example to adding video to a web page shows:

```
<video src="catz.mp4" width="400" height="300"></video>
```

Embedding an mp3 audio file onto your page is similar; for video and audio, you can add built-in player controls and preloading capabilities with the `controls`, `preload`, and `autobuffer` attributes:

```
<audio src="high_seas_rip.mp3" controls preload="auto" autobuffer>
    </audio>
```

This feature of HTML5 is helpful when compared with current available methods; for example, embedding video using Flash requires more code to implement. Additionally, there is currently a large category of mobile devices such as Apple's iPhone and iPad that do not support Flash, and in these cases the video element is the primary alternative. Although the simplicity of having `<video>` and `<audio>` tags is welcome, it does raise the question of how older browsers that do not recognize these tags are supposed to handle them. You will learn more about these complications and solutions in Lesson 9, *Working with the Video and Audio Elements*.

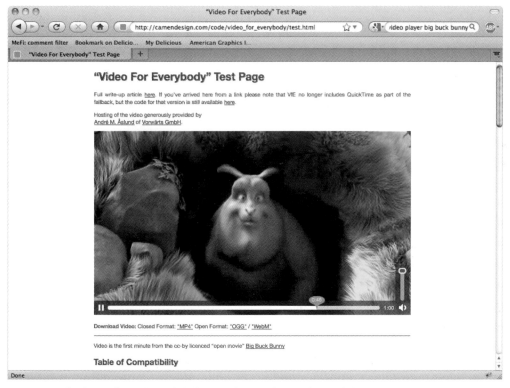

An HTML5 video player with controls is embedded into a web page; no browser plugin needed.

The `<canvas>` element provides drawing and animation features

The canvas element works as a drawing surface on your page. Within this drawing surface, you can create shapes with color, gradient, and pattern fills. You can interactively manipulate pixels onscreen, render text, and export these contents to a static image file, such as a .png. You can also add JavaScript or the new CSS3 animation features to make the objects you create move, fade, scale, and so on. Adding a canvas element to a page is simple:

```
<canvas id="myCanvas"></canvas>
```

JavaScript handles all of the work, and it provides a context for the object you create. For example, to create one of the simplest canvas objects, a black rectangle, the code might appear as follows:

```
<script>
    var canvas = document.getElementById ("myCanvas"),
context = canvas.getContext("2d");
    // x = 10, y = 20, width = 200, height = 100
    context.fillRect(10, 20, 200, 100);
</script>
```

This creates a simple rectangle filled with the color black. The code might seem longer than necessary for a simple result, but the canvas tag simply exposes the code within an HTML document and this model provides a number of benefits. Future uses include user interface elements such as player controls, illustration elements that can be animated, and data visualization uses, such as charts and graphs. You will learn more about creating content with the `<canvas>` tag in Lesson 10, *Working with Canvas*.

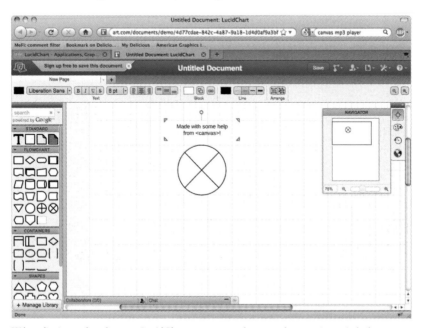

Web applications such as the one at LucidChart.com can use the canvas element to interactively draw charts and diagrams.

Web forms

The new form elements in HTML, when implemented, will make working with forms easier than at present. For example, many web designers need to create forms that require validation before the data is submitted. In order to do so, a user must enter a value in the email field of a form submission. Currently, most solutions to this problem require JavaScript or another scripting language, but HTML5 just adds the `required` attribute to the list of form input types, as shown below:

```
<input type="email" required>
```

There are many new form input types, such as `email` for email addresses, `search` to designate form fields used with search terms, `url` to specify a form field that uses a web address, and many more. These new web form elements will take time to become part of the official specification, but they are designed to regress to generic input forms. In other words, you can begin to use these new input types, and if a browser does not support the new form element, it will use a generic (supported) element. You'll learn how to work with forms in Lesson 7, *Creating HTML5 Forms*.

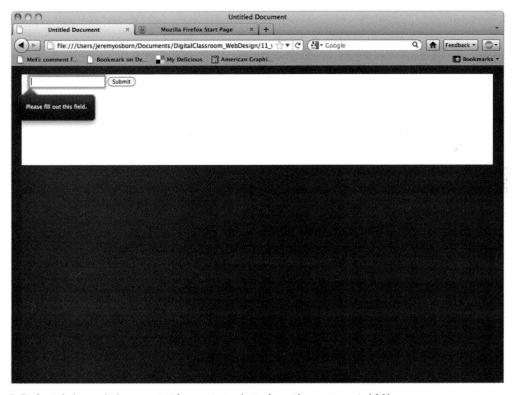

In Firefox 4, the browser displays a warning if a user tries to submit a form with an empty required field.

Many more new HTML5 elements

In addition to the new `<video>`, `<audio>`, `<canvas>`, and form elements, there are several more new elements for use in HTML5. Some examples are the `<figure>` and `<figurecaption>` elements used to label images on your pages, the `<hgroup>` element to group a set of heading elements into a logical section, and more. HTML5 also addresses existing tags found in HTML 4.0.1 that were outdated or needed refinement, such as `<i>`, `<b>`, `<small>`, `<strong>`, and `<abbr>`, which have new meaning and new uses in HTML5.

An overview of HTML5 APIs and supporting technologies

There are other developing web technologies related to the HTML5 specification on syntax. These techniques will help you perform tasks in the web browser and supported mobile devices that were not possible in previous versions of HTML.

What is an API?

APIs (Application Programming Interfaces) are a way to create applications using pre-built components and are not unique to web development, or even to scripting languages. Websites such as Twitter, YouTube and others provide APIs to the public so designers and developers can integrate features into their own websites (or for other purposes such as mobile or desktop applications). One of the main goals of an API is to standardize how certain mechanics work and to simplify otherwise complicated programming tasks. APIs are very significant in the world of HTML5 and there a number of them to explore, including Drag and Drop, Web storage, Microdata, and Geolocation, among others.

Knowing that the official documentation for these APIs is separate from the official documentation of HTML5 is the first step toward using them. Keep in mind that unless you are comfortable with the more technical side of web development, this documentation will not be intuitive at first. However, there are code examples here for you to examine.

Drag and Drop
http://developers.whatwg.org/dnd.html#dnd

Web Storage
http://dev.w3.org/html5/webstorage/#introduction

Microdata
http://developers.whatwg.org/links.html#microdata

Geolocation
http://dev.w3.org/geo/api/spec-source.html#introduction

Geolocation in action

Geolocation is an API that helps identify the web browser's geographic location. This information is then used to send you relevant data based on your position. Version 3.5 of Firefox was one of the first browsers to use geolocation. An example of the usefulness of geolocation is to connect a web search with map data to help you locate restaurants within walking distance of your hotel. Instead of manually entering your address, a geolocation-enabled browser could deliver local results based on your location.

Geolocation is currently enabled in some modern browsers. For an example of how this feature works, follow the instructions in the next procedure to visit Flickr, the photosharing site. (You need a browser that supports geolocation.)

At the time of this writing, Firefox 3.5 and above and Safari 5 and above support Geolocation.

1   Open your geolocation-enabled browser and type the following URL: **flickr.com/map**. This page displays a map of photographs around the world that users have uploaded with metadata that tags their images with the geographical coordinates of the location. (This information can be entered manually or automatically by some cameras. The term for images with this metadata is geotagged.)

2   Click the Find My Location button at the top right side of the map. (You will not see this button if your browser does not support geolocation.)

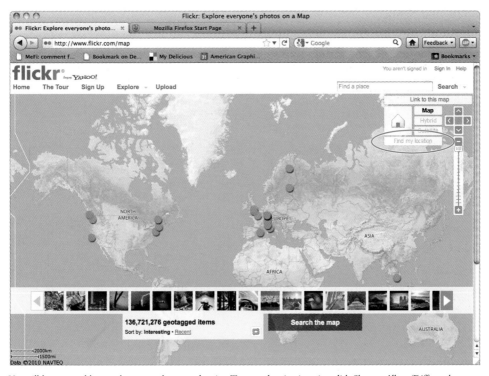

You will be prompted by your browser to share your location. To see geolocation in action, click Share or Allow. (Different browsers implement this differently.)

3   The Flickr map will update your geographic location. If there are geotagged images in your immediate area, you will see pink circles representing images on a local map. Additionally, a row of thumbnails representing these images appears at the bottom of the page.

The geolocation-enabled map displays thumbnails of images taken in your surrounding location.

For the last few years, smartphones have provided the ability of connecting geographical or GPS data with the device's browser or an application. When the geolocation feature becomes available to more web browsers, these benefits can be part of the desktop experience.

Web Workers

Web Workers is another API often grouped into the HTML5 family. Web Workers is a framework that addresses browser performance. When you access advanced web applications, such as mapping or applications that instantly generate charts and graphs, there are several processor-intensive computations that can slow down the performance of your application. Much of the slowdown occurs because there is competition between user interaction (clicking, dragging, and so on) and the need for the application to access resources (graphics, data, and more).

Web Workers are scripts that run in a separate thread. This separation means that processes, such as obtaining data from a database, occur independently from user behavior, which creates a more seamless environment for the user. Web Workers are in an early phase of development; at the time of this writing, there has been relatively little browser support.

Web storage

Web storage is an example of using pre-existing models of web technology in more powerful ways. Web storage improves browser cookies. Currently, browser cookies let websites store small pieces of data on your system so the site can save information for later use; for example, sites that recognize your login information when you return.

Cookies are a limited technology, and are not particularly easy for designers to use. Web storage updates the model to allow for greater storage space for modern web applications and makes the addition of storage features more accessible.

HTML5 provides two ways to store data: `localStorage` and `sessionStorage`. Data saved as `localStorage` is available to the browser at any point, even when the browser closes or the system is restarted. Data saved as `sessionStorage` is lost when the browser is closed.

An example of web storage currently in use is in Apple iPhones, which have a default storage space of five megabytes for data used in web applications. As this space begins to fill, you receive a prompt asking you to expand your storage.

Web pages request user permission to use offline storage.

CSS3 is not part of HTML5, but is closely related

As noted earlier, many of the examples labeled as HTML5 are a combination of the HTML5 technologies described above and JavaScript or CSS. CSS is an evolving language identified by version numbers, and the latest version of CSS (3.0) has evolved alongside the HTML5 specification. Some components of CSS3 are frequently mistaken as components of HTML5, such as animation or transitions. The confusion is understandable but it is important for professional designers and developers to understand the distinction. Below is a brief description of some of the most interesting CSS3 features.

CSS animations

Technologies such as Flash have traditionally been used to animate objects in the browser. You can now create some of the same functionality using CSS rules and properties. In the future, the HTML5 Canvas element and CSS3 transitions can help designers create interactive and animated elements on the page.

Visit http://animatable.com/demos/madmanimation/ *in a Webkit browser, such as Chrome or Safari, to see CSS animation in action.*

CSS transitions

CSS transitions are closely related to animation, but fundamentally different. A transition allows property changes in CSS values to occur smoothly over a specified duration. For example, a button that has a background color of green can smoothly animate to a different background color when the user rolls over the button. You can currently perform this type of animation with JavaScript and Flash, but as with much of CSS3, transitions give designers a tool to use without becoming a scripting expert.

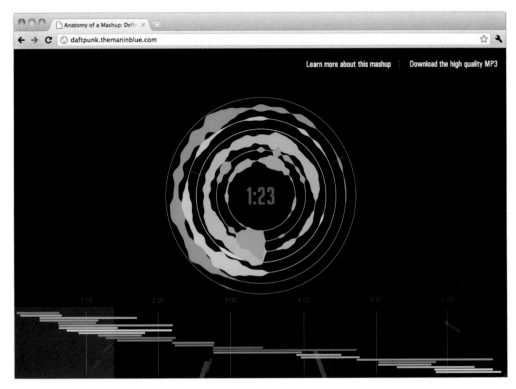

Visit http://daftpunk.themaninblue.com/ *to see an example of CSS transitions in action.*

CSS 2D- and 3D-transformations

The CSS transform property allows you to rotate, scale, or skew an element on your page. An example is the ability to rotate an image on the page slightly to one side for aesthetic effect. You can also animate transforms; for example, animating the scale property lets you create an enlarging or minimizing effect on an image or other element. You can also add the perspective property to the transformation effect to simulate an object positioned or animated in 3D space.

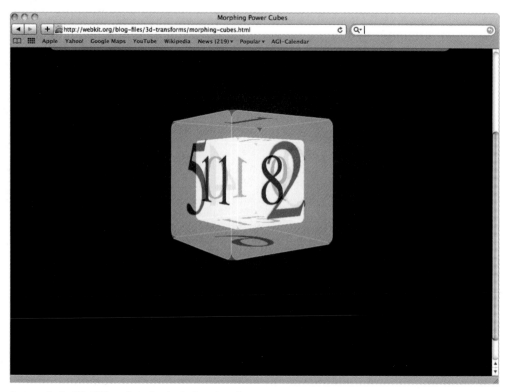

An example of a 3D-CSS transformation that is also animated.

CSS3 backgrounds, borders, RGBa colors, gradients, drop shadows, and rounded corners

There are several enhancements to the visual style of the page that are now possible with CSS3. A simple example is the border-radius property which allows you to add rounded corners to your boxes, but there are many other new effects you can create, such as native gradients and drop shadows. Traditional effects, such as the background-image and the border property, are improved in CSS3. For example, you can use the border-image property to apply images to style a border, or add multiple background images to a single container; this removes the current limitation of a single background-image.

`@font-face` **web fonts**

There is increasing support for the ability to add custom fonts to page designs using the `@font-face` property, which lets the designer specify a particular font and provide a source link for the font to allow the browser to download it. This feature could dramatically transform the appearance of web pages worldwide, but it has many of the same browser support issues as the various HTML5 features.

HTML5 is in a state of transition

The technologies behind HTML5 are in transition, so you need to determine when you can use them and when you should not. Throughout this book, we will guide you and offer a perspective on the kind of support you can expect in web browsers, and provide scenarios where HTML5 might be more appropriate to use than other languages.

Each of the major browsers in use today (Microsoft Internet Explorer, Mozilla Firefox, Apple Safari, Google Chrome, and Opera) have different support for HTML5 features in the syntax and the supporting family. In some cases, a page that has new functionality or appearance in one browser might not appear at all in another, or features might be missing, but the page continues to be functional. These scenarios might change in the future, but desktop web browsers evolve very slowly, so there will continue to be inconsistent browser support in the near future.

The timeline for browser support

The timeline for full HTML5 browser support cannot be accurately predicted, but the W3C has targeted the second half of the year 2014 as the date when the HTML5 specification will be finalized. Conservative web designers might choose to wait until then to use HTML5 in production environments, but the standard is separate from browser support. Most current web browsers support some HTML5 features. Some of these features are relatively well-developed and safe to use, others are still under development and designers can use them to experiment with the new features, or with the understanding that they might be exchanging reliability for innovation.

Who is using HTML5 today?

Mobile devices and smartphones are active platforms for HTML5 documents and web applications today. Browsers such as Apple Safari for iOS have supported features associated with HTML5 (for example, offline storage and CSS3 animations) for a few years. This is because iOS mobile devices, such as the iPhone and the iPad, have a distinctive hardware profile including screen size and memory capabilities as well as a consistent software profile (only one operating system needs to be supported). Within the controlled environment of a smartphone or mobile device, it is much easier to add advanced features when you know definitively they will be supported by the browser. In contrast, within the landscape of desktop computing, there are far too many variables to support easily, including multiple browsers, old browsers, different monitor resolutions and more.

The mobile Safari browser on Apple's iPhone has been using HTML5 features such as offline storage since 2009, and has internal preferences to set the storage size.

Users are also demanding content that is optimized for mobile devices, which HTML5 and its supporting technologies can deliver. For this reason, HTML5 support is a high priority for the manufacturers of these devices. This support, in turn, encourages designers and developers to build unique and compelling websites and web applications that leverage HTML5 features.

All of the major web browsers are committed to HTML5, and by learning these skills today, you can be a part of the exhilarating (and challenging) evolution of the Web.

Identifying HTML5 sites

The World Wide Web Consortium (known as the W3C) is a group that has been in existence since the beginning of the Web. This group has no formal power, but it provides the specifications, or rules, for the various technologies behind the Web. For example, formal specifications for HTML and CSS help browser manufacturers make browsers, and help designers and developers build reliable websites that work in these browsers.

In January 2010, the W3C introduced an HTML5 logo for public use to promote the new capabilities of HTML5 and related technologies.

*The HTML5 logo is free
to download and use.*

The logo is available as a graphic to display on websites and other media to indicate the use of this technology. Note that the W3C uses the term HTML5 in a broad sense and includes other technologies. In addition, HTML5 will become an official standard in 2014, but web developers and designers are encouraged to start using the specification today. For more information about HTML5 and the logo as discussed by the W3C, visit: *www.w3.org/html/logo/*

Self study

1 Browser manufacturers often promote HTML5 features. In addition to your primary web browser, download and install one or more of the following browsers: Microsoft Internet Explorer, Mozilla Firefox, Apple Safari, Google Chrome, and Opera. Visit the URL for your primary browser, and then explore the HTML5 features.

- Google Chrome (*www.chromeexperiments.com*)
- Apple Safari (*www.apple.com/html5*)
- Mozilla Firefox (*https://developer.mozilla.org/en/HTML/HTML5*)
- Microsoft Internet Explorer (*www.nevermindthebullets.com*)

2 Next, use a different browser for the same site. Can you identify any missing features? Does the primary website give you warnings about features that might not be supported?

Review

Questions

1 Name three components of HTML5 designed to reduce or replace web browser dependence on browser plugins such as Flash.

2 What is the difference between the HTML5 specification and the HTML5 family as defined in this lesson?

3 Where was the earliest adoption of HTML5 seen and why?

Answers

1 The `<video>` and `<audio>` tags let you embed multimedia directly in HTML without the need for a browser plugin. The `<canvas>` element lets you add a drawing surface to your page and create shapes, fills, gradients, and with the help of CSS, it can animate these objects.

2 The HTML5 specification features a number of new elements (or tags) that you can use to add new layout structure or functionality to web pages. The HTML5 family is composed of several related, but independent, technologies such as Geolocation, web storage, and CSS3.

3 The earliest adoption of HTML5 was seen on mobile devices, such as the iPhone, because the operating system and browser were based on a controlled environment (such as screen size and memory) that made it easier to introduce the new HTML browser features.

Fundamentals of HTML, XHTML, and CSS

In this lesson, you'll discover the fundamentals of HTML, XHTML, and CSS. Together, these form the structure and style of your web pages.

Starting up

You will work with several files from the HTML5_02lessons folder in this lesson. Make sure you have loaded the HTML5lessons folder onto your hard drive from the supplied DVD. See "Loading lesson files" in the Starting Up section of this book. We used the text editor Coda on the Mac to create the markup in this lesson, but you can use the text editor of your choosing and achieve the same results. Other popular text editors for the Mac include: BBedit, TextWrangler, and Textmate. For Windows, Microsoft Visual Web Developer Express, Microsoft WebMatrix, and E-Text Editor are good options. For more details see the sidebar on the next page.

See Lesson 2 in action!

Use the accompanying video to gain a better understanding of how to use some of the capabilities shown in this lesson. The video tutorial for this lesson can be found on the included DVD.

Web languages

In this lesson, you will discover two languages: HTML and CSS. Although they have different syntax and rules, they are highly dependent on each other. By the end of this lesson, you will understand how to create simple HTML pages, add images, create hyperlinks from one page to another, and add simple styling to pages using CSS.

This lesson covers a lot of ground, and many of the core principles introduced in this lesson are reinforced throughout the remaining chapters.

Web page structure is based on HTML

Hypertext Markup Language (HTML) documents use the .html or .htm extension. This extension allows a web browser or device, such as a smartphone, to understand that HTML content is on the page, and the content of the page is then rendered by the browser or device according to the rules of HTML.

Markup tags are used to define the content on an HTML page. Markup tags are contained between greater than (<) and less than (>) symbols, and they are placed at the start and end of an object or text that is used in an HTML page. Here is an example of two heading 1 tags for text. The tags are not seen by the viewer of the web page, but every web browser knows that the text between the tags is a heading 1.

```
<h1>New Smoothie Recipe!</h1>
```

In this example, the <h1> is the opening tag and the </h1> is the closing tag. So this entire line of code is an *element*. More specifically, it is referred to as the heading 1 element.

HTML and XHTML are closely related. There is a list of rules defined by the World Wide Web Consortium, or W3C that specify the perimeters of HTML and XHTML.

An overview of text editors

The following is a brief list of popular text editors for both Mac OS and Windows computers. These editors offer capabilities such as automatic code completion, code coloring, and code checking.

BBedit and TextWrangler (Mac) These text editors are similar and are developed by the same company. TextWrangler is free and has fewer features than BBedit. *www.barebones.com*

Coda (Mac) is a text editor that also provides site management, browser preview, and built-in web publishing. *www.panic.com/coda/*

TextMate (Mac) Along with being a text editor, its functionality can be extended by bundles that extend the capabilities of TextMate; for example, there are bundles that make adding JavaScript to your web pages much easier. *http://macromates.com*

E Text Editor (Windows) E Text Editor is a Windows-based text editor that supports many of the features of TextMate such as bundles and snippets. *www.e-texteditor.com*

Microsoft Visual Web Developer Express (Windows) provides a full featured text editor for web coding that supports HTML, CSS, and functionality for .NET programming. It also provides a basic visual layout environment for website design and development. *www.microsoft.com/express/Web/*

Microsoft WebMatrix A code editing tool that also allows you to code, test, and deploy websites. www.microsoft.com/web/webmatrix/

HTML code as rendered in the browser

To help you understand the relationship between the HTML code and what you see in your web browser, the following illustration will show you the connection between the two.

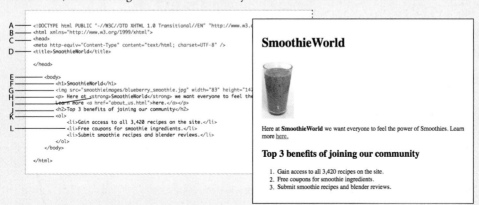

A. *Doctype. This line instructs the browser to interpret all the code that follows according to a unique set of rules.*

B. *HTML element. This element nests all the following elements and tells the browser to expect an HTML document.*

C. *Head element. This section includes information about the page, but nothing is rendered on the page itself.*

D. *Title element. Any content inside the title tags show up at the top of the browser. This is what is used when a user bookmarks a page in the browser.*

E. *Body element. All content within the body can be rendered in the browser's main window.*

F. *Heading 1 element. The first of six heading elements. Content that is a heading 1 is rendered very large and bold.*

G. *Image element. Links to a graphic file and displays it on the page.*

H. *Paragraph element. By default, the browser adds space before and after this element which often contains multiple lines of text.*

I. *Strong element. Formats the enclosed content as bold by default.*

J. *Heading 2 element. Compare the size of second largest heading to the first one.*

K. *Ordered list element. Defines the enclosed list items as numbered.*

L. *List element. Multiple list items will automatically be numbered by the browser.*

The details of XHTML syntax

There is little fundamental difference between HTML 4.0 and XHTML 1.0—the two standards previously released by the W3C (World Wide Web Consortium). As XHTML was defined, it was created so that pages written in XHTML also work in browsers that render current HTML. The tags and attributes of XHTML and HTML remained the same, but the syntax of XHTML code is more strict. The most significant differences between XHTML and HTML are as follows:

- In XHTML, all tags must be lowercase.

- XHTML requires all tags to be closed—meaning that there must be a tag at the start and end of the element being tagged—such as a headline, paragraph, or image.

 All tags in XHTML must close, even special tags that technically don't require an open and close tag. For example, the <br> tag, which creates a line break, uses a special self-closing syntax. A tag that self-closes looks like this (with a space and a forward slash):

```
<br />
```

- XHTML requires proper nesting of tags. In the following example, the <em> tag to emphasize text opens within the <h1> headline tag. As such, it must be closed before the <h1> is closed.

```
<h1>Smoothies are <em>great!</em></h1>
```

We've used XHTML-compliant code throughout this book as we provide HTML5 examples, which helps make your designs compatible with modern browsers and mobile devices.

Doctype lets the web browser know what to expect

The start of every web page should include a Doctype declaration. Declaring the doctype tells the web browser a little bit of information about what it is going to see on the page. Because there are different specifications for XHTML and HTML, the web browser knows which language it's about to see and render. Because a browser renders the page starting at the top line and then moves down, placing your doctype on the first line makes a lot of sense. While it's not required, it's good form to always use doctype at the start of your HTML pages. The doctype for HTML 4.0.1 looks like this:

```
<!DOCTYPE HTML PUBLIC "-//W3C//DTD HTML 4.01 Transitional//EN"
"http://www.w3.org/TR/html4/loose.dtd">
```

When a web browser sees a Doctype declaration, the browser expects that everything on the page that follows will use that language. If the page adheres to the specifications perfectly, it is considered valid.

The W3C and page validation

The W3C is the World Wide Web consortium—a non-profit group that helps guide the evolution of the Web. The W3C provides guidelines and rules for specifications including HTML and XHTML. One way to determine the validity of the HTML or XHTML code you generate is to use W3C's free online validation service.

You will need access to the Internet for this exercise. If you do not have Internet access, you may read through the exercise to understand the validation process.

1   Open your web browser and navigate to *http://validator.w3.org*.

2   Click the Validate by File Upload tab.

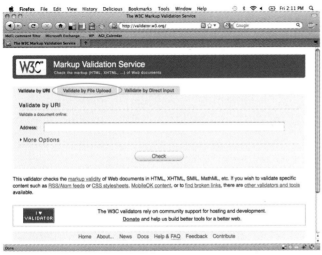

The W3C validator allows you to check your HTML code for errors.

3   Click Browse (depending on your browser, this may also read "Choose File"), and navigate to your HTML5_02lessons folder, and select the w3_noncompliant.html file. Click the Check button to validate the code.

4   The W3C site returns several errors. Scroll down the page and you can see in-depth information on the errors. Don't worry about the errors at this point. You will now upload a nearly identical file without errors.

5   Click the Browse button, navigate to your HTML5_02lessons folder, and select the w3_compliant.html file. The File Upload window appears. Press Open or Check, depending on how your browser labels the button.

6 Click the Revalidate button. You now see a Congratulations message that the page has been checked and found to be compliant as XHTML 1.0 Strict.

Although the page is valid, it may not look good to a viewer. This example uses a page that has missing styles and missing images to emphasize this point. It's important to understand that having valid code is only one step in a series to make certain your web pages can be viewed by the widest possible audience.

You can validate web pages that you've already placed online. Do this by using the Validate by URL option. You can also paste HTML code directly into the validator by choosing the Validate by Direct Input option.

7 In your web browser, choose File > Open, navigate to the HTML5_02lessons folder, and select the same w3_compliant.html document that you just confirmed was valid. If you are using Internet Explorer, navigate to the HTML5_02lessons folder on your computer and drag and drop the w3_compliant.html document into your browser window.

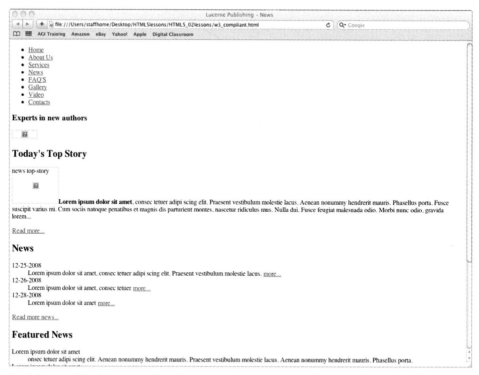

A "valid" page can have links to images that don't exist and may have a poor visual design.

Because we know that the page uses valid XHTML, we know that whatever problems there are with the page, they are not due to improper XHTML code. We know that there are no missing tags or misspelled tags. This can be useful for troubleshooting, allowing you to quickly identify any syntax problems.

Other benefits of standards-based design

W3C page validation is the most tangible aspect of standards-based web design, but there are also other benefits to creating well-structured pages, including:

Less code: Using HTML and CSS allows you to create similar pages with fewer lines of code—less work for you and faster download times for the viewer.

Ease of maintenance: Less code means a website that is easier to maintain. This helps you, the author of a page, as well as any members of a team working on maintaining or revising a website.

Accessibility: Web documents marked up semantically, meaning those that use the best HTML tag for the job, can be easier to navigate by users with visual impairments and the information they contain is more likely to be found by a visitor to the site.

Search engine optimization: Web pages with clear and logically named sections, both within the code and also within page content, are easier for search engines to index and categorize because content that is organized and well-labeled is easier for search engines to evaluate content and relevance of content on the page.

Device compatibility: Websites that separate the structure from the style are more easily repurposed for mobile devices and other browsers. CSS also allows for alternative style sheets that optimize the appearance based on the device being used to view the page.

HTML structure

One of the most important concepts to understand when designing web content is the nested structure of HTML documents. Elements are often nested within each other. You will often start with the HTML structure first and then begin to style it with CSS.

As an example, let's look at the basic elements that are in virtually every web page:

```
<html>
    <body>
    </body>
</html>
```

In this example, the <body> element is nested within the <html> element. In other words, <body> is placed between the opening <html> tag and the closing </html> tag, so nested tags are those that are placed between other opening and closing tags. These two elements, <body> and <html>, form the structure of all web pages; when a browser opens an HTML document, it looks for this structure.

Content within the body tag is visible on the page as it is displayed within the web browser.

```
<html>
    <body>
    Nobody knows who invented smoothies, but the world wouldn't be
    the same without them!
    </body>
</html>
```

In HTML documents, some of the content is displayed to the viewer in their browser, but there is also other code on the page that is hidden from view, but useful for the browser, search engine, or site developer. Examples of this hidden code include scripts to add interactivity, code to help search engines categorize the document, and the styles that define the appearance of the page. This code is often found inside of the <head> element, and the <head> element is nested within the <html> tags. An example of this is:

```
<html>
    <head>
    </head>
    <body>
    Nobody knows who invented smoothies, but the world wouldn't be
    the same without them!
    </body>
</html>
```

In the above example, there is no content in the <head> element just yet. Notice that the <head> element is nested within <html>, but is not nested within <body>. The <head> element opens and closes before the <body> element starts.

The <body> element contains text, but it is lacking context, so neither you nor a search engine can determine if it is a heading, list, quotation, or some other type of content. To define the text as a paragraph, the <p> tag is used:

```
<html>
    <head>
    </head>
    <body>
    <p>Nobody knows who invented smoothies, but the world wouldn't be
    the same without them!</p>
    </body>
</html>
```

The paragraph element is now nested within the <body> element, which, in turn, is now nested within the <html> element. You will now open this document in a text editor and add to the file:

1   Open your text editor and then choose File > Open and navigate to your HTML5_02lessons folder. Depending on which text editor you are using, you may need to select "All Files" instead of "Text Documents" in order to see the file. Choose the index.html file and then click Open.

To get a better understanding of the structure of HTML and nesting of tags, you will add a hyperlink to this document linking the word *SmoothieWorld* to an external website.

2   In the last paragraph that reads "All content on this site is the copyright of SmoothieWorld," click once before the word SmoothieWorld, and then type the following code: **<a>**. This <a> is the opening for the anchor element, which you use to link to other pages in your site or elsewhere on the Internet.

3   Click to the right of the word SmoothieWorld and type **</a>**. This is the closing tag for the anchor tag and is required in XHTML.

If you are using Dreamweaver, it may be set to automatically complete closing tags. To change this preset, choose Edit > Preferences (Windows), or Dreamweaver > Preferences (Mac). Under Category, click Code Hints, select Never under Code Hints, and choose OK.

To finish the job of creating a link, you need to add the destination of the link with the `href` attribute.

4   Click between the letter a and the closing bracket (>) in the opening tag. Press the spacebar once to add a space and type **href=""**. The complete code should now read `<a href="">`.

You now have an anchor tag and the href attribute. To finish the job of creating a hyperlink, you need to add the value of the attribute. In this case the value will be a URL—a web address.

5   Click inside the quotation marks and type **http://www.digitalclassroombooks .com/smoothieworld**. This completes the destination and with all the pieces in place, you now have a complete hyperlink.

```
    <p>All content on this site is the
    copyright of <a href="http://www.digitalclassroombooks.com/smoothieworld">SmoothieWorld</a></p>

</body>
</html>
```

Creating a hyperlink using the <a> tag and href *attribute.*

6   Choose File > Save, and then preview the page in your web browser by either opening your browser and choosing File > Open and navigating to the file you just saved, or by Ctrl + clicking (Mac OS) or right-clicking (Windows) the file and directing your operating system to open the file with a web browser. The link has the standard blue underlined appearance of a hyperlink that you have not yet visited.

7   Close your browser and return to your text editor.

Placing images in HTML

To add images to an HTML document, use the `<img>` tag. Like the anchor tag, the image tag does nothing by itself. The image tag relies on attributes and values that specify the image to display. Here you will insert an image into the HTML code.

1   Click once after the closing paragraph line `</p>` that follows the text indicating the site content is copyrighted. Press Return to go to the next line. Type **`<img />`**.

The image tag is in a special category of HTML tags that are self-closing. You do not need a pair of tags with the image tag; one tag is sufficient, but it is important that you type this tag correctly. There is a space between the `img` and the `/`. This satisfies the requirements of XHTML syntax, and you will specify the exact image to use in the space between the `img` and `/`.

```
<body>
    <h1>SmoothieWorld</h1>
    <p>Smoothies are the stuff of life. they get you going in the morning, refresh you when you're h

    <p>All content on this site is the
    copyright of <a href="http://www.digitalclassroombooks.com/smoothieworld">SmoothieWorld</a></p>
    <img />
```

Adding an image to to your page with the `<img>` tag.

2   Click once to the right of the text img, press the spacebar, and then type **`src=""`**.

`src` is the source attribute, and you will specify a value, which is the location (URL) of an image which will display on the page.

3   Click between the quotation marks that follow the `src=` code and type **images/ blueberry_smoothie.jpg**.

Your `img` code should now look like this:

```
<img src="images/blueberry_smoothie.jpg" />
```

This code tells a web browser to look inside the images folder and display the file blueberry_smoothie.jpg. In the next few steps, be sure to maintain the extra space between the last quotation mark and the closing tag. You will be adding an `alt` tag.

This `alt` attribute represents the text equivalent for the image and is required if you want your page to be valid. `Alt` attributes help those who use screen readers to navigate the Web. They also appear in browsers if the image is broken or missing for some reason.

4   Click to the right of the last quotation mark that follows the blueberry_smoothie.jpg file name and press the spacebar. Type **`alt=""`**.

5   Click inside the quotation marks you added in step 4 and type **Blueberry smoothie**.

Both the `src` attribute and the `alt` attribute are required for fully valid XHTML. There are also optional attributes that you should consider. We'll look at two of these option's attributes: `height` and `width`.

6   Click to the right of the last quotation mark following the `alt` attribute, press the spacebar, then type **width="180" height="320"**. These attributes tell the web browser how large the image should be displayed on the page. The values used are pixels. Keep this document open as you will be working with it in the next exercise of this lesson.

```
<p>All content on this site is the
copyright of <a href="http://www.digitalclassroombooks.com/smoothieworld">SmoothieWorld</a></p>
<img src="images/blueberry_smoothie.jpg" alt="Blueberry Smoothie" width="180" height="320" />
```

Adding `Width` *and* `Height` *values to your image is not required, but is a good idea.*

Using optional attributes

Many of HTML's optional attributes fall under the category of best practices. *Best practices* is an umbrella term used to describe the accepted way of doing something in web design. There are generally logical reasons behind best practices; for example, setting the width and height creates a placeholder for the images even if they haven't loaded due to a slow Internet connection. Without the placeholder created by the width and height values, the page layout will change as the images load.

7   Choose File > Save, and then preview your page in the browser to see your image.

The result of an embedded image as displayed in the browser.

The role of CSS

Cascading Style Sheets (CSS) use a separate language from HTML. CSS allows you to apply consistent styling of elements across all pages on your site, so that all headings, lists, and paragraphs look and act the same on every page of a site.

How we refer to CSS syntax in this book

Before you begin to work with CSS, we need to explain how we will refer to the various parts of CSS syntax throughout this book. This is not as easy as it sounds because there is a gap between the official specification of the CSS language and the way designers often refer to CSS in the "real world." Nevertheless, here are the fundamentals: all the following code is what we refer to as a rule in CSS:

```
h1 {
    color:blue;
    margin-top:1em;
}
```

There are various components to this rule, as follows:

```
A ——
      h1 {
B ————————
              color:blue;
C ——————————
              margin-top:1em;
                              — D
      }
```

A. Selector. B. Declaration. C. Property. D. Value.

We will refer to each of the various components from time to time throughout the book, so if we ask you to change the value "blue" to "red", you should know what to do. Or, if we ask you to locate and change the h1 selector to a h2 selector, it should make sense.

On a day-to-day basis, most designers aren't always so specific. For example, the rule above might be referred to as a "style," "style rule," "the h1 rule," or "the CSS rule for h1." Also, as you can see above, the official name for the pair of the property and the value is called a declaration. Again, in everyday use, the use of the term "declaration" is not common and most designers will use the term property or properties interchangeably.

Styling a heading

To get a sense of how CSS works, you'll create a simple CSS rule that changes the style of a heading in your page. In your index.html page, you already have the content "SmoothieWorld" nested inside an `<h1>` tag. Perhaps one of the best ways to begin thinking about how CSS works is to consider how the default style of this heading is rendered in the browser.

1   Examine the heading of the file you previewed in the last step of the previous exercise. The style and formatting instructions are being provided by the browser. The size, color, and font are provided by the browser because exact formatting instructions are not specified. The browser only knows that this is a headline. You will redefine this style with a CSS rule.

2   In your code, locate the `<title>` tag on line 5, click once at the end of the line following the closing tag, then press return to add a new line of code. Type the following:

```
<style type="text/css">
```

3   Press Return three times and then type **</style>**. This is a style element which you will use to place your rule for the style of the `<h1>` element.

```
<!DOCTYPE html PUBLIC "-//W3C//DTD XHTML 1.0 Transitional//EN" "http://www.w3.org/TR/xhtml1/DTD/xhtm
<html xmlns="http://www.w3.org/1999/xhtml">
<head>
<meta http-equiv="Content-Type" content="text/html; charset=UTF-8" />
<title>Untitled Document</title>
<style type="text/css">


</style>
```

The `<style>` element is nested within the head section of the page, and is where the CSS rules will be placed.

The `<style>` element is nested within the `<head>` tags of your page. In HTML, everything nested inside the `<head>` section is not rendered by the browser on the page. For example, there is also a `<title>` element inside this section; this title appears at the top of the web browser, not on the actual page.

4   In the empty line below the opening `<style>` tag, type the following:

```
h1 {
```

This is your selector. The selector is the HTML element you want to style, in this case, the Heading 1 element.

5   Press Return and then press Tab to place your cursor below the curly bracket. The tab is optional, but it helps make your CSS more readable. As you will soon see, the number of lines in this rule will grow and it's worthwhile keeping the code easy to read.

6   Type the following code below the h1 {:

```
color:purple;
```

The word *color* is referred to as a property in CSS syntax and the word *purple* is a value. The combined pair of a property and a value is called a *declaration*.

```
<title>Untitled Document</title>
<style type="text/css">
h1 {
    color:purple;

</style>
```

The combination of the property (color) and the value (purple) is often referred to as style rule.

7   Press Return again and on the next line, type } which is the right curly bracket character.

This closes the curly bracket you added in step 4.

You now have three lines in this rule:

```
h1 {
    color:purple;
}
```

8   Choose File > Save, and then preview your page in the browser. The head is now a light purple color and you have successfully created your first CSS rule. Close your browser and return to your text editor.

Your H1 color is now being styled by a CSS rule.

9   In the HTML file, select the word `purple` and type the following for the color value: **#800080**. This hexadecimal color is the equivalent of purple. You can use either named colors or hexadecimal colors when defining colors using CSS.

Save your file and then preview it in the browser. The color remains the same. Hexadecimal colors are a more common method for describing colors.

Hexadecimal colors

Color in both HTML and CSS is referred to by a six-character code preceded by a pound sign. This code is called hexadecimal code, and is the system used to identify and apply color to elements. You can reproduce almost any color using a unique hexadecimal code. For example, the following code is dark-red: `a#CC0000`.

The first, middle, and last pair of digits in the hexadecimal code correspond to values in the RGB spectrum. For instance, white, which is represented in RGB as R:255 G:255 B:255, is represented in HTML as #FFFFFF (255|255|255). A program like Photoshop will allow you to choose a specific RGB color in the Color Editor and give you the equivalent hexadecimal color for use in your code.

There are also online references you can use to locate or "mix" hexadecimal colors, such as: *www.w3schools.com/Html/html_colorvalues.asp*

The rule you just created uses what is officially known as a "type selector" since it targets every instance of the h1 element type in your document. Type selectors assign CSS properties to an existing HTML tag. In this case, the <h1> tag. All <h1> tags on this page will be displayed as purple. Type selectors are more commonly known as tag selectors. It is rare that you will actually hear someone use the phrase "type selector", but that is the official name for it, so we mention it here.

You will now get an introduction to another category of CSS styles known as a class. You will also work with the <span> element, which separates and controls inline content, such as a sentence within a paragraph, or an individual word within a sentence.

Understanding class styles and the `<span>` element

Tag selectors are frequently used, but they can only be applied to HTML elements. When you want to style something that does not map directly to a tag, for example, change the color of a single word within a paragraph, standard HTML tags are not a good option. In this case, you can use a class selector, which is a CSS rule that you can apply to any number of items on a page. Class selectors have flexible naming options, but you should choose names that describe what they do. For example, you may wish to name class selectors as `caption`, `imageborder`, or `redtext`. In this exercise, you will create a class style that applies the color purple to the word Smoothies in your paragraph.

1   Place your cursor on the line immediately below the closing curly bracket for the `h1` rule, then type the following:

```
.purple {
    color:purple;

}
```

Note the period at the beginning of the class selector. The text following the period is the class name. You can use any name you wish, but the period is required at the start to identify it as a class. The rule is the same as in the last exercise, only here the selector is not the h1 element. The class name can be anything you want, but it must have the period at the beginning to identify it as a class. Next, you'll apply this class to the word Smoothie in order to style it purple. To do this, you will use an HTML tag `<span>`.

2   In the paragraph within the `<body>` tag, locate the word Smoothies, click once to the left of it, and then type:

```
<span>
```

```
<body>
    <h1>SmoothieWorld</h1>
    <p><span>Smoothies</span> are the stuff of life. they get you going in the morning, refresh you

    <p>All content on this site is the
    copyright of <a href="http://www.digitalclassroombooks.com/smoothieworld">SmoothieWorld</a></p>
    <img src="images/blueberry_smoothie.jpg" alt="Blueberry Smoothie" width="180" height="320" />
```

The `<span>` tag allows you to define the portion of a paragraph you'd like to style.

3   Click to the right of the word Smoothies and add a closing span tag `</span>`.

Your code should look like this:

```
<p><span> Smoothies</span> are the ...
```

Save your file. If you were to preview the page in the browser, you would see no change. The `<span>` tag in HTML is an empty tag; it does nothing on its own and needs to be paired with a style. The `<span>` tag defines the beginning and end of where the style will be applied within the paragraph, but it does not apply the style on its own, and does not define the style.

4   Close the browser and return to your text editor. Locate the opening `<span>` tag you inserted before the word Smoothies. Click once after the word span but before the `>` bracket, then type the following:

```
class="purple"
```

The code should now read:

```
<span class="purple">Smoothies </span>
```

5   Locate the word Smoothies in the second sentence and before it type:

`<span class="purple">` and after the word Smoothies type: `</span>`.

6   Save your page and preview it in your browser. The text is now styled purple. Keep the document open in the text editor, as you will be working with it in the next exercise.

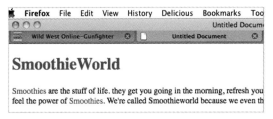

The word Smoothies is styled using an HTML span tag and a CSS class style.

Three ways to use styles

In this exercise, your styles were located within the head section of the page. This type of style is called an *internal style sheet*. In addition to internal (or embedded) style sheets, there are external style sheets and inline styles.

An *external style sheet* is a separate document with the file extension .css. When using an external style sheet, all styles reside inside the style sheet document and you link it to your HTML pages. While internal style sheets affect only the page on which they exist, external styles can be applied to multiple pages.

Inline styles are used infrequently. With inline styles, the style rules are nested inside the HTML tags. An example of an inline style that colors a heading purple would look like this:

```
<h1 style="color:purple">Smoothies</h1>
```

Inline styles are powerful because they override both internal and external styles, although they only apply to a single tag at a time. This embedded nature of inline styles means they are not easily re-used. In the simple example illustrated above, you can see the style for the color purple is nested inside the `<h1>` tag. If you had 50 `<h1>` elements throughout your website and were using inline styles, you would add this style code 50 times. If you decided to change the color to green, you would need to locate and modify all 50 uses of the style. Inline styles are useful for single overrides, or when an internal or external style sheet may not be available; a good example of this is HTML-based e-mail.

You will not be using inline styles very often in this book, which is a reflection of the current state of web design. Working with a combination of internal and external styles is the most common practice of web designers today.

Internal versus external style sheets

Internal style sheets are CSS rules contained directly within a document, using the `<style>` tag. The entire style sheet is contained within the opening and closing `<style>` tags.

External style sheets are CSS rules saved in a separate document with the file extension .css. With internal style sheets, CSS rules apply only to the HTML in the current document. For example, if you had a 20 page website and were using internal style sheets, you would need to create a separate style sheet in each of the pages. A change to the style would require you to update the internal styles in each of the 20 separate pages.

External style sheets place all the CSS rules for a site in a single document. You can attach the .css file to an unlimited number of HTML pages. This provides more flexibility. If a style rule is changed in the external style sheet, all paragraphs across the site are modified with a single step. You will make an external style sheet and then attach it to a new HTML page.

Creating an external style sheet

An HTML page does not have to be limited to just one style sheet, and many large websites will break-up their styles into separate pages, making them easier to organize and maintain. You can even use style sheets for specific functions such as printing a page or for displaying a site on mobile devices. Specific style sheets can even be used to make sites compatible with older web browsers when they are used to visit sites you create.

In this exercise, you will create a new external style sheet, move the style rules from your current document to the external style sheet, and then attach the style sheet to a new HTML page.

1   Choose File > New Text Document.

The text editor you are using may have a different menu command. You may need to choose the equivalent command. For example, many editors will allow you to choose File > New CSS document.

2   Choose File > Save. Name the document **styles.css** and save the file into the HTML5_02lessons folder. An external cascading style sheet has a specific .css file extension, but it is simply a text file.

3   Switch to the HTML document from the last exercise, but keep the style sheet open as well.

4   In the HTML document, locate the rules you created within the `<style>` tags, and then select them. Do not select the style tags themselves, just the rules that start with `h1` and end with the closing bracket `}`.

```
<style type="text/css">
h1 {
    color:purple;
    }

.purple {
    color:purple;
    }

</style>
```

Select just the style rules, not the `<style>` tag.

5   Choose Edit > Cut, then switch to the styles.css file and choose Edit > Paste to paste the rules into the external style sheet document. Choose File > Save to save your style sheet.

The entire external style sheet acts as a substitute for the `<style>` tags in the HTML document. Now that you have moved the rules to this document, you need to link it to your HTML page so that a web browser knows where to find the style rules that apply to the HTML.

6   Switch back to the index.html page and choose File > Save. You will add the `<link>` tag, pointing to the styles.css document. If you do not link to the external styles, the HTML page will have no styles.

7   Place your cursor *after* the closing style tag `</ style>` then press return to start a new line. Now type the following:

`<link rel="stylesheet" type="text/css" href="styles.css" />`

You have added the `rel`, `type`, and `href` attributes. You may recall the `href` attribute from when you added the hyperlink in an earlier exercise. In order for your external style sheet to work properly, the name of the file, and the path to the file must both be accurate.

8   Choose File > Save and then preview the HTML page in your browser. The page should not change, as the same style is being used; it is simply being applied from outside the document.

9   Close the browser and return to your text editor. You'll now create a new HTML document, and add the same link to the external CSS file, seeing how the rules are applied.

10 Choose File > Open and locate the file test.html in the HTML5_02lessons folder. This is an empty HTML document.

11 Continuing to work in your text editor, switch back to the index.html file and select the entire `<link>` element you typed in step 7:

`<link rel="stylesheet" type="text/css" href="styles.css" />`

and then choose Edit > Copy.

12 Switch back to the test.html document, and then click below the `<title>` element and Choose Edit > Paste to place the `<link>` element, then save the the file by choosing File > Save.

```
<!DOCTYPE html PUBLIC "-//W3C//DTD XHTML 1.0 Transitional//EN" "http://www.w3.org/TR/xhtml1/DTD/xhtml
<html xmlns="http://www.w3.org/1999/xhtml">
<head>
<meta http-equiv="Content-Type" content="text/html; charset=UTF-8" />
<title>Untitled Document</title>
<link rel="stylesheet" type="text/css" href="styles.css" />
</head>
```

Attaching an external style sheet using the `<link>` *element.*

The external style sheet is now attached to this HTML document. Any HTML tags you add to this new document will be styled if there is a corresponding rule in the CSS file. For example, the `<h1>` tag has a style of the color purple.

13 Click inside the `<body>` element and type:

`<h1>The Benefits of Smoothies </h1>`

Save the file and preview it in your web browser.

The `<h1>` *tag gets its style from the external CSS style sheet you created.*

The heading is purple because the style rule for the `<h1>` element is `color:purple` and because this rule is located in an external sheet and linked in two places: the index.html and test.html pages. Because of this, you can control the style of both HTML documents from a central location.

What makes styles cascading

You've seen three different places where CSS rules are found: inline, internally, and externally. If there are conflicting definitions of styles between inline, internal, and external styles, the inline style will be used because it is closer to the HTML source. The internal style sheet takes precedence over an external style sheet, and definitions used in an external style sheet are used only if they don't conflict with either inline or internal styles.

In this lesson, you've discovered many ways to format text. When you want to style text, it is almost always best to use actual text rather than an image of text. Using actual text rather than a picture of text created in programs like Photoshop or Illustrator makes your sites more accessible to the widest audience of users, devices, and search engines.

In this lesson, you discovered three categories of styles: internal, external and inline. You also created an element style and a class style, and then moved them into an external style sheet. Additionally, you explored how to link an external style sheet to a new HTML page.

Self study

1   Add another heading below the last paragraph in your completed file as follows:

```
<h2> Smoothies have flavor </h2>
```

2   Create a tag style in your external style sheet that defines this heading as the color orange.

Review

Questions

1   What is a doctype and how does it relate to page validation?

2   In the following XHTML code, what is the attribute and what is the attribute value? What other attributes would you often find in an img element such as this?

```
<img src="images/blueberry_smoothie.jpg"/>
```

3   Define the purpose of an external style sheet and one of the benefits of using an external style sheet.

Answers

1   A doctype is a declaration at the start of your HTML document. It is used by a web browser to determine what markup language and version is used on the page. Page validation tests the syntax of your code against the specifications of your doctype. Page validation is a good way to check your page for problems such as missing tags or typographical errors in your code.

2   In this line of code, `src` is the attribute and the attribute value is `images/blueberry_smoothie.jpg`. Nested inside the `<img>` tag is the `src` attribute and its value. It links to an image that is then rendered on the page. Other examples of image attributes are the `alt` attribute, which provides a text version of an image to devices such as screen readers, and the `width` and `height` attributes, which define the size of the image on the page.

3   An external style sheet is a text document with the extension .css. This document contains CSS rules that define the appearance of HTML elements. Because external style sheets can be linked to multiple HTML pages, they provide one central location for your styles. One benefit to this is the ability to update the style of an entire site with a single change to a CSS rule. Other benefits include the ability to use multiple style sheets for organizational purposes, and to specify specific style sheets for printing or optimize the display for mobile devices.

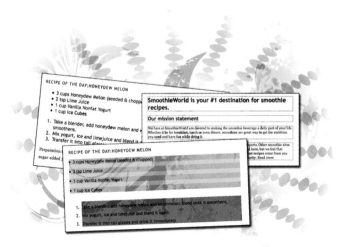

What you'll learn in this lesson:

- Using the `font-family` property
- Setting text size
- Working with the em measurement
- Changing text properties
- Using HTML lists

Formatting Text with CSS

In this lesson, you'll learn how to control the appearance of text on your web pages using CSS styling.

Starting up

You will work with several files from the HTML5_03lessons folder in this lesson. Make sure you have loaded the HTML5lessons folder onto your hard drive from the supplied DVD. See "Loading lesson files" in the Starting Up section of this book.

See Lesson 3 in action!

Use the accompanying video to gain a better understanding of how to use some of the features shown in this lesson. The video tutorial for this lesson can be found on the included DVD.

Although this lesson uses the TextWrangler text editor to create the markup, you can use any text editor and get the same results..

The importance of typography on the Web

> Typography is two-dimensional architecture, based on experience and imagination, and guided by rules and readability. And this is the purpose of typography: The arrangement of design elements within a given structure should allow the reader to easily focus on the message, without slowing down the speed of his reading.
>
> —*Hermann Zapf*

Typography has a starring role in graphic design, including web design. Most user interaction on the Web starts with text. Users spend a great deal of time on the web scanning, navigating, and reading text. As a result, it is extremely important that the web designer understands how to control the placement, appearance, and style of text.

For purposes of clarity, it is worth pointing out that the words *typeface* and *font* are mistakenly used interchangeably. A typeface is a more abstract term for the character design of an alphabet; it is a term that preceded the invention of computers and digital typesetting. An example of a common typeface is Helvetica, which also includes different styles including Bold, Condensed, and Light, among others. A font is the digital system file that resides on a computer and is used in print design to set text. In web design, web browsers use a font to display text on the screen (as well as when printing).

The challenges of fonts on the Web

When designing for the Web, you can format text in a way that is similar to desktop publishing and word processing applications, but there are important differences to keep in mind. When you specify that a specific font be used, that font needs to be installed on the user's computer when the web page is rendered on the viewer's computer or device. If the user does not have this font, the browser replaces it with another font.

Because you don't know what fonts are installed on viewers' computers, and because the web browser of a viewer might substitute fonts, your design intentions for text might not be faithfully reproduced. One option is to use fonts that you are sure will be found on most computers. Unfortunately, only a handful of fonts can reliably be found on virtually all computers around the world.

Web-safe fonts

Following is a list of the most reliable fonts for web use:

- Arial
- Verdana
- Georgia
- Times New Roman
- Courier
- Trebuchet
- Lucida
- Tahoma
- Impact

The list is small because it takes into account both Mac and Windows platforms and assumes that there may still be older computer systems that are active and accessing the Web. These older systems had a more limited font selection than today's systems, and so a designer needs to consider this when choosing fonts.

The above list is also limited for stylistic reasons. Both Courier and Impact, for example, are used infrequently because although they are widely available, their distinctive styles limit their everyday use.

One of the solutions to the lack of fonts on the Web is to use a *font stack*. In CSS, a font stack is a list of multiple fonts that the web browser uses in an attempt to display text onscreen. The following CSS code shows an example of a font stack:

```
font-family:"Helvetica Neue", Helvetica, Arial, sans-serif;
```

In this example, the browser first looks for the Helvetica Neue font on the user's system. Notice the quotation marks in this example. In most cases, when specifying a font, quotation marks are unnecessary, but in some cases, the quotation marks are needed to help the user's computer choose the right version of the font. If the user doesn't have Helvetica Neue, then the browser looks for the more generic version of Helvetica. If Helvetica is absent, the browser uses Arial, which is a font that is extremely similar to Helvetica. If for some reason Arial is not on the system, the last choice is sans-serif, which allows the system to use any sans-serif font it can find on the system. Sans-serif is the generic definition for all fonts that do not have small strokes (called serifs) at the end of each character. Examples of serif fonts are Times New Roman and Georgia.

Setting a `font-family`

In this exercise, you will set your `font-family` for an entire page, and then set the `font-family` for your headings.

1 In your text editor, choose File > Open and navigate to the HTML5_03lessons folder. Locate the 03_fonts.html file and click OK. This file has four blocks of text: a heading 1 `<h1>`, a heading 2 `<h2>`, and two paragraphs `<p>`. Additionally, in the `<style>` section, empty style rules are added to save you time. In this exercise, you will add the CSS properties. You will start by adding the `font-family` property for the body element.

2 In the style rule for the body, type the following line:

```
body {
    font-family:"Trebuchet MS", Tahoma, Arial, sans-serif;
}
```

3 Choose File > Save, and then preview your page in the browser. As noted above, your web browser renders Trebuchet if you have it on your system; if you do not, it displays Tahoma; and if you don't have Tahoma, you still see a sans-serif font.

When you define the font family Trebuchet for the body rule, all your text is set in this font.

All of the text on your page is rendered in Trebuchet because the only style set is for the body. Remember that the HTML body tag defines all of the elements on the page. Now you will set a specific font family for the paragraph element.

4 In the style rule for the paragraph (p), type the following line:

```
p {
    font-family:Georgia, "Times New Roman", Times, serif;
}
```

5 Save your document and preview it in your browser. Now that there is a specific rule for paragraphs, they are styled as Georgia. The two headings are still using Trebuchet, which you defined in the body style.

6   In the style rule for heading 2 (h2), type the following line:

```
h2 {
    font-family:Zapfino;
}
```

7   Save your document and preview it in your browser.

Styling the heading 2 as Zapfino will only show up if that font is on a user's system.

If you have the Zapfino font on your system, you see a calligraphic script for your heading. The Zapfino font is installed with Adobe applications such as Photoshop, so it is very likely that designers will have this font on their system. Because many web users do not have this font on their system, using it is not a good idea.

8   Select the entire font-family line in your h2 rule and delete it.

The promising future of web fonts

The lack of choices for using fonts on the Web has been a source of frustration for web designers for many years. The situation is improving as several companies have created solutions to enable your pages to display on a browser with the fonts you've specified as a designer.

Some of the methods use paid services, but free options are also available. Here are some resources to get you started:

- *http://code.google.com/webfonts*
- *http://typekit.com/*
- *http://fontdeck.com/*
- *www.fontsquirrel.com/fontface*

Sizing text with CSS

When using CSS to style text for the Web, you have a few options for the unit of measurement. The CSS property that controls the size of your text is named `font-size`.

You can control the `font-size` property in a few different ways:

- **Absolute-size:** A set of keywords that indicate predefined font sizes. Named font sizes scale according to the user's font setting preferences. Possible values include `xx-small`, `x-small`, `small`, `medium`, `large`, `x-large`, and `xx-large`.

- **Length:** A number followed by an absolute units designator (`cm`, `mm`, `in`, `pt`, or `pc`) or a relative units designator (`em`, `ex`, or `px`).

- **Percentage:** An integer followed by a percent sign (`%`). The value is a percentage of the font size of the parent object.

- **Relative-size:** A set of keywords that are interpreted as relative to the font size of the parent object. Possible values include `larger` and `smaller`.

Choosing the unit of measurement for the `font-size` in a web page is an important decision and not as easy as it is in print design. The main difficulty in selecting a size has to do with monitor resolution. Text on smaller monitors looks different than text on larger monitors; with a bit of forethought, you can correct this. In addition to the monitor resolution issue, you must also consider the way that different web browsers interpret how text is rendered. For example, unlike print, the Web allows users to resize their text manually. Furthermore, there is a growing audience that browses the Web with mobile devices, which makes sizing your text even more important.

Pixels and points are not the best choices

Setting font size in points might come naturally to you if you have worked in print design, or if you have created web graphics, you might be comfortable measuring using pixels. The `font-size` property in CSS allows you to use both forms of measurement. In the following example, the first CSS selector shows you a paragraph rule for points, while the second one shows you a paragraph rule for pixels:

```
p {
    font-size:12pt;
}
```
Points

```
p {
    font-size:12px;
}
```
Pixels

Even though points are supported, it is bad practice to use them and not advised for web design. Points are a system of measurement designed for print, and although available for use, they indicate an absolute unit of measurement and they don't translate well to the screen.

Pixels, on the other hand, are the unit of measurement often used for screen-based graphics. Monitor resolution sizes are measured in pixel units. In an ideal world, designers could reliably use pixel sizes for their fonts because they are relative units and are designed to scale natively. Unfortunately, web browsers such as Internet Explorer 6 and 7 do *not* resize pixel-based text if the user chooses to override the default settings.

Web browsers include a text resize option. This option is often found in the View menu. In some modern browsers, the text-resize option is located in a submenu called Zoom. *Many browsers also use the keyboard shortcut Ctrl + + (plus) and Ctrl + − (minus) to increase and decrease the text size, respectively. On the Mac OS, these shortcuts are Command + + [plus] (and Command + − [minus]).*

Using a combination of percent and the em measurement

Here you will create reliable font sizing using a combination of percents and ems. To get a sense of how these work, you will apply some CSS styling to a page of text for the SmoothieWorld site.

1   In your text editor, choose File > Open and navigate to the HTML5_03lessons folder. Locate the 03_sizing.html file and click OK. This file has four blocks of text: a heading 1 <h1>, a heading 2 <h2>, and two paragraphs <p>. The font-family styles are included from the last exercise as well. You will start by setting different properties for the body to see their effect.

2   Before making any changes, you should know what the page looks like in its default state. Preview the page in your default browser. Browsers need to set some default size for the text if there is no rule defined; in most cases 16 pixels is the value used for the body (in this case, the paragraphs are inheriting the body's value). Close your browser and return to your text editor.

Some browsers allow you to view the default font and font size and even to change it. In Firefox 3 and later, for example, this setting is found in the Content section of the preferences.

3   In the style rule for the body, type the following line:

```
body {
    font-family:"Trebuchet MS", Tahoma, Arial, sans-serif;
    font-size:10px;
}
```

4   Save your file and then preview your page in the browser. Note that all your text is smaller. This is because the body style defines the baseline size for text on your page.

Remember that the HTML body tag contains all the rendered content on the page, so this style is simply targeting your entire page.

5   Return to your text editor and change the following value in your `font-size` property:

`font-size:` **`small`**`;`

6   Again, save your file and preview the page in your browser. All your text is slightly larger than the 10-pixel value you set in step 3. As noted above, the value `small` is an absolute-size unit of measurement called a *keyword*. Web browsers have pre-defined sizes assigned to keywords, and though keywords can be useful because they avoid the whole issue of using units, they often don't offer the level of control that designers prefer.

7   Return to the text editor and change the following value in your `font-size` property:

`font-size:100%;`

8   Save your file and preview the page in your browser. You might notice that there is no difference between this size and the size of the text at the beginning of the exercise (when no `font-size` was defined). This step explicitly defines the `font-size` for the body to be the same size as the browser-defined `font-size`.

You will have to take a small leap of faith here and realize that the technique you are learning addresses some particular resizing problems in two popular web browsers (IE6 and IE7). Taking care of these problems now will mean fewer problems in the future.

9   In the style rule for the paragraph, type the following line:

```
p {
    font-size:1em;
}
```

The unit of measurement called an *em* is very similar to pixels in that it is designed to scale; the main difference is that ems are not tied to the monitor resolution, while pixels are related to the monitor resolution. Ems may not be intuitive at first, but understanding how to use them will pay off in the future.

10   Save your file and then preview the file in your browser. Depending on which browser you are using, you will probably not see any changes in your page. This is because an em value of 1 is tied to the `font-size` of 100% that you defined in the body.

It may help to understand this relationship in an equation form: **1 em = 100% = 16 pixels**. Here, the paragraph size is the `1em` value, the `font-size` for the body is 100%, and the default `font-size` for the web browser is 16 pixels. Once you understand this relationship, you can begin to change the value of the em in order to enlarge or reduce the size of your text.

11 Close your browser and return to the text editor. In the rule for the paragraph, change the following value:

```
font-size:0.875em;
```

12 Save your file and preview the page in your browser. Your paragraph text is now smaller. The reason for using the precise 0.875 value is because it is the font-size equivalent to 14 pixels.

If you're starting to think that web design is all about math, don't worry too much. It all gets easier from here. If you are interested in understanding the math more deeply, you multiply the em value (0.875) by the browser's default pixel value (16) to arrive at the 14-pixel number.

13 You will now size your headings using ems as well. For the `h1` property, add the following line:

```
h1 {
    font-size:1.5em;
}
```

This scales the top heading to 1.5 times the size of your body text; in this case, it is the equivalent of 24 pixels. Save your file and preview the page in your browser to see the effect.

Your heading 1 element is set to 1.5em, the equivalent of 24 pixels.

Now the `h1` is approximately the same size as the `h2`, which isn't particularly logical, so you will reduce the size of the `h2` heading as well.

14 For the `h2` property, add the following line:

```
h2 {
    font-size:1.25em;
}
```

This scales the top heading to 1.25 times the size of your body text, which is the equivalent of 20 pixels.

15 Save your file and preview it in the browser. You now have text proportioned as needed.

Remember that one of the main reasons why ems are used is to adjust for users who resize the text in their browser. You can simulate this by going into your browser and enlarging the text size. You can see that the text responds well to this enlarging and reducing. When you are finished, be sure to return the text size to the default setting. Most browsers have a command to allow you to do this.

The issue of browsers resizing text is a bit more complicated because some browsers use a zoom feature that increases or decreases magnification of the entire page. Zoom-enabled browsers may also have a text-only resize option.

There is another benefit of using ems, and this has to do with the scaling relationship between all elements that use ems.

16 In your body property, modify the following value:

```
font-size:85%;
```

17 Save your file and preview your page. All your text is now smaller, even though you just changed one value! This is because of the linked relationship the em has to the body element. Some designers adjust this base size if, for example, a client wants larger or smaller text across the entire site. Rather than modifying all the individual properties, having one rule control multiple font-sizes makes it easy to do.

18 Return the `font-size` value to the original 100% value:

```
font-size:100%;
```

Save your document.

Pixels-to-em conversion table

The following chart can help you make easy conversions from pixels to ems. Keep in mind that this chart is based on two constants: that your default browser text size is 16 pixels and that your body `font-size` is set to 100%.

Pixel font-size	Em equivalent
11	0.689
12	0.750
13	0.814
14	0.875
15	0.938
16	1.000
17	1.064
18	1.125
19	1.188
20	1.250
21	1.313
22	1.375
23	1.438
24	1.500
25	1.563
26	1.625
27	1.688
28	1.750

There are also free pixel-to-em calculators to help you with on-the-fly conversions:

- *http://pxtoem.com/*
- *http://jameswhittaker.com/projects/apps/em-calculator-air-application/*

Using margins to modify the space between your text

In this exercise, you will work with the CSS `margin` property in order to change the amount of space between your various text elements. Understanding how the `margin` property works and how to control it is key to understanding CSS, and in fact is the first step toward CSS layout. In order to better understand all the effects of using margins for text, you will first add the `margin` property to your body style.

1   In the body style, add the following line:

```
body {
    font-family:"Trebuchet MS", Tahoma, Arial, sans-serif;
    font-size:100%;
    margin:0 20%;
}
```

This `margin` property sets the margins of the page in shortcut form. The 0 value is for the top and bottom margins. The 20% value is for the left and right margins.

2   Save your page and preview it in your browser. You can see that your text is centered in your browser window. Change the width of your browser window and you see the text reflow.

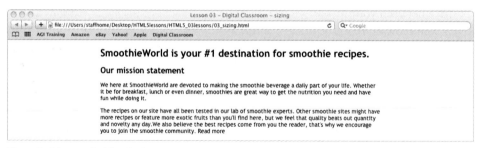

The result of changing the left and right margins of the body to 20%.

Return to your text editor.

You will now work further with margins in order to begin controlling the space between your elements. First, you will add temporary borders to your text elements in order to better understand how margins work.

3   In the style for your paragraph element, add the following lines:

```
p {
    font-family:Georgia, "Times New Roman", Times, serif;
    font-size:0.875em;
    border:thin red solid;
}
```

This is the CSS `border` property, which allows you to add borders around your elements. You will eventually use borders as decoration in your layout, but here they are being used to help you understand how elements, such as headings and paragraphs, interact with each other. You will now add this same code to your `h1` and `h2` elements.

4   Select the `border:thin red solid;` code from your paragraph rule and press Ctrl + C (PC) or Command + C (Mac) to copy the code.

5   Click inside the `h1` style and press Ctrl + V (PC) or Command + V (Mac) to paste the code. Repeat this step for the `h2` style.

6   Save your file and preview it in your browser. With the red borders applied, you can now see the space between the elements more clearly.

> **SmoothieWorld is your #1 destination for smoothie recipes.**
>
> **Our mission statement**
>
> We here at SmoothieWorld are devoted to making the smoothie beverage a daily part of your life. Whether it be for breakfast, lunch or even dinner, smoothies are great way to get the nutrition you need and have fun while doing it.
>
> The recipes on our site have all been tested in our lab of smoothie experts. Other smoothie sites might have more recipes or feature more exotic fruits than you'll find here, but we feel that quality beats out quantity and novelty any day. We also believe the best recipes come from you the reader, that's why we encourage you to join the smoothie community. Read more

Applying borders to your elements helps you see the default margins more clearly.

This space between your paragraphs and headings is a result of the default margins as defined by your web browser. You have learned about browser defaults before in the `font-size` exercise, and this is very similar. HTML elements have default styles associated with them that include properties such as pixel size, margins, bold styling, italic styling, and many others. You need to set specific rules to override the default styles for these properties. In this case, you will adjust the space between the heading 2 and the first paragraph.

7   Return to your text editor and add the following line to your h2 element:

```
h2 {
    font-size:1.25em;
    border:thin red solid;
    margin-bottom:0em;
}
```

The `margin-bottom` property affects the margin spacing on the bottom of the h2 element only. This is not enough to affect the spacing between your heading and the paragraph. You also need to set the top margin of the paragraph.

8   Add the following code to your p element:

```
margin-top:0em;
```

9   Save your file and preview it in the browser.

> **SmoothieWorld is your #1 destination for smoothie recipes.**
>
> **Our mission statement**
> We here at SmoothieWorld are devoted to making the smoothie beverage a daily part of your life. Whether it be for breakfast, lunch or even dinner, smoothies are great way to get the nutrition you need and have fun while doing it.
>
> The recipes on our site have all been tested in our lab of smoothie experts. Other smoothie sites might have more recipes or feature more exotic fruits than you'll find here, but we feel that quality beats out quantity and novelty any day. We also believe the best recipes come from you the reader, that's why we encourage you to join the smoothie community. Read more

With the bottom margin of the heading and the top margin of the paragraph set to 0, the space between them has collapsed.

You can now see that the space between your heading 2 and the first paragraph has collapsed. To increase space between elements, you can increase margin values. For example, you will now increase the space between your paragraphs.

10   Add the following code to your paragraph (p) element:

```
margin-bottom:1.5em;
```

Remember that 1 em in this style sheet is equal to 16 pixels, so setting a value of 1.5 ems is the same as adding 24 pixels.

11   Save your file and preview it in the browser.

You can now see the space between your paragraphs increase. At this point, the borders around the elements have served their purpose; you don't want to lose them completely, so you will comment them out. Commenting is a process that deactivates a style without removing the code.

12   Add the following code to the border rule in your paragraph element:

```
/*border:thin red solid;*/
```

The forward slash and the asterisk at the beginning and end of the code will disable this rule. The original code is always available in case you want to enable these borders again.

13 Repeat step 12 by adding the commenting code to the two other `border` properties in your `h1` and `h2` styles.

14 Save your file and view the page in your browser to see your page without any borders.

The final result of modifying your margins by deactivating the borders.

Setting paragraph `line-height`

To improve readability of your text, you can change `line-height`, which is the amount of space between lines. In the world of print design this is called *leading*, but the concept here is the same: changing the amount of space between sentences can affect the readability of your text. A `line-height` that is too small results in cramped text, while a `line-height` that is too high risks losing the reader's focus. Unfortunately, you can't just set a universal `line-height` value and be done with it; `line-height` is connected to a number of factors, including the amount of text and the width of the text block, as well as the color, size, and choice of font. In this exercise, you will set the `line-height` of your current paragraphs.

1 Add the following code to your `p` element:

```
p {
    font-family:Georgia, "Times New Roman", Times, serif;
    font-size:0.875em;
    /*border:thin red solid;*/
    margin-top:0em;
    margin-bottom:1.5em;
    line-height:1.75em;
}
```

2   Save your file and preview it in your browser. You now have extra space between the lines in your paragraph.

> **SmoothieWorld is your #1 destination for smoothie recipes.**
>
> **Our mission statement**
> We here at SmoothieWorld are devoted to making the smoothie beverage a daily part of your life. Whether it be for breakfast, lunch or even dinner, smoothies are great way to get the nutrition you need and have fun while doing it.
>
> The recipes on our site have all been tested in our lab of smoothie experts. Other smoothie sites might have more recipes or feature more exotic fruits than you'll find here, but we feel that quality beats out quantity and novelty any day. We also believe the best recipes come from you the reader, that's why we encourage you to join the smoothie community. Read more

Increasing the line-height values will increase the amount of space between paragraph lines.

`Line-height` works on any multiple-line body of text. For example, if your heading 1 SmoothieCentral is your #1 destination for smoothie recipes is broken over multiple lines, you can set the `line-height`.

3   Add the following code to your `h1` element:

```
line-height:1.5em;
```

4   Save your file and preview it in your browser.

Depending on your monitor resolution, you may need to narrow the width of your browser in order to force the heading to break. The type in the heading is much larger than the paragraph, so it wouldn't do as well with the same `line-height` value.

You can feel free to override the browser defaults in order to control the look of your page.

Transforming text with CSS

As discussed earlier, the lack of choices when it comes to type (or text) on the Web is a bit constraining; fortunately, you have other options. There are a number of CSS properties that allow you to control the appearance of your text in visually interesting ways. In this exercise, you will work with several styling techniques to create unique headings for your page, including `font-weight`, `text-transform`, and `letter-spacing`.

The first setting you will modify is the `font-weight` for your main heading in order to decrease the thickness of the characters.

1   Add the following code to your `h1` element:

```
h1 {
    /*border:thin red solid;*/
    font-size:1.5em;
    line-height:1.5em;
    font-weight:normal;
}
```

2   Save your file and preview the page in your browser.

By setting the `font-weight` to normal, you have decreased the thickness of the heading. The default browser styling for a heading 1 is actually bold, so you are essentially resetting this bold style to normal. The default browser styling for all headings is bold, and you can see this by comparing the styles of your heading 1 to your heading 2. The heading 2 has thicker letterforms and, even though it is smaller in size, it appears more dominant on the screen.

There are additional values for the `font-weight` property. Here, you'll lighten the value for the heading 2, and then add a new `text-transform` property.

3   Add the following code to your `h2` element:

```
font-weight:lighter;
text-transform:uppercase;
```

The value *lighter* for the `font-weight` reduces the thickness of the letterforms further, and the value for `text-transform` converts your text to uppercase.

4   Save your file and preview the page in your browser.

Your heading is now in uppercase. This is a good example of how CSS controls style. The HTML code shows that the source text is still lowercase; the display of the characters is controlled by the CSS.

5   Return to your text editor and add the following code to the same `h2` style:

```
letter-spacing:0.2em;
```

`Letter-spacing` controls the amount of space between characters. In print design this is called *kerning* and *tracking*. Save your page and preview the page in your browser. By increasing letter-spacing, you can add a bit more space around the letters in condensed headlines. You should be careful about adding too much `letter-spacing`, as it can make headlines harder to read.

It is even possible to set negative values for most of these CSS properties (`letter-spacing: -0.4em`, for example), although you will not be doing this as often. Experiment with different combinations of fonts and styles, and you might be surprised with what you can come up with.

Often times, experimenting with styles such as `text-transform` and `letter-spacing` will require you to return to your initial `font-size`. In your heading 2, for example, using all capital letters makes the heading look bigger, so you will reduce the size a bit.

6 Modify the `font-size` value of your h2 style as follows:

`font-size:1.125em;`

7 Save and close your file.

Working with HTML lists

Lists are found on many web pages and it is important that you learn how to control their appearance. Examples of where you might find lists include recipes, frequently asked questions, and navigation menus. In this exercise, you will learn the three categories of lists and how to control their styles. The three categories are *unordered lists*, *ordered lists,* and *definition lists*.

Unordered lists are also called bulleted lists because the default style adds a bullet to the left of each item in the list. Ordered lists are also called numbered lists because the default style adds a number to the left of each item in the list. Definition lists have two default styles: a bold style for a definition term and an indented style for the definition description.

1 In your text editor, choose File > Open and navigate to the HTML5_03lessons folder. Locate the 03_lists.html file and click OK. This file has the styled text from the previous exercise, as well as three new paragraphs that you will be converting to lists.

   Before starting on the exercise, note a few changes that are made to the new <h3> style. In this example, you want all the attributes of the h2 without having to write them again, so a comma and the code h3 are added to the h2 selector. Because the h3 element needs to be smaller, a new `font-size` property of `0.875em` is set. To adjust the `letter-spacing`, this property is set to `0.1em`. Because these are the only two properties for h3, they override the properties for h2.

2   Preview the page in your browser to see the default paragraph styling. Keep this formatting in mind as you begin converting the paragraphs to lists. Close your browser and return to your text editor.

SmoothieWorld is your #1 destination for smoothie recipes.

OUR MISSION STATEMENT
We here at SmoothieWorld are devoted to making the smoothie beverage a daily part of your life. Whether it be for breakfast, lunch or even dinner, smoothies are great way to get the nutrition you need and have fun while doing it.

The recipes on our site have all been tested in our lab of smoothie experts. Other smoothie sites might have more recipes or feature more exotic fruits than you'll find here, but we feel that quality beats out quantity and novelty any day. We also believe the best recipes come from you the reader, that's why we encourage you to join the smoothie community. Read more

RECIPE OF THE DAY: HONEYDEW MELON
3 cups Honeydew Melon (seeded & chopped) 2 tsp Lime Juice 1 cup Vanilla Nonfat Yogurt 1 cup Ice Cubes

Take a blender, add honeydew melon and watermelon; blend until it smoothens. Mix yogurt, ice and limejuice and blend it again. Transfer it into tall glasses and drink it immediately.

Preparation time 10 Minutes Number of servings (12 oz) 2 Calories per serving 250. 295 if 1 tbs sugar added 315 if 1 tbs honey added

---

You will convert the last three paragraphs to lists.

3   In the list of ingredients in the first paragraph, change the opening `<p>` and closing `</p>` paragraph tags to an opening `<ul>` and closing `</ul>` unordered list tag to change this element to an unordered list.

You now need to separate the ingredients into list items. The `<ul>` tag is rarely used by itself, as the whole purpose of lists is to have separate items.

4   Add an opening `<li>` tag at the beginning of the first line and a closing `</li>` tag at the end:

```
<ul>
    <li>3 cups Honeydew Melon (seeded & chopped) </li>
    2 tsp Lime Juice
    1 cup Vanilla Yogurt
    1 cup Ice Cubes
</ul>
```

Preview this page in your browser and note the bullet point on the first line. Close your browser.

5   Repeat step 4, and add the list tags to the next three ingredients. Each list item will have its own bullet point.

Now you'll convert the next paragraph, which describes the steps for making the smoothie, into an ordered list.

6   In the next paragraph, change the opening <p> and closing </p> paragraph tags to opening <ol> and closing </ol> ordered list tags to change this element to an ordered list. Then, as in steps 4 and 5, add <li> tags to create three list items:

```
<ol>
    <li>Take a blender, add honeydew melon and watermelon; blend
until it smoothens.</li>
    <li>Mix yogurt, ice and lime juice and blend it again.</li>
    <li>Transfer it into tall glasses and drink it immediately.</li>
</ol>
```

7   Save your file and then preview it in the browser. The ordered list now displays numbers for each list item.

RECIPE OF THE DAY: HONEYDEW MELON

- 3 cups Honeydew Melon (seeded & chopped)
- 2 tsp Lime Juice
- 1 cup Vanilla Nonfat Yogurt
- 1 cup Ice Cubes

1. Take a blender, add honeydew melon and watermelon; blend until it smoothens.
2. Mix yogurt, ice and limejuice and blend it again.
3. Transfer it into tall glasses and drink it immediately

Preparation time 10 Minutes Number of servings (12 oz) 2 Calories per serving 250. 295 if 1 tbs sugar added 315 if 1 tbs honey added

---

The second paragraph has been converted to an ordered (or numbered) list.

Close the browser and return to your text editor.

One of the advantages of ordered lists is that the numbers are rendered in the browser. This allows you to add or remove list items in your HTML and to not have to worry about keeping track of the numbers.

8   Add the following line between list items 2 and 3:

```
<li> Sample your smoothie and add honey or sugar if needed. Blend
again.</li>
```

Save the file and preview it in your browser. Note that the steps have automatically been renumbered. Close your browser and return to your text editor. Now you'll convert the last paragraph into a definition list.

9   In the last paragraph, change the opening <p> and closing </p> paragraph tags to opening <dl> and closing </dl> definition list tags to change this element to a definition list.

Definition lists are used less often than ordered and unordered lists. One way to think of them is to visualize a listing in a dictionary. A dictionary is just a big list of words; for any given word, there may be a number of different definitions. A definition list has two types of list items: the definition term <dt> and the definition description <dd>.

10   Add the following code to separate this list into terms and descriptions:

```
<dl>
    <dt>Preparation time</dt>
    <dd>10 Minutes</dd>
    <dt>Number of servings (12 oz)</dt>
    <dd>2</dd>
    <dt>Calories per serving</dt>
    <dd>250</dd>
    <dd>295 if 1 tbs sugar added</dd>
    <dd>315 if 1 tbs honey added</dd>
</dl>
```

Save the file and preview it in your browser. The definition terms act as a type of a heading with the definition description indented below. Note that you may have multiple descriptions, as you can see in the last definition term for Calories.

Styling HTML lists

You can easily modify the styling for lists with CSS. The indentation and spacing of a list (as well as the list items) are controlled by margins and padding. There are also a few CSS properties that are unique to lists; for example, later in this exercise, you will learn how to customize the bullet appearance in the unordered list. First, it's important to understand the default styles of both the parent list and the list items. A specific goal of this exercise is to make you aware of the differences between margins and padding; these two properties are often confused by beginners and your future as a web designer will be much happier if you avoid this confusion!

One thing you may have noticed is that all your lists are bigger than your paragraphs, and they also have a different font family. This is because you have not set any rules for them yet, so they are inheriting their style from the body. As you go through styling each list, you will add font-size and other properties as needed.

1   Type the following code to add a `font-size` as well as a new background color to the unordered list style:

```
ul {
    font-size:0.875em;
    background-color:#E5DAB3;
}
```

2   Save the file and preview it in your browser. You can see that the background color defines the area of the unordered list. Although you can use background colors to make your lists more attractive, here you are using a background color to illustrate how lists work. Close your browser. You will now style the list items.

> **RECIPE OF THE DAY: HONEYDEW MELON**
>
> - 3 cups Honeydew Melon (seeded & chopped)
> - 2 tsp Lime Juice
> - 1 cup Vanilla Nonfat Yogurt
> - 1 cup Ice Cubes

Using a `background-color` *helps you see the boundaries of the* `ul` *element.*

3   Add this code to the empty list item style:

```
li {
    background-color:#AA6C7E;
}
```

Save the file and preview it in your browser.

You can see that the background color of the list items overrides the color of the unordered list, but it's not a complete overlap; the list item `background-color` stops at the bullet points (and at the numbers in the ordered list). Equally important is the fact that both the unordered list and the ordered list use `<li>` tags, so they are all styled equally. If you want to specifically change the color of the list items in the unordered list, you must target them with a more specific rule.

4   Add this entire section of code to create a specific rule for list items in an unordered list only:

```
ul li {
    background-color:#ABC8A5;
}
```

This rule is known as a *descendant selector* because the list item is a descendant of the unordered list in your HTML. Because this rule is more specific, the rules of CSS state that it will override the more general rule for the `<li>` element.

5   Save the file and preview it in your browser. The background color for the list items in the unordered list is green because of that `ul li` rule, while the background color for the ordered list is purple based on the `li` rule.

RECIPE OF THE DAY: HONEYDEW MELON

- 3 cups Honeydew Melon (seeded & chopped)
- 2 tsp Lime Juice
- 1 cup Vanilla Nonfat Yogurt
- 1 cup Ice Cubes

1. Take a blender, add honeydew melon and watermelon; blend until it smoothens.
2. Mix yogurt, ice and limejuice and blend it again.
3. Transfer it into tall glasses and drink it immediately

Only the list items in your unordered list are colored green.

6   Close your browser and return to your text editor. You'll now focus on controlling the spacing of your lists. First you'll correct the fact that your ordered list is bigger than your unordered list by adding a `font-size` property.

7   Add the following code to make the ordered list the same size:

```
ol {
    font-size:0.875em;
}
```

In order to add space between the unordered list and the ordered list, you can add a bottom margin to the unordered list:

```
ul {
    font-size:0.875em;
    background-color:#E5DAB3;
    margin-bottom:2em;
}
```

This works much like the earlier exercises where you controlled the space between your headings and paragraph. However, it is also important that you understand the role of padding when it comes to lists.

8 Add the following code to your `ul` style:

```
padding-left:0em;
```

Save the file and preview the page in your browser.

> **RECIPE OF THE DAY:HONEYDEW MELON**
>
> - 3 cups Honeydew Melon (seeded & chopped)
> - 2 tsp Lime Juice
> - 1 cup Vanilla Nonfat Yogurt
> - 1 cup Ice Cubes

The unordered list with a left padding of 0 places the bullet points outside the box by default.

By zeroing-out the left padding, you collapse the default padding; all the list items shift to the left, and the bullet points are now hanging outside the unordered list! Close the browser and return to your text editor. Using a CSS rule, you can force the bullet points to be inside the unordered list.

9 Add the following code to your `ul` style:

```
list-style-position:inside;
```

This causes the bullets to be nested within the unordered list.

10 The spacing of lists is also determined by the margins and padding of the individual list items. Here you will modify both properties of the unordered list in order to see the difference. First you will add a top margin value:

```
ul li {
    background-color:#ABC8A5;
    margin-top:1em;
}
```

Save the file and preview it in your browser. `Margin-top` adds 1 em of space to the top of each list item. Because the margin value adds space on the outside of an element, you see the `background-color` of the unordered list.

Now you'll add padding to the ordered list.

12 Add the following code:

```
ol li {
    padding-top:10px;
}
```

13 Save the file and preview it in your browser.

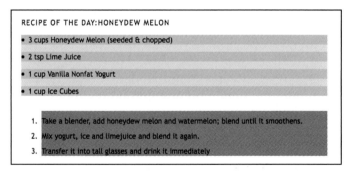

RECIPE OF THE DAY: HONEYDEW MELON

- 3 cups Honeydew Melon (seeded & chopped)
- 2 tsp Lime Juice
- 1 cup Vanilla Nonfat Yogurt
- 1 cup Ice Cubes

1. Take a blender, add honeydew melon and watermelon; blend until it smoothens.
2. Mix yogurt, ice and limejuice and blend it again.
3. Transfer it into tall glasses and drink it immediately

The list items in the first list are spaced using margins, while the list items in the second list are spaced using padding.

`Padding-top` adds 1 em of space to the top of each list item, but because padding adds space to the inside of an element, you do not see the background color.

14 Return to your text editor and comment out all three of your background color properties.

15 Save the file and preview it in your browser.

Notice that without the background colors, it would be impossible to know that the spacing of the first list used margins and the spacing of the second list used padding. Using margins and padding indiscriminately can lead to problems, especially as your lists become more complicated.

In this lesson, you learned the different ways you can set the `font-size` of your text with an emphasis on using the em unit of measurement. You also learned how to control the appearance of your text with CSS properties, including `margins`, `padding`, `line-height`, `text-transform`, `letter-spacing`, and `font-weight`. Finally, you learned the three types of HTML lists and how to style them.

This lesson involved the most coding you have done up to this point. If you would like to compare your work with a finished version, open the final page, named 03_final.html, which is located in your HTML5_03lessons folder.

Self study

To practice styling lists, create new style rules for the definition list. Here are some ideas to help you get started:

1 Make the entire definition list smaller than the other two lists and create an italic style for the definition definitions `<dd>`.

2 Experiment with some of the other properties you learned in this lesson, such as `text-transform`, `letter-spacing`, and so on.

3 Remember that with definition lists, you have an extra item to work with (the `<dt>` element).

Review

Questions

1 What is the em measurement when referring to `font-size`? What are its advantages?

2 Jennifer has defined the paragraph rule in her CSS the following way:

```
p {
    font-family:Baskerville;
}
```

Is this the best way for her to define her paragraph style? Explain your answer.

3 What is the best way to increase or decrease space between two text blocks (for example, the space between a heading and a paragraph)?

Answers

1 The em as it applies to `font-size` in CSS is a relative unit of measurement. A unit of 1 em is equivalent to the default `font-size` of the web browser (traditionally 16 pixels). Because em units are relative, they scale well when resized in a browser. They also allow the designer to link elements such as paragraphs and headings to a specific value in the body. This allows for easy resizing of text if needed.

2 This is not the best way for Jennifer to define her paragraph style. Because fonts defined in a style sheet only appear on the user's page if they have the font installed on their system, it is best to use a font-stack. A font-stack lists two or more fonts in the preferred order of display (based on their availability on the user's system). Furthermore, this font-stack should include fonts that are generally accepted as being on most systems.

3 The best way to increase or decrease space between two text blocks is to use `margins`, `padding`, or some combination of the two. All CSS elements are based on a box model, and the space *outside* of the element is controlled by an invisible margin on all four sides. The space *inside* the element is controlled by invisible padding. In the case of a paragraph that is below a heading, you would only need to set the top or bottom values, not the right or left values.

What you'll learn in this lesson:

- Understanding CSS reset files

- An overview of CSS layout options

- How to use margins and padding to add space to your pages

- Working with the `float` and `clear` properties

Introduction to CSS Layout

In this lesson, you will learn the fundamentals of how to create a two column, fixed-width CSS layout.

Starting up

You will work with several files from the HTML5_04lessons folder in this lesson. Make sure you have loaded the HTML5lessons folder onto your hard drive from the supplied DVD. See "Loading lesson files" in the Starting Up section of this book.

See Lesson 4 in action!

Use the accompanying video to gain a better understanding of how to use some of the capabilities shown in this lesson. The video tutorial for this lesson can be found on the included DVD.

The examples in this lesson use the TextWrangler text editor to create the HTML markup, but you can use any text editor and achieve the same results.

Working with a CSS reset file

Before you start building your page layout, you will learn to use a CSS reset file. In Lesson 3, you learned that virtually all HTML elements (such as paragraphs and headings) have default styles rendered by the browser. For example, the heading 1 default style has top and bottom margins of 10 pixels. If you want to style a heading so there is no margin, you must explicitly set the style rules to zero.

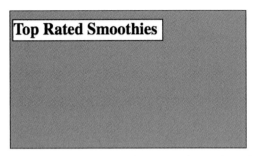
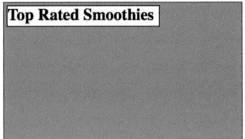

On the left is a heading 1 with default margins of 10 pixels. On the right is a heading 1 with the margins set to zero.

The CSS rule for setting the margins to zero is as follows:

```
h1 {
    margin-top:0px;
    margin-bottom:0px;
}
```

All HTML elements have default margins; unfortunately, web browsers use their own rules for rendering content, and interpret the appearance of these margins differently. For example, the 10-pixel margin in browser A might be rendered as 15 pixels in browser B. These differences can introduce inconsistencies in your page layouts. Fortunately, you can use the CSS reset file to remove the default styles from the most commonly used HTML elements. With the CSS styles reset, you have a reliable and consistent foundation on which to base your new styles. To get a better sense of how styles work, open a page that contains a number of default styles and link the CSS reset style sheet to this page.

1   In your text editor, choose File > Open. In the dialog box that appears, navigate to the HTML5_04lessons folder, choose the 04_reset.html file, and click Open.

    This file has a number of generic HTML elements, such as headings, paragraphs, lists, and forms; it has no CSS styles.

2   Preview the page in your web browser and notice the space between the headings as well as the appearance of the lists and the form. Your next step will be to a link to your CSS reset style sheet to see how this affects the appearance of these elements. Close your web browser and return to your text editor.

3   Add the following line of code to attach the reset.css style sheet located in the HTML5_04lessons folder:

```
<head>
    <meta charset="utf-8" />
    <title>Digital Classroom Lesson 04 CSS Reset</title>
    <link href="reset.css" rel="stylesheet" type="text/css">
</head>
```

Save the file and preview it in your browser.

```
Heading 1
Heading 2
Heading 3
Heading 4
Heading 5
Heading 6

Lorem ipsum dolor sit amet, test link adipiscing elit. This is strong. Nullam dignissim conv
Nunc iaculis suscipit dui. Nam sit amet sem. Aliquam libero nisi, imperdiet at, tincidunt ne
eget sapien fringilla nonummy. Mauris a ante. Suspendisse quam sem, This is small conseq
quis tellus.
HTML and CSS are our tools. Mauris a ante. Suspendisse quam sem, consequat at, commo
Praesent mattis, massa quis luctus fermentum, turpis mi volutpat justo, eu volutpat enim di

List Types
Definition List
Definition List Title
This is a definition list division.
Definition
Another dd tag>
Ordered List
List Item 1
List Item 2
Nested list item A
Nested list item B
List Item 3
Unordered List
List Item 1
List Item 2
Nested list item A
Nested list item B
List Item 3

Table
    The caption tag defines the caption of a table
Table Header 1  Table Header 2  Table Header 3
Cell 1          Cell 2          Cell 3
Cell 1          Cell 2          Cell 3
Cell 1          Cell 2          Cell 3
```

A page of common HTML elements that have been reset.

Many of the elements on your page have had the margins and padding set to zero. As a result, all the space between them has collapsed. There are a number of other reset styles; for example, your list-styles are set to "none," which removes the default bullet points from unordered lists and the numbers from ordered lists. Close your browser and return to your text editor.

4   Choose File > Open. In the dialog box that appears, select the reset.css file and click Open. Take a few moments to look through the file.

This group of rules removes the default margins, padding, and borders from most of your HTML elements.

You will not change this style sheet, but will attach it to your pages. Remember that reset style sheets are optional. They help standardize your layout across browsers, and some designers also add their most frequently used styles to their reset style sheets.

Extending the reset style sheet

Eric Meyer was the first designer to develop reset style sheets, which he then released into the public domain. You will use his style rules in this exercise. For more information on the reset technique, visit *http://meyerweb.com/eric/thoughts/2007/04/18/reset-reasoning/*.

Many designers customize this reset style sheet to fit their needs. For example, if the most common font-family you use is Verdana, you can add this rule to your body style. If you like more space between the lines in your paragraphs, you can set a standard line-height value that best works for you. The point is to have a consistent set of rules that you can use to quickly start up a project.

Using CSS reset style sheets has some potential disadvantages, especially for beginners: you must constantly remember that the reset style sheet is there and be aware of how it affects the appearance of different elements in your site. If you are using the reset style sheet across the entire site, you might be surprised by some of its effects, especially when using elements you are not familiar with. For example, a CSS reset file strips out the margins and padding for most form elements, and when you start working with forms for the first time, you might be confused as to why your buttons, form fields, and other elements appear the way they do.

A brief history of layout techniques on the Web

Although you will be learning how to build your page layout using CSS styles, you should note that this was not always a standard practice. As web design developed in the mid-1990s, the only method available for sophisticated page layout, such as adding multiple columns to a page, was to use the HTML `<table>` tag. The HTML table was originally designed to present data in a logical format using rows, columns, and cells.

Designers adopted this table element and used it as the foundation for their page structure. At the time, this technique made perfect sense: tables were the only tool available to create the sort of designs required at the time.

Designers often used techniques such as nesting tables. For example, the code for a standard two-column page might start with a table consisting of three rows and two columns.

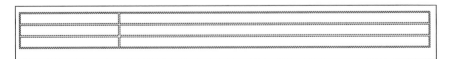

A three-row and two-column table.

Because the first row would become a header section, the column being defined would be in the way. The HTML `<colspan>` tag allowed the designer to merge the two cells.

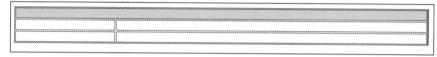

A table with two merged cells in the first row.

In this merged first row, a designer might want an independent three-column section for a logo and other elements, such as navigation or a user login. To add this section, the designer would add a new table (with three columns) into the top row.

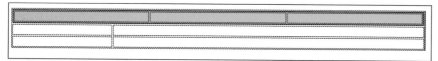

Nesting a new three-column table into the top row of the original table.

To give this table structure, the designer might set the original table to a fixed width and height. Assume the designer also wanted a thin, black border around the entire layout. The border property for HTML tables is very basic and does not allow the addition of colors. One common solution was to insert the existing table into another table, which would consist of a single cell with a background color of black. By modifying the padding and background color and merging additional cells, the designer was able to create a table-based layout with some basic styling.

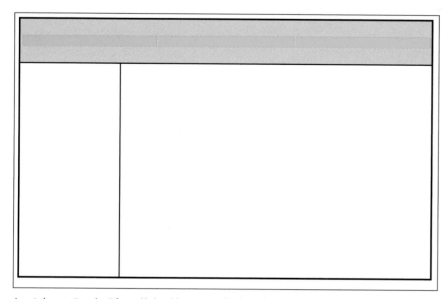

A typical empty "template" for a table-based layout as rendered in a browser.

This review of web layout is relevant today because a vast number of websites were built and continue to be built using the table method. CSS has been replacing the use of tables for page layout, but the process is a slow, gradual one. Table layouts have an advantage of being reverse-compatible with older browsers. This advantage has diminished as people update to newer browsers.

CSS layouts were also not well supported (if at all) in early web browsers, and so for web designers, there was no real incentive to discard table layout techniques for CSS layout. One of the disadvantages of table-based layouts was the amount and type of code required to build a page. The layout described in the previous paragraphs would have required code similar to the following:

```
<table width="799" border="0" cellspacing="1" cellpadding="1">
    <tr>
        <td bgcolor="#000000">
        <table width="800" height="485" border="0">
            <tr>
            <td height="81" colspan="2" bgcolor="#CCCCCC">
            <table width="100%" border="0">
                <tr>
                    <td bgcolor="#FF9966"> </td>
                    <td bgcolor="#FF9966"> </td>
                    <td bgcolor="#FF9966"> </td>
                </tr>
            </table>
            </td>
            </tr>
            <tr>
                <td width="191" bgcolor="#FFFFFF"> </td>
                <td width="599" bgcolor="#FFFFFF"> </td>
            </tr>
        </table>
        </td>
    </tr>
</table>
```

This is a relatively simple layout with no content or navigation. Defining the relationship between all the various elements is very confusing, and it requires multiple lines of code.

 If you want to look at this code in your text editor, you can find it in the 04_table.html file within the HTML5_04lessons folder.

Remember that one of the main goals of CSS was to separate the style from the structure of HTML. In the table code above, note that values for width and height, as well as the background color and a few other values, are embedded within the HTML. Although this practice was unavoidable before CSS, you can now set these values using CSS.

The HTML table element is slowly returning to its original function of presenting data, and not being used for layout. You might still find examples of these layouts on the Web, but you will not learn to build them in this book. Instead, you will learn the basics of layout using CSS.

An overview of page layout options

Before building a page layout, there are a few decisions you should make. The first is the width of the layout. There are two main categories of layout widths: *fixed-width layouts* and *flexible layouts*. Fixed-width layouts are much more common: in a fixed-width layout, all page elements are nested within a container that has an explicit width (in this example, you will use 960 pixels, but the unit of measurement is often in ems as well). A fixed-width layout is useful for the designer because it offers a way to reliably position the various layout elements (such as headers, sidebars, and footers). It also provides a reliable structure for elements, such as the width of a paragraph on a page or the placement of images.

Fixed-width layouts have explicit widths and have a defined space on a web page.

Flexible layouts are so named because they are designed to adapt to the width of the browser window. This style of layout is useful when users have different monitor resolutions, making it impossible to build a fixed-width layout that looks the same on every screen. A properly designed flexible layout can automatically adjust to fit the user's browser window.

Flexible layouts readjust as the browser window changes size.

Flexible layouts are appropriate for the Web because both text and images on a web page can reflow. Mobile devices also make up a substantial proportion of web browsers, and flexible layouts are often better suited to these new interfaces than are fixed-width layouts.

Flexible-width layouts are more difficult to build. There are additional decisions for the designer consider. For this reason, you will learn how to create a fixed-width layout in this lesson. See Lesson 12, *CSS3 Media Queries and the future of CSS3* for more discussion on flexible layouts.

Understanding the `<div>` element: creating a two-column fixed-width CSS layout

In this exercise, you will build a two-column fixed-width layout. To begin, you will work with a basic page that has been set up for you. This page uses a series of HTML `<div>` elements as the basic structure. Think of the `<div>` element as a container into which you'll place logically related elements on a page. Opening and closing `<div>` tags are often placed around other elements on a page, thereby nesting the related items inside the container. You may have multiple `<div>` elements on a page and they are often used to create the layout structure of a page. A `<div>` element often has either a CSS class or ID attribute, which are used to style the container. By using `<div>` elements, you can make it easier for others to identify the sections of your pages, and it can make it easier to control and style a section of a page. Here you will combine the `div` element with CSS IDs.

1   In your text editor, choose File > Open. In the dialog box that appears, navigate to the HTML5_04lessons folder. Select the 04_layoutstart.html file and click OK.

2   Choose File > Save As and name this file 04_layoutwork.html. This preserves the original structure of the page for you. This page has a series of HTML `<div>` elements with some placeholder content. Analyze and style this page to understand how it was set up. The HTML page contains several comments to guide you through the file.

The structure of the page was established for you; you will go through each section to get an understanding of how it works. The first step is to understand the function of the HTML `<div>` tag and its central role in CSS layout.

3   In your HTML, locate the line `<div id="wrap">`. This is the beginning of a section of your page that will nest all your other page elements. By itself, the HTML `<div>` tag does nothing, which makes the tag unique, since all the other HTML elements, such as paragraphs (`<p>`) and lists (`<ul>`, `<li>`, `<dl>`), have some effect on their content.

The `<div>` tag as well as paragraphs and lists, among others, is a block-level element. Block-level elements usually start new lines of text when they are used. The `div` tag is often paired with either a CSS class or a CSS ID. Once you pair the CSS class or ID with a `div` tag, you can begin to add rules to control its appearance. Before doing this, you should take a look at the page before you style it.

4   Preview the page in your browser. The reset.css file you examined earlier is causing the elements on your page to be collapsed.

Top Rated Smoothies
The Funky Orange
Submitted by user iosborn22, this smoothie has recieved over 200 5 star ratings and its **orange juice** and **banana** base make this a great choice for breakfast!
The Tropical KickBack
Submitted by user smoothj282, this smoothie combines the exotic ingredients passionfruit and mango. The result is an invgorating and delicious beverage that is great any time of the day.
SmoothieWorld is your #1 destination for smoothie recipes.
Our mission statement
We here at SmoothieWorld are devoted to making the smoothie beverage a daily part of your life. Whether it be for breakfast, lunch or even dinner, smoothies are great way to get the nutrition you need and have fun while doing it.
The recipes on our site have all been tested in our lab of smoothie experts. Other smoothie sites might have more recipes or feature more exotic fruits than you'll find here, but we feel that quality beats out quantity and novelty any day. We also believe the best recipes come from you the reader, that's why we encourage you to join our smoothie community. Learn more
Footer

This page has a number of pre-built `div` sections and the HTML elements have been reset.

To understand `div` tags, you will style the `wrap` div to begin your fixed-width layout. Close your browser and return to your text editor.

5   Locate the `<style>` tag that was added to your document. Add a style rule for the ID named wrap. The following code shows how:

```
<style type="text/css">
    #wrap {
        background-color:#E0B3B9;
    }
</style>
```

Save the file and then preview it in your browser. The `wrap` div encompasses all the other content on the page, as shown by the background color you added. Currently, this div stretches from one side of the browser to the other. This is a very basic flexible-width layout. Resize your browser window and notice how the text reflows. You will now define the width of the `wrap` div.

6   Return to your text editor and add the following two lines of code to your `#wrap` style:

```
#wrap {
    background-color:#E0B3B9;
    width:960px;
    border:thin solid black;
}
```

Save the page and preview it in your browser. The `wrap` div now occupies 960 pixels of space on your page.

Your wrap *div is now 960 pixels wide and has a thin, black border.*

The border is there to help illustrate the boundaries of the `wrap` div. Resize your browser window again. The text no longer reflows, and if your browser window is narrower than 960 pixels, your content is cropped. When the browser window is wider than 960 pixels, the box defined by the `wrap` div is aligned to the left. There is a simple way to position this div so it will always be centered in the browser window.

7   Return to your text editor and add the following line of code:

```
#wrap {
    background-color:#E0B3B9;
    width:960px;
    border:thin solid black;
    margin:0 auto;
}
```

This is a margin shorthand rule; the value '0' defines the top and bottom margins of the `wrap` div, and the value `auto` defines the left and right margins. The auto value automatically calculates equal amounts of margin on both sides of the `wrap` div. As a result, the box is always centered.

Save the file, and then preview it in your browser to see how the margin shorthand rule works. Close your browser and return to your text editor. You will work with the other `div` elements, but you must first apply a basic style to the header.

8   In your HTML, insert an image into the `masthead` div—in this case, the site's logo. To begin, allow the height of the image to set the height of the `header` div by adding the following code to link to the logo image located in the HTML5_04lessons folder.

```
<div id="masthead">
    <img src="images/smoothieworld_logo.png" width="200" height="150"
alt="smoothieworld_logo" />
</div>
```

The `div` tag has no style, even though the height of the `header` div is controlled by the image. This is why you can see the color of the wrapper, for example, but if you set the background color of the header, it will be visible.

9   Below your rules for #wrap, add the following rule for the `masthead` div:

```
#masthead {
    background-color:#FFF;
}
```

Save the file and preview it in your browser. The entire `masthead` div now has a white background color, and this overrides the background color of the `wrap` div.

Your `masthead` section now has a logo and a background color.

10 The navigation section will require some more advanced work later in this lesson. For now, you will set a few basic style rules in order to define this section on the page. Add the following selector and style rules below the `#masthead` rule:

```
#mainnav {
    background-color:#C2C895;
    height:40px;
}
```

Save your page and preview it in the browser.

Your `mainnav` section with a background color and defined height.

You have now reached the inner wrap section, which contains the sidebar and the main content sections. You will learn to create columns by positioning them with divs. The current CSS specification does not have a column element; "columns" are styled divs that are often taller than they are wide. To understand how columns are made, you need to understand the concept of the CSS `float` property.

Understanding the CSS `float` property

The `float` property in CSS allows text to wrap around an image. This style was borrowed from print design, where the effect is called text wrap or runaround. CSS achieves this effect by allowing elements following a floated element in the HTML markup to surround the element, effectively changing their position. This behavior also makes it possible to create columns on a page.

In the left image below, there is an inline graphic nested inside a paragraph. This is the default behavior of the graphic, as there is no `float` property. In the right image, nothing changes except that the rule `float:right` has been applied to the graphic. The graphic shifts as far to the right as posssible and the text wraps around the left side automatically.

We here at SmoothieWorld are devoted to making the smoothie beverage a daily part of your life. Whether it be for breakfast, lunch or even dinner, smoothies are great way to get the nutrition you need and have fun while doing it.

The recipes on our site have all been tested in our lab of smoothie experts. Other smoothie sites might have more recipes or feature more exotic fruits than you'll find here, but we feel that quality beats out quantity and novelty any day. We also believe the best recipes come from you the reader, that's why we encourage you to join our smoothie community. Learn more.

We here at SmoothieWorld are devoted to making the smoothie beverage a daily part of your life. Whether it be for breakfast, lunch or even dinner, smoothies are great way to get the nutrition you need and have fun while doing it.

The recipes on our site have all been tested in our lab of smoothie experts. Other smoothie sites might have more recipes or feature more exotic fruits than you'll find here, but we feel that quality beats out quantity and novelty any day. We also believe the best recipes come from you the reader, that's why we encourage you to join our smoothie community. Learn more.

An image in the default flow of HTML (left). The same image floated to the right (right).

You can also have a float value of `left`. In the above example, this would place the graphic at the left-most margin and wrap the text on the right.

The only values possible for a float are `left`, `right`, or `none`. You cannot center an object using the `float` property.

If you have multiple floated elements within the same element, they align beside each other. This behavior is often used for common web page features such as horizontal menus or image galleries.

Understanding how multiple floated elements interact with each other is crucial to using them effectively. Consider the following example: there are six images inside a div that is 360 pixels wide. Each image is 50 pixels wide, and also has 10 pixels of margin space (5 on the left and 5 on the right). By adding the values, you can see that 6 × 50 is 300 pixels for the images and 6 × 10 is 60 pixels of margin. Consequently, the images plus the margins fit inside the div, with a total width of 360 pixels.

If you have defined an explicit width for the container, adding another image causes the new image to break to the next row.

This behavior might work well for a thumbnail image gallery, but not for navigation.

| Home | About Us | Recipes | Submit a Recipe |
| Forum | Contact Us | | |

You will learn more about using floats in the next exercise when you build a two-column layout.

Creating columns with the `float` property

You will apply the `float` property to the `sidebar` and `main` content divs to see how they are affected.

1   Add the following selector and style rules below the `#mainnav` rule:

```css
#sidebar {
    float:left;
    width:300px;
    background-color:#CCC;
}
```

Save the page and preview it in your browser. The page has become "broken"; you will learn to recognize the reasons behind a "broken" page such as this one, because this behavior teaches you how floats work.

When you float an element (in this case, the `sidebar` div), it is removed from the normal flow of the HTML. This is why the sidebar extends over the entire container. The two divs that have content are contained within boundaries of the sidebar.

Top Rated Smoothies
The Funky Orange
Submitted by user iosborn22, this smoothie has recieved over 200 5 star ratings and its **orange juice** and **banana** base make this a great choice for breakfast!
The Tropical KickBack
Submitted by user smoothj282, this smoothie combines the exotic ingredients passionfruit and mango. The result is an invgorating and delicious beverage that is great any time of the day.

SmoothieWorld is your #1 destination for smoothie recipes.
Our mission statement
We here at SmoothieWorld are devoted to making the smoothie beverage a daily part of your life. Whether it be for breakfast, lunch or even dinner, smoothies are great way to get the nutrition you need and have fun while doing it.
The recipes on our site have all been tested in our lab of smoothie experts. Other smoothie sites might have more recipes or feature more exotic fruits than you'll find here, but we feel that quality beats out quantity and novelty any day. We also believe the best recipes come from you the reader, that's why we encourage you to join our smoothie community. Learn more
Footer

The sidebar is floated, but is also overlapping the boundaries of other page elements.

This containment can be deceptive because it is affected by the amount of content in each div. To illustrate, you will add more content into the `main` div by duplicating the current paragraph.

2   In your HTML, select the entire paragraph element within the main div and press Ctrl + C (Windows) or Command + C (Mac OS) to copy it. Click once after the element and press Ctrl + V (Windows) or Command + V (Mac OS) to paste it.

3   Save the file and then preview it in your browser. When additional content is added to the `main` div, it expands and pushes the `footer` div downwards. Now the `footer` div appears below the sidebar because there is space for the div above it. Close your browser and return to your text editor.

4   These three divs (`sidebar`, `main`, and `footer`) currently appear to be interdependent. Removing (or adding) content from the sidebar also has an effect. In your HTML, select the "tropical kickback" paragraph within the sidebar and delete it. Save the page and preview it in your browser. Now that the height of the `sidebar` is shorter than both the `footer` and the `main` divs, they "flow" beneath it. This can lead to some layout problems; you will learn strategies for solving these problems in a later section, but now, you will float the main container as well.

5   Close your browser and return to your text editor. Press Ctrl + Z (Windows) or Command + Z (Mac) to undo the deletion of the paragraph in the sidebar. Additionally, select the paragraph in the `main` div that you duplicated in step 2 and delete that as well.

6   Add the following selector and style rules below the `#sidebar` rule:

```
#main {
    width:600px;
    float:right;
    background-color:#ADA446;
}
```

Save the file and preview it in your browser.

The `main` div floats to the right, but the footer has moved upwards in the flow of the page.

Floating this div to the right solves the problem of the content appearing below the `sidebar`; although the amount of content in the `main` div forces it to extend outside the entire container. This is a problem when you consider the `footer` element: footers should appear at the bottom of the page, and this one is not.

To force the `footer` div to the bottom of the page, you will assign a new property called `clear` to this div.

Working with the `clear` property

When you add the CSS `clear` property to an object, you add a rule that says, "No floated elements are allowed to my sides." You can specify whether you want to clear floated elements on the left side, the right side, or both. In the case of the footer, you will choose both.

1   Add a new selector and style rules below your `#main` div:

```css
#footer {
    clear:right;
    background-color:#BA2B22;
}
```

2   Save the file and preview it in your browser. Your footer is now placed at the bottom of the `main` div. This is because the `clear:right` rule does not allow any floated elements to the right of the footer. The `main` div was floated, and so the footer moves to the next available spot on the page. Close your browser and return to your editor.

As in the earlier examples, the amount of content in your divs can affect your floated and cleared elements. For example, if the amount of text in the sidebar expands to the point of reaching the footer, you have a problem again as the sidebar extends outside. For this reason, elements are often set to clear on both sides.

3   Change the value of your `clear` property as follows:

```css
clear:both;
```

This code ensures that no floated elements are allowed on either side of the footer.

Creating a list-based navigation using floats

Now that you have learned the basics of floating and clearing, you will return to your navigation section and add a simple navigation bar based on an unordered list. The list items inside your navigation should be floated to override the default vertical appearance of a list. CSS navigation menus are used frequently in standards-based design because they can easily be updated and modified, and because they are text-based (not images), which improves accessibility in devices such as screen readers and can even help a website's search engine rankings.

1   In your HTML, locate your `mainnav` div and add the following unordered list and list items:

```html
<div id="mainnav">
    <ul>
        <li><a href="index.html">Home</a></li>
        <li><a href="about.html">About Us</a></li>
        <li><a href="recipes.html">Recipes</a></li>
        <li><a href="submitrecipe.html">Submit a Recipe</a></li>
        <li><a href="forum.html">Forum</a></li>
        <li><a href="contact.html">Contact Us</a></li>
    </ul>
</div>
```

The list items are linking to pages that do not exist yet. Nevertheless, you are linking the items because they need to be hyperlinked to be styled correctly.

2   Preview the page in your browser.

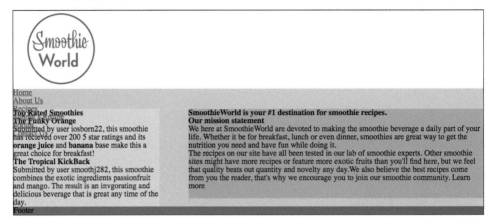

Your list is in the default vertical position and is overlapping your sidebar.

Notice that your page appears "broken" again. This is because your list is overlapping your floated sidebar. Also, the list has no bullet points. Remember that your CSS reset style sheet is attached to this page and one of the rules has a property of `list-style:none`, which removes the bullet points. For this example, the lack of bullet points is acceptable because you are using this list for navigation.

3   Return to your text editor and locate your `#mainnav` rule. Add a new rule between this one and the sidebar by pressing Return a few times to add some space and then adding the following code:

```
#mainnav li {
    float:left;
}
```

This is a new type of CSS rule called a *contextual selector*; it targets *only* list items that are inside the `mainnav` div. If you were to define a new rule just for list items, all the list items on the page would be affected, which would not work for this example.

4   Save the page and preview it in your browser. All the list items are now stacked side by side. Notice that the list inside the main content has not been affected. Add space between the list items and add other styles, as indicated in the following step.

Floating the list items causes them to be stacked side by side.

5   Add the following code to your `mainnav li` rule:

```
#mainnav li {
    float:left;
    width:120px;
    height:25px;
    background-color:#CCC;
    text-align:center;
    border-left:1px black solid;
    border-right:1px black solid;
}
```

In this code, you have done the following: defined the box around each list item as 120 pixels wide by 25 pixels high, added a background color, aligned each list item to the center, and added a border to both sides of the item. Save the file and preview it in your browser.

When you define the width and height of the box, the text naturally sits at the top. Unfortunately, while there is a `text-align:center` property that centers the text horizontally, there is no simple way to *vertically* center objects in CSS. In this case, you will use the `line-height` property to move the nav text downwards.

6 Add the following line of code below your `border-right` declaration:

```
line-height:25px;
```

Save the file and preview it in your browser. Your text is now centered within the box. Remember that the line-height number is based on the font size; it will likely change if you change the font size.

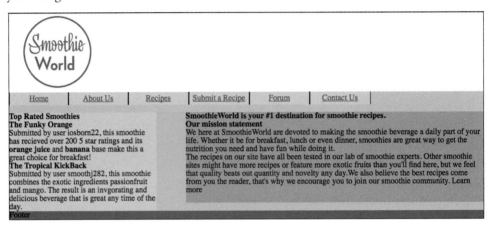

Adding line-height to the list items positions them vertically within the navbar.

Adding text styles

Before continuing with your layout, you will import the text styles you worked on in Lesson 3. Until now, you have added your styles to an internal style sheet instead of an external one. When building a layout, using an internal style sheet is a matter of convenience: creating and modifying style rules is easier to do by scrolling up the page than by accessing an external style sheet. Eventually, you will move the layout rules you have created to an external style sheet. For now, you will attach a style sheet that sets the base rules for elements, such as your headings, lists, and paragraphs.

1 At the top of your HTML, locate the `<link>` tag for your reset.css style sheet. To add another external style sheet, select this line, and then press Ctrl + C (Windows) or Command + C (Mac OS) to copy it. On the next line, press Ctrl + V (Windows) or Command + V (Mac OS) to paste the line. Now replace the value "reset.css" with the following value:

```
<link href="reset.css" rel="stylesheet" type="text/css" />
<link href="base.css" rel="stylesheet" type="text/css" />
```

2   Save the file and then preview it in your browser to see the effect of the new values.

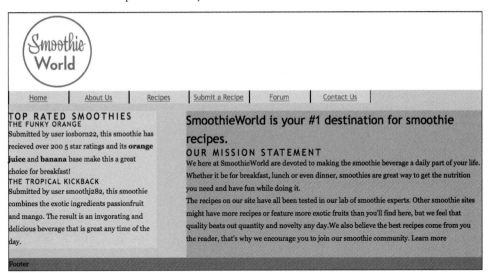

Your page now uses an external style sheet for the text elements.

3   Return to your text editor and choose File > Open. In the dialog box that appears, navigate to your HTML5_04lessons folder, select the base.css file, and click Open. Review the styles in this CSS file. They should be familiar to you from Lesson 3, but the margin and padding styles were removed because these styles made sense in the context of that lesson, but not in the new layout. You can add a style to these elements.

The effect of margins and padding on your fixed-width layout

In this section, you will add space between the sections of text on your page (which have margins of zero from the reset style sheet). You will learn some strategies for controlling the layout. The goal of this exercise is not to show you a single method of CSS layout, but to help you understand the different options, which should help you in your future projects to decide which method to use.

In this first exercise, you will add padding to the `sidebar` element.

1   Preview the page in your browser and notice the lack of space between your text and the edge of your sidebar. Also, notice the width of this sidebar: if you measure it based on the navigation bar above, the sidebar ends approximately one-third of the way through the "Recipe" list item.

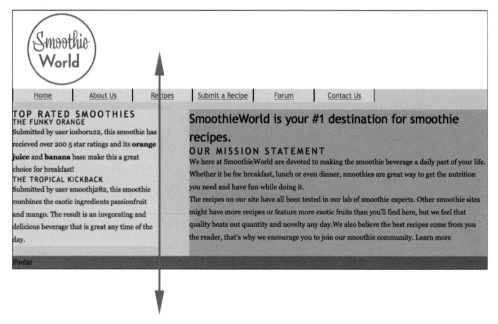

A guide is added in this screenshot to show where the sidebar ends in relation to the navigation bar.

The width of this sidebar is set to 300 pixels. Increase the padding of the sidebar by following the instructions in the next step.

2   Return to your text editor, locate the rule in your CSS for the sidebar, and add the
    following code:

```css
#sidebar {
    float:left;
    width:300px;
    background-color:#CCC;
    padding:0px 20px 0px 20px;
}
```

Remember that this is a CSS shortcut and you should read the values in a clockwise
manner. The first value (`0px`) is the top padding, the second value (`20px`) is the right
padding, the third value (`0px`) is the bottom padding, and the last value (`20px`) is the left
padding. Save the page and preview it in your browser.

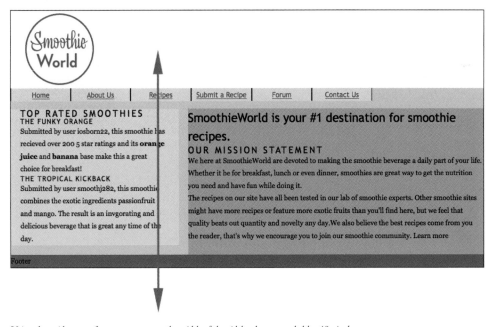

Using the guide as a reference, you can see the width of the sidebar has expanded by 40 pixels.

By adding 20 pixels of left padding and right padding to the `sidebar` div, you can increase the amount of space inside the column. Notice the end of the sidebar now lines up at the end of the Recipe item. This is because increasing the padding has increased the width of the sidebar by 40 pixels. This means the absolute width of the sidebar is 340 pixels, where 300 pixels comes from the width property in the `sidebar` rule and 40 pixels comes from the padding that you add.

3 Return to your text editor. Add an equivalent amount of padding to the `main` div because it also needs space for the text.

Locate your `#main` rule and add the following padding:

```
#main {
    width:600px;
    float:right;
    background-color:#ADA446;
    padding:0px 20px 0px 20px;
}
```

Save the file and preview it in your browser. A new problem arose: the total width of your two columns when you include the padding is wider than the container they are nested in. If you scroll down the page in your browser, you see the `main` div has slid into the only space it is allowed, underneath the `sidebar`.

You can fix this problem in several ways: you could expand the overall width of the `wrap` div, you could reduce the width value of the `sidebar` or the `main` div (or both), or you could reduce the padding values. All these methods are based on using padding, and there is an alternative method of adding space to columns that does not rely on padding at all. You'll take a look at this technique now.

4 Return to your text editor and locate the padding rules you added in steps 2 and 3. Select and delete these rules. You can achieve a similar effect by adding margin rules to the text elements inside the columns, as described in the following step.

5 Below the `#footer` rule in your CSS, add the following rule:

```
p, h1, h2, h3 {
    margin-left:20px;
    margin-right:20px;
}
```

This rule places 20 pixels of margin on the left and right of all paragraph and heading elements on the page. Save the file and preview it in your browser.

TOP RATED SMOOTHIES
THE FUNKY ORANGE
Submitted by user iosborn22, this smoothie has recieved over 200 5 star ratings and its **orange juice** and **banana** base make this a great choice for breakfast!
THE TROPICAL KICKBACK
Submitted by user smoothj282, this smoothie combines the exotic ingredients passionfruit and mango. The result is an invgorating and delicious beverage that is great any time of the day.

Adding margins to the elements within the sidebar increases the amount of space, but does not increase the width of the sidebar.

As in the earlier padding example, the result is extra space between the text and the columns. A crucial difference is that when you add margins to the text elements, the width of the columns is *not* affected. This can be advantageous, as you no longer have to add width to the padding. You only need to consider the width property for the column.

This technique has its own disadvantages, because the rules you set currently apply to *all* paragraphs and headings 1, 2, and 3 elements on the page. For example, notice that the footer was pushed 20 pixels to the right because the content is a paragraph. In cases where you only want to specify the elements within the sidebar and main ID, the contextual selector you used earlier for the navigation is useful.

6   Return to your text editor and delete the `margin-left` and `margin-right` properties you added in step 5 (but leave the rule intact). Add the following group of rules:

```
p, h1, h2, h3 {

}
#sidebar p, #sidebar h2, #sidebar h3, #main p, #main h1, #main h2,
#main h3 {
    margin-left:20px;
    margin-right:20px;
}
```

This is a CSS shorthand to select any paragraph, heading 1, heading 2, or heading 3 element child of the sidebar ID or the main ID, and apply left and right margins of 20 pixels.

7 Save the file and preview it in your browser. Scroll to the footer paragraph and notice that it no longer has margins. Close your browser and return to your text editor.

This method of styling requires a bit more attention to detail than the padding method. For example, when new elements are added inside a div, they do not use the same margins. The next step shows an example of this problem and then the solution, which involves adding a heading 4 element to the sidebar.

8 In the HTML of your `sidebar` div after the last paragraph, add the following code:

```
<h4>Submit a Recipe</h4>
```

Save the page and preview it in your browser. This heading 4 uses its zero margins (inherited from the reset.css style sheet), so it is flush against the column. Close your browser and return to your text editor.

9 In your group of rules for the sidebar and main columns, add a new rule in the sidebar for heading 4 (h4):

```
#sidebar p, #sidebar h2, #sidebar h3, #sidebar h4, #main p, #main h2 {
    margin-left:20px;
    margin-right:20px;
}
```

Save the page and preview it in your browser. The heading 4 element now has the same margins as the others.

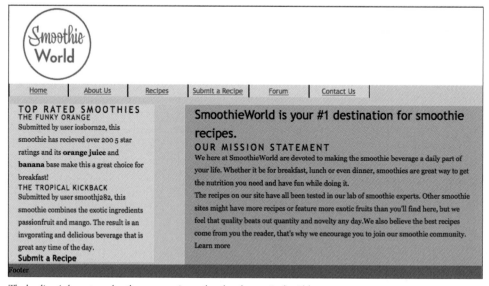

The heading 4 element now has the same margins as the other elements in the sidebar.

You can add a different margin to one of the elements. For example, you might want to move the paragraphs inside the sidebar to the right so they are indented. In this case, add another rule specifically for the p elements in the sidebar, as indicated in the next step. Close your browser and return to your text editor.

10 Add a new rule immediately below your previous rule set for the sidebar paragraph,

```
#sidebar p, #sidebar h2, #sidebar h3, #sidebar h4 #main p, #main h1,
    #main h2, #main h3{

    margin-left:20px;

    margin-right:20px;

}

#sidebar p {

    margin-left:30px;

}
```

This rule overrides the rule you set in step 9. Save the page and preview it in your browser. The paragraphs in the sidebar now have a left margin of 30 pixels, and in contrast to the other elements, are now indented.

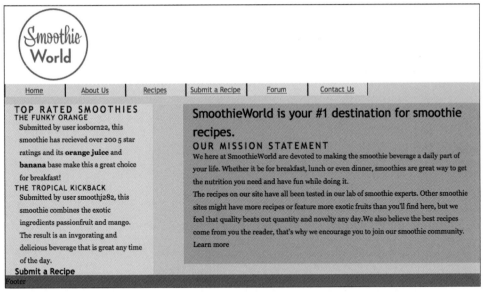

The paragraphs in the sidebar have specific rules for a left margin of 30 pixels.

With the exceptions of the changes you made in this exercise, all the margins and padding for the elements on your page are set to zero based on the reset style sheet. Add new values to the top and bottom margin values for most of your elements, as indicated in the next step.

11 Locate the empty p, h1, h2, and h3 rules in your style sheet. Also add the h4 selector to cover the elements on your page, and modify this rule set as follows:

```
p, h1, h2, h3, h4 {
    margin-bottom:20px;
}
```

Save the page and preview it in your browser. Most of your elements now have some added space from these margins. To add a top margin to the heading 2 in your sidebar, you could add another rule as shown in the next step.

12 In your text editor, add the following rule set:

```
#sidebar h2 {
    margin-top:15px;
}
```

Save the page and preview it in your browser. Your heading 2 in the sidebar has been pushed down by the top margin.

TOP RATED SMOOTHIES

THE FUNKY ORANGE

Submitted by user iosborn22, this smoothie has recieved over 200 5 star ratings and its **orange juice** and **banana** base make this a great choice for breakfast!

THE TROPICAL KICKBACK

Submitted by user smoothj282, this smoothie combines the exotic ingredients passionfruit and mango. The result is an invgorating and delicious beverage that is great any time of the day.

Submit a Recipe

Your sidebar, with a top margin of 15 pixels, applied.

A review of using margins and padding for layout

In this lesson, you have learned two methods for adding space between the elements in a page. The first method is to add padding to a `div` element. The advantage with this method is that all the elements inside the div are affected simultaneously, making it quick and efficient. A disadvantage to using padding for a div container is that increasing padding changes the width; to compensate, you must take into account the extra width.

The second method is to add margins to the elements inside the divs. The disadvantage to this method is that it requires more code and attention to detail, because you must notice how individual elements are positioned. The advantage is that column behavior is more predictable, since there is only one width property to consider.

There is another less obvious advantage to the second method that has not been discussed. This method is more reliable for achieving similar layouts across browsers, and it solves a bug found in Internet Explorer 6.

Finally, you should note that a combination of methods (using margins and padding) might be necessary for some situations. Consequently, you should understand the cause and effect of each method you use.

Styling your footer with a background image

So far, the structure of your page has been defined by the background colors of your `div` elements. In this section, you will learn to add images. To do this, you will add a CSS background image to your footer.

1 Locate the `#footer div` and replace the placeholder content inside the div with the following code:

```
<div id="footer">
    <p>Copyright SmoothieWorld 2011 </p>
    <p>Registration on or use of this site constitutes acceptance of
    our <a href="useragreement.html"> user agreement </a> and
    <a href="privacy.html">Privacy Policy.</a></p>
</div>
```

2 Save the page and preview it in your browser. Each paragraph is styled based on the current rules for paragraphs. You will adjust the rules for the footer, but you must know the size of the footer, which will be based on the dimensions of the background images you will add.

3 In your internal style sheet, locate the current rule for the footer. Add a new rule to apply a background image from your images folder:

```
#footer {
    clear:both;
    background-color:#BA2B22;
    background-image:url(images/footer_background.jpg);
    background-repeat:no-repeat;
}
```

Save the page and preview it in your browser.

Your footer now has a background image applied.

Your background image is now applied to the footer. This allows the footer text to be visible above it. Notice the `background-repeat` property in the code above. CSS background images tile by default, so setting a value of `no-repeat` ensures that this image will *never* tile. This code might seem redundant when your background image is the same size as your footer; if the footer expands, the code will ensure the image does not tile.

Set the footer dimensions to match the background image as indicated in the next step.

4 Modify your footer rule as follows:

```
#footer {
    clear:both;
    background-color:#BA2B22;
    background-image:url(images/footer_background.jpg);
    background-repeat:no-repeat;
    width:960px;
    height:128px;
}
```

Save the file and preview it in your browser. Your footer is sized correctly and you can adjust your paragraphs. Use another contextual selector, as shown in the next step.

5   In your text editor, add a new rule for paragraphs inside the `footer` div:

```
#footer p {
    margin:10px 0 0 20px;
    width:280px;
    font-family:Verdana, Geneva, sans-serif;
    font-size:0.689em;
}
```

This rule adds 10 pixels to the top margin and 20 pixels to the left margin of each paragraph in your footer. By defining a width for the paragraphs, you can force a break approximately where you need it: inside the white space of the image. The font properties define a different font family and a smaller font-size.

6   Save the page and preview it in your browser.

Your footer paragraphs with new styles.

In the previous section, you learned that applying padding and margins is a common technique. You could add more space between the first paragraph and the top of the footer, but increasing the top margin of the `#footer p` rule affects the second paragraph. In this case, add padding to the top of the footer as indicated in the next step.

7   Add the following declaration to your `#footer` rule:

```
#footer {
    clear:both;
    background-color:#BA2B22;
    background-image:url(images/footer_background.jpg);
    background-repeat:no-repeat;
    width:960px;
    height:128px;
    padding-top:10px;
}
```

Save the file and preview it in your browser. Notice that the additional padding increased the true height of the footer, but the red background color is extending out. You can solve this problem in several ways, but the simple solution is to subtract 10 pixels from the height of the footer.

8　Change the height of the `footer` div to 118 pixels:

`height:118px;`

Save the file and preview it in your browser. Your footer is now positioned correctly.

The final appearance of the footer.

In this lesson, you learned the difference between table and CSS layouts. You also learned to use the `float` and `clear` properties to create columns on your page. Finally, you explored the advantages and disadvantages of using margins and padding to control your layout. Although you have a strong foundation for your page, in the next lesson, you will continue working on this design, add more images, upgrade the style of your navigation bar, and add other elements to your page.

To compare your work with a complete version of the final page, open the file named "04_final.html" in your HTML5_04lessons folder.

Self study

1   To practice styling with margins and padding, add new content to your main section. For example, add a new heading 3 and an unordered list between your two paragraphs:

```
<h3>Recipe of the Day: Honeydew Melon</h3>
    <ul>
        <li>3 cups Honeydew Melon (seeded & chopped)</li>
        <li>2 tsp Lime Juice</li>
        <li>1 cup Vanilla Nonfat Yogurt</li>
        <li>1 cup Ice Cubes</li>
    </ul>
```

2   After adding this HTML, use what you learned in this lesson to experiment with positioning these elements on the page.

Review

Questions

1   What is a fixed-width layout and what is a flexible layout? What are some of the advantages and disadvantages of each?

2   What is the CSS float property and where would you use it?

3   Cheri added a paragraph to the sidebar div she created. The paragraph is flush against the side of the sidebar. Name two options Cheri could use to move the paragraph away from the edges of the sidebar.

Answers

1   A fixed-width layout has a defined width (usually in pixels or ems) for the primary container. One of the main advantages to this type of layout is that this primary container provides a reliable way to position the other page elements. One disadvantage to this type of layout is that it does not resize with the web browser, and some features, such as text reflowing, are lost. Flexible layouts resize based on the browser or device; this creates a more challenging layout for the designer.

2   The CSS float property lets you remove an element from the default flow of HTML and move (or float) it to either the left or right of its containing element. You would use floats when you want to wrap text around images, create horizontal navigation menus, or use columns for page layout.

3   Cheri could add some padding to the sidebar (which would move any content inside away from the edges). She could also add a rule for paragraphs inside the sidebar; specifically, Cheri could add margin values that would move the paragraphs away from the edges. (Cheri could also use a combination of padding and margins.)

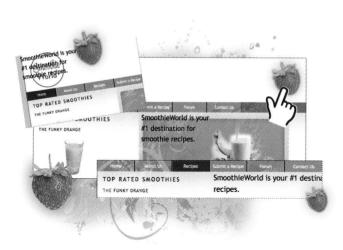

What you'll learn in this lesson:

- Using comments in cascading style sheets
- Using background images
- Creating navigation styles
- Working with absolute positioning

Advanced CSS Layout

In this lesson, you'll learn how to refine the appearance of your page layout by adding graphics, color, and additional page sections.

Starting up

You will work with several files from the HTML5_05lessons folder in this lesson. Make sure you have loaded the HTML5lessons folder onto your hard drive from the supplied DVD. See "Loading lesson files" in the Starting Up section of this book.

See Lesson 5 in action!

Use the accompanying video to gain a better understanding of how to use some of the capabilities shown in this lesson. The video tutorial for this lesson can be found on the included DVD.

This lesson uses the TextWrangler text editor to create the markup, but you can use any text editor and get the same results..

Building your page layout

In this lesson, you will be working with the two-column fixed-width layout from Lesson 4. In Lesson 4, you added background colors to the various page elements. In this lesson, you will remove the background colors to unify the appearance of the page.

You will also create a more attractive and useful navigation bar, add more images, create a styled data table, and add form elements for a contact page. At the end of the lesson, you will look at a few alternative page layouts based on the one you create.

Removing the background color

Your first task is to remove the background colors from the page. You do not need to delete the CSS properties for these elements, just comment them out in the code.

1   In your text editor, choose File > Open. In the dialog box that appears, navigate to the HTML5_05lessons folder, choose the 05_start.html file, and click Open. Preview this page in your browser to see the current layout.

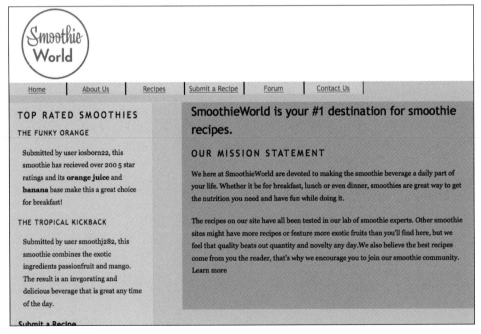

Your page in its initial state.

2   Return to your text editor. Choose File > Save As, and in the dialog box that appears, go to the HTML5_05lessons folder. Name this file 05_layoutwork.html, and then click Save. This ensures you have a backup file.

3   Locate the `#wrap` rule in your CSS, and then add the following commenting code to the `background-color` property:

```
#wrap {
    /*background-color:#E0B3B9; */
    width:960px;
    border:thin solid black;
    margin:0 auto;
}
```

This code disables the style so the browser ignores it. You can remove these comments at any time to activate the style. Designers often keep either background-colors or borders in the code to help them identify layout elements in the future. Save the file and preview it in your browser. The purple background for the wrap is now gone.

4   Return to your text editor and repeat step 3, but this time add the commenting code for the `#sidebar` and `#maincontent background-color` properties. Save the file and preview it in your browser. Your page no longer uses color to define the two columns.

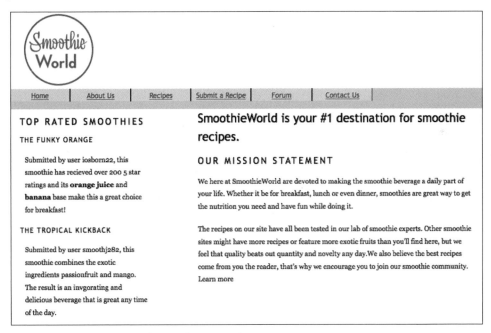

Your page with the background-colors for your columns removed.

Now that you have disabled the background colors of the columns, you'll add other colors, starting with the page itself. The CSS body selector allows you to do this; you need to open your external style sheet to modify it.

5   In your text editor, choose File > Open. Navigate to your HTML5_05lessons folder, select the base.css file, and then click Open.

Remember that your page is currently using three sources for the styles: the internal styles, which you have already modified; an external style sheet named reset.css, which applies margins and a padding of 0 to most of your HTML elements; and the base.css style sheet, which contains common styles, such as font family and font size.

Style sheet management

Learning to manage multiple style sheets is increasingly important in modern web design. Placing all your styles in a single style sheet can cause confusion and inefficiency, especially as the number of rules increases. Modern websites often use multiple external style sheets: one for the reset, one for layout, one for text, one for older browsers, one for mobile devices, and so on.

It is important to know when to use internal and external style sheets. On most completed websites, internal styles are used to style a unique page; the majority of the styles are in the external style sheets. During development, it is more convenient to experiment and refine the layout using internal styles; all the designer needs to do is scroll up the page and add or modify a rule. The point at which internal styles are moved over to an external style sheet is a matter of preference. Designers often do this when the design is approved and they are beginning to build new pages.

6   In your base.css file, locate the body rule and add the following property:

```
body {
    font-family:"Trebuchet MS", Tahoma, Arial, sans-serif;
    font-size:100%;
    background-color:#B3BBCA;
}
```

This adds a light-blue background color to the page. Save the file and preview it in your browser. You can see that with no background colors applied, your columns are transparent and the body background is visible. You'll fix that by applying a white background to the wrap div.

7   In your text editor, return to 05_layoutwork.html. Locate the rule for the `#wrap` div. Modify the color value and remove the commenting code:

```
#wrap {
    background-color:#ffffff;
    width:960px;
    border:thin solid black;
    margin:0 auto;
}
```

Save the file and preview it in your browser. With the `wrap` div using the white background, your page is beginning to take shape. Now you'll add some images.

Working with CSS background images

There are two ways to add images to a web page. The first way uses HTML to insert an inline image. You have already added an inline image when you inserted your site logo. Inline images rely on the HTML image tag, and the code is similar to this:

```
<img src="images/smoothieworld_logo.jpg" width="200" height="150"
alt="smoothieworld_logo" />
```

The second way to add images to a web page is by using CSS background images. You should generally use CSS background images as decorative elements and not primary content. In the following steps, you will add a CSS background image to the div container named `#innerwrap` that is nesting your two columns.

1   In your 05_layoutwork.html file, locate the `div` tag with the ID `innerwrap`. Here is a list of the containers currently on your page, from the top of your HTML code to the bottom: `wrap` div, `masthead` div, `mainnav` div, and `innerwrap` div. Currently, the `innerwrap` div is the parent container of the `sidebar` and `maincontent` div, which are the columns you created in Lesson 4.

The `innerwrap` is currently unstyled. Its function right now is to provide a container for the two columns. Note the behavior of this container in the next few steps.

2   In your internal style sheet, locate the `wrap` rule and below it add a new rule for the `innerwrap`:

```
#innerwrap {
    background-image:url(images/inner-wrap_bg.png);
    height:450px;
}
```

The background-image property is pointing to a small gradient image located in your images folder. The height property gives the innerwrap some structure; this value of 450 pixels is arbitrary, and you will return to this shortly. For now, save the file and preview it in your browser.

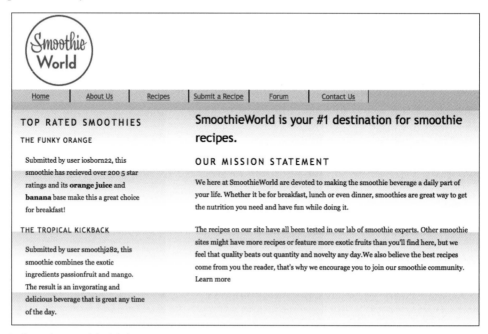

Background-images tile by default.

Your page looks strange because by default, background images tile both horizontally and vertically. In order to correct this, you need to tile the image horizontally (the direction of the x-axis).

3   In your text editor, add the following property and value to the innerwrap rule:

```
#innerwrap {
    background-image:url(images/inner-wrap_bg.png);
    background-repeat:repeat-x;
    height:450px;
}
```

Save the page and preview it in your browser. Your background image now tiles across the top of the innerwrap div, which creates the intended effect.

The many wonders of the background image

You can find CSS background images everywhere in web design, so you need to understand how they work. The following are some of the properties associated with background images.

To tile an image horizontally within the parent container, use the following value:

```
background-repeat:repeat-x;
```

To tile an image vertically only, use this value:

```
background-repeat:repeat-y;
```

To add a single instance of the graphic (in other words, with no tiling), use this value:

```
background-repeat:no-repeat;
```

Background-position

Another useful property is background-position. The default position for background images is the top-left corner of the containing element, as shown in the following figure:

A background image with the no-repeat *value.*

You can position this image in the bottom-right corner by adding this property:

```
background-position:right bottom;
```

You can use the keywords left, right, and center to position an image horizontally; by combining it with the keywords top, bottom, and center, you can also position the image vertically.

You can position background images even more precisely by using either unit or percentage values. The most common unit values are pixels, but you can also use other units, such as ems. When using unit values, the first value is the horizontal position and the second value is the vertical position, as the following example shows:

```
background-position:10px 40px;
```

The background image is positioned 10 pixels horizontally and 40 pixels vertically from the top-left corner of the box (the box itself is 100 pixels high by 300 pixels wide).

(continues)

The many wonders of the background image (continued)

You can use percentages for background images, particularly if the parent container has a flexible width. When using percentage values, the top-left corner is 0% 0% and the bottom-right corner is 100% 100%. The following example uses percentages:

The image above, as indicated by the following code, is positioned 20 percent away from the top and 40 percent away from the left:

```
background-position 20% 40%;
```

Using hacks to solve layout problems

CSS layouts that rely on floated boxes sometimes have unexpected results because various browsers render the same content differently. When an elegant solution does not exist, you need to resort to *hacks*. A hack is a solution where you use elements or properties within HTML or CSS for a purpose other than their intended application. You'll use a hack in the following exercise to properly apply the background image that spans across your two columns.

In the previous exercise, you applied a background image to the `innerwrap` div and you defined a height of 450 pixels. The problem with this method is that the two columns inside the `innerwrap` div are longer than 450 pixels, and it's against best practices to have a containing element smaller than its content. To address this problem, you will remove the height value and then add new code to make the innerwrap work well in any situation.

1   In your 05_layoutwork.html page, locate the rule for the innerwrap and delete the entire `height:450px;` line.

Save the page and preview it in your browser. Your background image disappears because without a defined height, there is no content inside the `innerwrap` div.

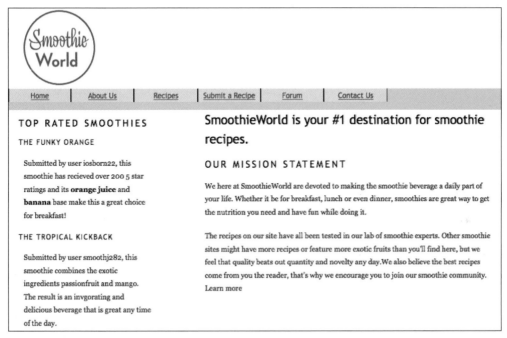

Your `innerwrap` div has no defined height, so it collapses and hides the background image.

The `sidebar` and `maincontent` divs are contained within the `innerwrap` div; note that these elements are floated, and floated elements are removed from the flow of HTML. Also, the `sidebar` and `maincontent` div do not have height values, so the `innerwrap` cannot expand. You will now add code that solves this problem.

2   In the CSS below the `#innerwrap` rule, add a new empty rule:

```
#innerwrap {
    background-image:url(images/inner-wrap_bg.png);
    background-repeat:repeat-x;
}
#innerwrap:after{

}
```

The `:after` is a special CSS property that allows extra content to be added at the end of an element using CSS. You will now add a series of rules that force the innerwrap to act as though there were content inside.

3   Add the following properties to this rule:

```
#innerwrap:after{
    content:".";
    display:block;
    clear:both;
    height:0;
    visibility:hidden;
}
```

Save the file and then preview it in your browser. Your innerwrap now displays properly. (If you are viewing this page in Internet Explorer 6 or 7, you might not be able to see the intended result; you will address this shortly.) It goes beyond the scope of this lesson to explain exactly what each one of these properties is doing, but essentially they are forcing the innerwrap to behave as a true container with content, not just a background image.

For more information about how this code works, go to www.positioniseverything.net/easyclearing.html.

The solution from the previous step will not work reliably in Internet Explorer 6 or 7, so you have to add a special set of rules for these browsers.

4   In your 05_layoutwork.html document, scroll to locate the links to your external style sheets. Type the following code below the link to the base.css style sheet:

```
<link href="reset.css" rel="stylesheet" type="text/css" />
<link href="base.css" rel="stylesheet" type="text/css" />
<!--[if IE ]>
<link href="iefixes.css" rel="stylesheet" type="text/css">
<![endif]-->
```

This section of code is called a *conditional comment*. A conditional comment uses a special syntax that only Microsoft browsers will understand. For now, think of this as a link to an external style sheet that will only be used if the browser is Internet Explorer. All other browsers will ignore this code. The next step explains the content of the iefixes.css style sheet.

5   In your Text Editor, choose File > Open. Navigate to your HTML5_05lessons folder, select the iefixes.css file, and then click Open. It contains the following rule:

```
#innerwrap {
    zoom:1;
}
```

This is a special rule that forces Internet Explorer 6 to render the page as you intend. (You will learn more about these details in the next lesson.) Close this file without making any changes.

Enhancing your CSS navigation bar

Now you'll make your navigation bar more aesthetically pleasing. Currently, it uses the positioning and colors you added in Lesson 4 to understand how floats work. You'll now use CSS to add styling and interactivity. To review how the menu works, modify some of the properties to create a navigation menu better suited for the style of your page, as indicated in the following steps.

1   In your 05_layoutwork.html internal style sheet, locate the `#mainnav` rule. This rule sets the height of the div to 40 pixels and gives it a pale-green background color. Below this rule is the `#mainnav li` rule, which is floating the list items to the left as well as setting styles such as width, height, background color, and more.

Preview the page in your browser to see how the navigation bar is currently styled. The list items (with a background color of grey) are not the same height as the `#mainnav` div, which is why there is a gap. You'll fix this now.

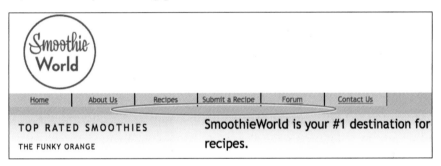

Your list items are not the same height as the surrounding navigation section; this accounts for the visual gap.

2   Return to your text editor. To make the list fit into the mainnav, both elements need to be the same height. Make the following changes to your rules:

```
#mainnav {
    background-color:#60668B;
    height:35px;
}
#mainnav li {
    float:left;
    width:120px;
    height:35px;
    background-color:#7D83A4;
    text-align:center;
    border-left:1px black solid;
    border-right:1px black solid;
    line-height:35px;
}
```

Save the page and then preview it in your browser. By making the heights the same value, you now have a narrower navbar. By changing the background colors to shades of blue, you now have colors that are more compatible with the background color of the page. Unfortunately, the default hyperlink color is also blue, and the rule below the links is not very attractive. You'll now change the link color and remove the underline next.

3   Below your `#mainnav li` rule, add the following rule:

```
#mainnav ul li a {
    color:#ffffff;
    text-decoration:none;
}
```

This rule is necessary because you are targeting hyperlinks inside the `mainnav` div. The `color` and `text-decoration` properties set the style of these links to white and also remove the underline. Save the page and preview it in your browser.

Styling the appearance of the hyperlinks by removing the underline and setting the color to white.

This navbar is aesthetically pleasing. You can improve its usability by making the nav items change color when the user moves the mouse cursor over them and by providing a visual indicator of which page the user has navigated to. See the next step for instructions.

4   In your text editor, add the following rule below your `#mainnav ul li a` rule:

```
#mainnav ul li a:hover {
    background-color:#29336B;
    color:#F8F068;
}
```

The `a:hover` property is an example of a *pseudoclass*, which are special properties of elements (links, in this case) based on user interaction. The `a:link` property defines the default appearance of a hyperlink before it is first clicked by a user. The `a:hover` property defines the appearance of a link when a user hovers the mouse cursor over it (this action is sometimes known as a rollover). The `a:visited` property defines the appearance of a link on the page after it has been visited. (This helps the user identify the links she already clicked.) The last pseudo-class is `a:active`, which defines the appearance of a link when it is being clicked (when the user is pressing down but not releasing the mouse).

You do not have to create styles for all these properties, but you will often see them in groups of four. To see the `a:hover` property in action, save your page and preview it in your browser.

Move the mouse cursor over your links to see the effect. The behavior appears odd because the background color is defined by the size of the text. Fill the entire block with color, as instructed in the next step.

5 In your text editor, add the following property to your `#mainnav ul li a` rule:

```
#mainnav ul li a {
    color:#ffffff;
    text-decoration:none;
    display:block;
}
```

This property and value override the default inline value of links in the mainnav, so the entire block expands. Save your file and check the menu in your browser.

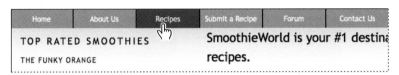

Setting the hyperlink element to display as a block element forces it to fill the menu area.

Return to your text editor. You will now set a style that defines the appearance of the menu when a user is on a specific page; this will help him identify which page he is on.

6 In your HTML, locate the code for the mainnav list. Add the following class names to each list item:

```
<ul>
        <li><a class="nav-home" href="index.html">Home</a></li>
        <li><a class="nav-about" href="about.html">About Us</a></li>
        <li><a class="nav-recipe" href="recipes.html">Recipes</a></li>
        <li><a class="nav-submitrecipes" href="submitrecipe.html">Submit a Recipe</a></li>
        <li><a class="nav-forum" href="forum.html">Forum</a></li>
        <li><a class="nav-contact" href="contact.html">Contact Us</a></li>
</ul>
```

The purpose of assigning a unique class to each list item is to target the list items with a style. You must also find a way to identify the page the user is on. You can do this by creating a unique ID style for each page.

7   In your HTML, scroll up to locate the `<body>` tag, and add the following code:

```
<body id="home">
```

By adding an ID to the body tag, you can set a style that applies to this page only. In this case, the style is for the appearance of the Home link on this page.

8   In your internal style sheet, add the following rule:

```
body#home .nav-home {
    background-color:#29336B;
    color:#F8F068;
    display:block;
}
```

This rule targets the class `nav-home` on the page with the ID "home." Save your page and preview it in your browser.

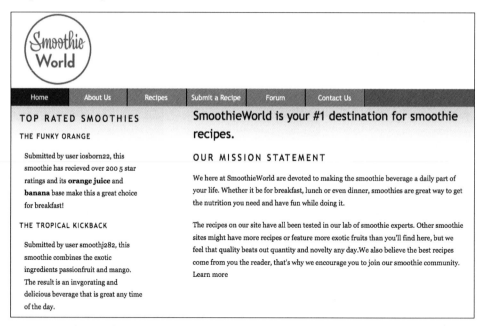

Setting a unique class name for the home page allows you to create distinct styles for it.

Notice that the Home link is permanently set to the same style as the hover effect. You can style it completely differently, for example, by choosing different values for the background color and color properties.

You will now add another page to your site and then style the navigation accordingly.

Moving internal styles to the external style sheet

Currently, the majority of the layout styles for this page are internal. These styles will not automatically apply to new HTML pages that you might want to add. To avoid this problem, you will cut the styles from this page and paste them into your base.css external style sheet.

1   In your 05_layoutwork.html document, select all the rules between your opening `<style>` and closing `</style>` tags. Press Ctrl + X (Windows) or Command + X (Mac OS) to cut the style rules.

2   Choose File > Open, navigate to your HTML5_05lessons folder, and select the base.css style sheet. This style sheet currently contains the style rules for your text. At the bottom of the style sheet, after the last `<ol>` rule, press Return a few times to add some space, and then press Ctrl + V (Windows) or Command + V (Mac OS) to paste all your rules. Choose File > Save to save your changes.

3   Keep this file open because any future additions or modifications that you make to your pages will be made here. Switch to your 05_layoutwork.html page and choose File > Save. Preview it in your browser to ensure you followed the steps correctly. There should be no change in the page. Your styles are now contained in the base.css page, not the 05_layoutwork.html page.

Creating a style for the active page

Now that you have saved your styles in an external style sheet, you will create two new pages that will use these styles: the Contact page and the About Us page. You'll create additional pages at the end of this lesson.

1   In your 05_layoutwork.html page, choose File > Save As and rename this file **about.html**. Scroll to locate the heading 1 content: *SmoothieWorld is your #1 destination for smoothie recipes.* You'll change this heading to help you identify this page, and later, you'll add more content to this page. Type the following:

```
<h1>About Us</h1>
```

2   Add an ID to identify this page as the About Us page, as you did with the home page, by adding the following code to the body tag:

```
<body id= "aboutus" >
```

Choose File > Save. Now, you'll add a rule to your style sheet to target the `nav-about` class attached to your About Us link, as instructed in the next step.

3 Choose File > Save to save the HTML file, and then toggle to your base.css file. Locate the rule you created for the home page and add to it as follows:

```
body#home .nav-home, body#aboutus .nav-about {
    background-color:#29336B;
    color:#F8F068;
}
```

This appends the new rules for the About Us page (make sure you include the comma after the `.nav-home` class). Choose File > Save, and then preview about.html in your browser.

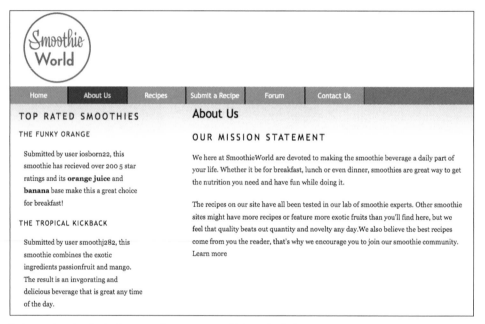

Setting a unique class for the about page allows you to create distinct styles for it.

Repeat the steps above for the Contact Us page, as instructed below.

4 In your about.html page, choose File > Save As and rename this file **contact.html**. Scroll to locate the heading 1 content, *About Us*, and change it to **Contact Form**.

5 Add an ID to identify this page as the Contact page by adding the following code to the body tag:

```
<body id= "contact" >
```

Choose File > Save. Add the necessary rule in your base.css file to highlight the Contact link, as instructed in the next step.

6 Locate the rules you have been working with and modify them as follows:

```
body#home .nav-home, body#aboutus .nav-about, body#contact
.nav-contact {
    background-color:#29336B;
    color:#F8F068;
}
```

Choose File > Save and preview the page in your browser. The Contact link is now active. Click the About Us and Home links to activate them.

In the On Your Own section, you will repeat these steps for the Recipes, Submit a Recipe, and Forum pages.

Adding images to your sidebar

In the Home page, add two images to the sidebar and one to the main section, as instructed below.

1 Open your 05_layoutwork.html page. In your HTML, locate the `sidebar` div, and below the heading 3 code, add the following:

```
<h3>The Funky Orange</h3>
<p><img src="images/FunkyOrange.png" width="235" height="130"
alt="FunkyOrange Smoothie" /></p>
```

2 Add another image further down in the sidebar as follows:

```
<h3>The Tropical KickBack</h3>
<p><img src="images/TropicalKickback.png" alt="" width="235"
height="130" /></p>
```

Note that these images have been sized to the same dimensions of 235 pixels wide by 130 pixels high. These images are located in your images folder so they will be correctly linked, but ensure you type the file name correctly so the links to the images are not broken.

3 Save the file and then preview it in your browser. The two images you added are inside the sidebar. You'll now use a more advanced technique to add another image into the main area.

Working with absolute positioning

You now need to place a large splash image in the main column and place it below your heading 1 (currently labeled "*SmoothieWorld is your #1 destination for smoothie recipes*"). You can create this layered effect of text on an image in several ways, but nothing you have learned up to this point would be ideal. The following paragraphs describe the methods you have learned, and explain why they would not work.

Method 1

Open Photoshop, add a text layer to your splash image, and save it as an optimized web graphic. The problems with this method are:

- Text in a graphic becomes invisible to search engines.

- You lose accessibility for other devices, such as screen readers.

- The method is inefficient when updating text, since it requires access to the original Photoshop file.

Method 2

Place the splash image as a background image within the main column and position the heading 1 over it. The problems with this method are:

- CSS background images are to be used as decoration, not as replacement for content.

- You can only use one background image for any given div; multiple background images are not possible in CSS.

The method you will learn in this subsection takes advantage of relative and absolute positioning in CSS. Following this method, you will first insert your splash image as a standard inline image in HTML and add a new `div` container for the text. You will then position this new container as needed.

Start by adding the inline image into the `maincontent` div, as explained below.

1   Type the following code between the heading 1 and heading 2 in the `maincontent` div:

```
<h1>SmoothieWorld is your #1 destination for smoothie recipes.</h1>
<img src="images/frontpage_splash.png" width="551" height="270"
alt="frontpage_splash" />
<h2>Our mission statement </h2>
```

Save the page and preview it in your browser. The image is located between the two headings.

Superimpose the `<h1>` text on the image (similar to a layer in Photoshop) by wrapping a new `div` container around it with the name splash, as indicated below.

2   Add the following code around the heading 1:

```
<div id="splash">
<h1>SmoothieWorld is your #1 destination for smoothie recipes.</h1>
</div>
```

Add a new style rule for this ID, as shown below.

3   Open the base.css external style sheet, scroll to the bottom, and add the following:

```
#splash {
    position:absolute;
    width:290px;
    height:230px;
    top:0px;
    left:0px;


}
```

Absolute positioning allows you to define the width and height of the div (as you did earlier), and then it allows you to move this box along a set of coordinates (in this case, a top value of 0 pixels and a left value of 0 pixels). Note that the default coordinates of 0 top and 0 left are defined as the top-left corner of the page.

Save the file and preview it in your browser.

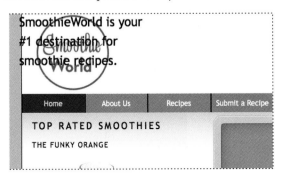

Your heading is absolutely positioned, but it is incorrectly using the entire page as a reference.

Your browser may have the text positioned differently. This should have no impact on the final result.

Recall that you nested the `splash` div inside the `maincontent` div, but this box appears in the top-left corner of the entire page. This is because absolutely positioned items are positioned independently of their containers by default, but you can change the position so it appears relative to the container.

4 Locate the `maincontent` rule in your base.css style sheet. Add the following property and value at the top of your list of rules:

```
#maincontent {
    position:relative;
    width:600px;
    float:right;
    /*background-color:#ADA446; */
}
```

Save the file, and then preview it in your browser. Although not positioned exactly where you need it, the `splash` div is now positioned in the top-left corner of the `maincontent` div.

By setting a `position:relative` *property on the* `maincontent` *div, your heading is using this div as a reference.*

Setting this div to `position:relative` instructs the absolutely positioned `splash` div to use the top-left corner of the `maincontent` div, not the top-left corner of the page. To position the box exactly where you want it, you can change the top and left coordinates.

5 Modify the `top` and `left` values as follows:

```
#splash {
    position:absolute;
    width:290px;
    height:230px;
    top:35px;
    left:35px;

}
```

Save the file and preview it in your browser. Your `splash` div and the enclosed heading have now been pushed down 35 pixels from the top-left corner of the `maincontent` div.

The advantage of this technique is that your text is not a graphic, so it will be readable by search engines and by users browsing with images turned off. Also, the image and the text are independent from each other, which makes them easy to modify. For example, the text may be resized a bit smaller to avoid the crowding effect.

Positioning models in CSS

In addition to absolute and relative positioning, there is a property called `fixed positioning` that is used less frequently than the other two. Here is a brief description of each of the properties:

Absolute positioning: An element that is set to `absolute` strictly follows the positioning values given to it, relative only to its containing element. The containing element can be another div or the actual page. Absolutely positioned elements are pulled out of the normal flow of HTML content, and regardless of the elements that surround them (such as, text content or neighboring divs), they always appear at the exact coordinates assigned to them.

Relative positioning: A relatively positioned element accepts values for position properties, such as top and left, but it also takes the normal flow of neighboring HTML content into account. For example, a value of `left:35` would add 35 pixels to the element's left position.

Fixed positioning: This property generates an absolutely positioned element that is positioned relative to the browser window. In other words, by fixed positioning an element, you are anchoring it to your browser window. This effect is used for elements, such as footers or menus, that you want to stay in the same position in the browser window (even when the user scrolls down).

Self study

1 In the *Creating a style for the active page* exercise, you learned how to add IDs to the body tag of your Home, About Us, and Contact pages. Create a fully functional navigation bar by following the directions in that exercise to add similar code for the Recipes, Submit a Recipe, and Forum pages.

2 Try experimenting with different background images and applying them to your sidebar and maincontent columns. Although this requires an image editor such as Adobe Photoshop for best results, you can use the background graphic supplied for you in your images folder. Add the following code to your `#sidebar` rule:

```
background-image:url(images/sidebar_bg.png);
background-repeat:repeat-x;
background-color:#EAB8C3;
```

Note that the `background-color` property seamlessly matches the color in the sidebar_bg.png graphic, thereby creating a transition between the image and the sidebar background color. This effect is often used to keep your graphic files small. In addition, this technique avoids the problem of predicting how tall a column needs to be.

Review

Questions

1 What is the difference between an HTML inline image and a CSS background image? Indicate the optimal conditions for each use?

2 What is the purpose of the `a:hover` property in CSS?

3 What is the default behavior of an element that is absolutely positioned?

Answers

1 An HTML inline image is an image on your page that originates from the HTML `<img>` tag. A CSS background image is an image that originates from the `background-image` property in CSS. Inline images are most suited for important content within a page (such as a product image). CSS background images are generally reserved for decorative elements (such as a pattern).

2 The `a:hover` property allows you to choose a style for a hyperlink that is triggered when a user rolls over, or "hovers" over a link.

3 If you add the `position:absolute` property to an element in CSS, you can specify positional values for it (most often, top and left). These values will always position the object based on the corners of the browser page.

Section Two: HTML5 with CSS3 and JavaScript

This section covers the fundamentals of HTML5 and CSS3 syntax, along with HTML5 techniques involving JavaScript and the jQuery JavaScript library. This section includes ten lessons. You should have an understanding of coding XHTML/HTML and CSS prior to starting these lessons. If you are new to coding HTML/XHTML and CSS, we suggest you start with section one of this book, which covers the fundamentals of web design and development with XHTML/HTML and CSS.

What you'll learn in this lesson:

- How to define the different HTML5 content categories

- How to replace div elements with new HTML5 elements

- Understanding sectioning content and HTML5 outlines

Using HTML5 Markup

In this lesson, you will learn how to update existing HTML pages using the new HTML5 sectioning elements and other new elements.

Starting up

You will work with several files from the HTML5_06lessons folder in this lesson. Make sure you have loaded the HTML5lessons folder onto your hard drive from the supplied DVD. See "Loading lesson files" in the Starting Up section of this book.

See Lesson 6 in action!

Use the accompanying video to gain a better understanding of how to use some of the capabilities shown in this lesson. The video tutorial for this lesson can be found on the included DVD.

To accurately preview the HTML5 content that you will create in this lesson, you need a browser that supports the relevant HTML5 tags. See "Using web browsers that support HTML5 tags" in the Starting Up section of this book to determine whether you are using such a browser and for instructions on downloading one, if needed.

A review of semantic markup

In this lesson, you will learn some of the new HTML5 elements that have been added to the language. To successfully complete the lesson, you should know the fundamentals of HTML and CSS and have experience building web pages with these languages.

This lesson begins with a brief review of *semantic markup*, which is a formal way of saying "always choose the best tag for the job." A more technical explanation of semantic markup is syntax that makes sense to humans as well as programs, such as a web browser. Semantic markup tries to explicitly attach meaning to content, most often through the use of tags.

At first glance, choosing the right tag seems fairly straightforward. For example, consider headings in HTML, of which there are 6 levels: `<h1>`, `<h2>`, `<h3>`, `<h4>`, `<h5>`, and `<h6>`. Rendered in the browser, the `<h1>` element is the largest and the `<h6>` element is the smallest.

Heading 1

Heading 2

Heading 3

Heading 4

Heading 5

Heading 6

The 6 heading elements, rendered in default styles, from top to bottom.

The content within an `<h1>` element should have greater importance than the content in an `<h3>` element. Likewise, if a font style is set for the headings, the font size of an `<h1>` element should be set larger than the `<h3>` element. There is no technical reason that prevents you from creating a style making the `<h3>` element larger than the `<h1>`. From the web browser's perspective it would make no difference, but to a human looking at the code for the first time it would be semantically confusing: an `<h3>` element is not supposed to be larger than an `<h1>`.

One of the goals of semantic markup is to make the code on a page logical and consistent. Logically chosen and consistent code is easier to update and modify for the designer, and it makes the web page more flexible and adaptable for different uses, such as websites for mobile devices. Semantic markup ensures that even pages with no style still display elements that are comprehensible and usable.

HTML5 fundamentals

Before creating an HTML5 page, you will review the different categories of content within an HTML document. Although the changes made to HTML5 are numerous, the fundamentals of HTML (and XHTML) have not changed dramatically. One interesting development is that the syntax in HTML5 is very forgiving, especially if you compare it to XHTML 1.0 syntax. For example, all of the following is currently true in HTML5:

- HTML5 is case insensitive, meaning that you can use uppercase tags, lowercase tags or even a mixture of the two and the page will still validate. For example, the following code is technically valid:

  ```
  <H1> Breaking news from Boston </h1>
  ```

- The closing tags for elements are not required. For example, adding multiple paragraphs in the following way is technically valid:

  ```
  <p> There is an accident on Interstate 95 between Woburn and
  Burlington.
  <p> Travelers should seek alternative routes.
   <p> The speed limit is 55 mph.
  ```

- Attribute quotes are optional. For example, the following code is technically valid:

  ```
  <img src=trafficjam.jpg alt=traffic jam>
  ```

If you have learned how to create webpages with code over the last 10 years or so, you might be scratching your head a bit because the preceding rules fly directly in the face of the "best practices" of web design that you may have been taught. If this is the case, why does HTML5 allow these practices? The answer is perhaps best summarized by the architects of the language as an attempt to "pave the cowpaths." In other words, when a practice is already widespread by designers and developers, "consider adopting it rather than forbidding it or inventing something new." In HTML5, there is an emphasis on backwards compatibility, and many of the practices mentioned above (such as using uppercase tags) were used by document creators in the early days of the Web. The W3C decided to fold this variety of coding practices into the specification to ensure that future browsers would continue to render as many pages on the Web as possible.

For a more detailed explanation of the W3C's philosophy for HTML Design Principles, visit http://www.w3.org/TR/html-design-principles/.

Just because HTML5 allows this syntax, it does not mean you need to change the way you currently write code. If you are used to closing your elements using lower-case tags and adding quotation marks for attributes, this remains a very good idea. By having a standardized way of writing code, you will tend to reduce the number of errors you make, and have a way to isolate problems when they do occur.

The HTML5 DOCTYPE declaration

A significant change in the HTML5 specification can be seen on the very first line of an HTML5 document. A web browser renders a page from the top of the document to the bottom. The opening line of most HTML files is called a DOCTYPE, which indicates to the browser the type of document to expect. For example, when a designer uses the transitional version of HTML (4.0.1), the DOCTYPE is:

```
<!DOCTYPE HTML PUBLIC "-//W3C//DTD HTML 4.01 Transitional//EN"
"http://www.w3.org/TR/html4/loose.dtd">
```

When a designer uses the strict version of XHTML 1.0, the doctype is:

```
<!DOCTYPE html PUBLIC "-//W3C//DTD XHTML 1.0 Strict//EN"
"http://www.w3.org/TR/xhtml1/DTD/xhtml1-strict.dtd">
```

In HTML5, a DOCTYPE is much simpler:

```
<!DOCTYPE html>
```

DOCTYPE is used to validate documents. Current and future browsers can check the syntax of documents that declare themselves as HTML. Any incorrect syntax (for example, a misspelled tag or missing attribute) returns an error. Validation is an optional process, but it is often used by designers and developers to find incomplete or missing code.

To learn more about validation, visit the W3C Markup Validation Service at http://validator.w3.org/about.html.

In this exercise, you will convert an older HTML page to HTML5. The document you'll convert is an HTML 4.01 document, so you will need to update the DOCTYPE to use the simpler HTML5 DOCTYPE.

1   In your text editor, choose File > Open and navigate to the HTML5_06lessons folder. Choose the 06_index.html file, and then click Open. Save the document with a new name to ensure you have a backup copy:

Choose File > Save As, name this file **06_index_work.html**, and save it within the HTML5_06lessons folder.

2   Preview this page in your browser to see the current layout. This layout is classified as a two-column fixed-width column layout. The basics are simple: there is a div element with the ID attribute wrap containing the other div elements that compose the layout of the page. The CSS style for the container div sets the width as 960 pixels and sets the left and right margins with the auto value to ensure the container is centered within the browser window.

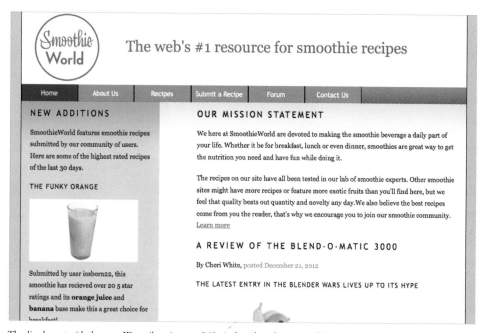

The div element with the wrap ID attribute is set to 960 pixels wide and contains all the other layout sections.

3   Close the browser and return to your text editor. Select the entire first line at the top of your page and delete it. Then type the following:

```
<!DOCTYPE html>
```

4   Save your file and preview in the browser. You should notice no change, but the browser recognizes this file as HTML5, not HTML 4.01.

5   Close your browser. You will replace some of the div elements with the new HTML5 elements, but first you'll review how to categorize the different types of content in HTML5.

The different categories used for HTML5 content

You can divide the content of a web page into categories that, for the most part, are not new to HTML5 and should be familiar to designers with experience building web pages.

- Metadata content
- Flow content
- Sectioning content
- Heading content
- Phrasing content
- Embedded content
- Interactive content

These categories are helpful for grouping the elements available for use. For example, the Flow content category describes all the elements available for use in the body of a page, but you can sub-divide flow content into smaller categories, such as phrasing and heading content.

Metadata content

Content that sets up the presentation or behavior of the rest of the content on the page is called metadata content. You can also use it to set up the relationship of the document with other documents. One obvious example of metadata content is the <meta> element, which often contains keywords or a description about the page, and is used by search engines to help categorize the page. Elements, such as <style> and <script>, are also considered metadata content since they contribute to the appearance and behavior of the primary content. Metadata content is located in the <head> section of a document.

```
<head>
    <title> SmoothieWorld: Providing access to the best smoothie
recipes anywhere. </title>
    <meta charset=utf-8>
    <link rel="stylesheet" href="styles.css" media="all">
    <script src= "jquery-1.4.2.min.js"></script>
</head>
```

Flow content

Flow content represents the elements that are considered the content of a web page. In other words, all the tags used to mark up content are placed in this category; for example, <p>, <h1>, <ol>, <table>, and so on. Flow content is traditionally text or an embedded file, such as an image or video. In HTML5, there are several new elements in this category; for example, <article>, <aside>, <audio>, <canvas>, <hgroup>, and many more.

```
<h3> This is flow content </h3>
    <p> Lorem ipsum dolor sit amet, consectetur adipisicing elit, sed
    do eiusmod tempor incididunt ut labore et dolore magna aliqua. Ut
    enim ad minim veniam, quis nostrud exercitation ullamco laboris
    nisi ut aliquip ex ea commodo consequat. </p>
```

Sectioning content

This category is new to HTML5 and currently includes four elements: `<article>`, `<aside>`, `<nav>`, and `<section>`. The W3C explains sectioning content as "defin[ing] the scope of headings and footers." Sectioning content is a subset of flow content; you will learn more about sectioning later in the lesson.

You can find the definitions of sectioning content and the other categories at: http://developers.whatwg.org/content-models.html#kinds-of-content.

```
<aside>
    <h1> New Additions </h1>
    <p> SmoothieWorld features smoothie recipes submitted by our
community of users. Here are some of the highest rated recipes of
the last 30 days.</p>
</aside>
```

Heading content

Heading content contains all the standard heading elements currently used in HTML 4.0: `<h1>`, `<h2>`, and so on. In addition, HTML5 includes the `<hgroup>` element, designed to group two or more headings. Heading content is a subset of flow content.

```
<hgroup>
    <h2>Top Rated Smoothies</h2>
    <h3>The Funky Orange</h3>
</hgroup>
```

Phrasing content

Phrasing content is the text of the document, which includes elements that mark up the text within a paragraph. Phrasing content is a subset of flow content.

```
<p> The advantage of having <strong> good </strong> hiking boots
becomes <em>extremely</em> clear after your third day of walking.</p>
```

Embedded content

Embedded content is content that imports another resource into your document page, such as an image or video.

```
<audio src="high_seas_rip.mp3" controls preload="auto" autobuffer>
</audio>
```

Interactive content

One of the most basic elements, the `<a>` tag (used for hyperlinks), is considered an interactive element. Other elements specifically intended for user interaction are also included in this category; for example, the `<textarea>` (used in forms) and the `<button>` elements.

```
<input type="button" value="Am I interactive?"
onClick='alert("Yep  I am interactive")'>
```

Clicking a button with a JavaScript alert attached.

In the next exercise, you will learn how to use some of the new HTML5 elements by converting an existing div-based layout to one that uses new sectioning elements and other new tags.

Using the new header element in HTML5

The HTML5 specification expands the current set of elements used today to give the designer and developer more precise semantic markup options. An example is the HTML `<div>` element used to divide a page into sections. The opening `<div>` tag is often paired with a class or ID attribute, which is then styled in CSS with various properties, such as `width`, `height`, and `background-color`. On its own, the `<div>` element is meaningless. Designers and developers give it meaning by adding ID and class names, but these names are arbitrary and not meaningful to a web browser. One of the goals of HTML5 is to add new elements that have inherent meaning within the structure of the document.

In this exercise, you will examine this structure by opening an existing layout that uses the current HTML framework, and then convert it to an HTML5 page.

1   In your text editor, choose File > Open, navigate to the HTML5_06lessons folder, select the base.css file, and choose Open.

2   Located approximately in the middle of the stylesheet is the following ID rule for the original header:

```
#masthead{
    background-color: white;
}
```

This is a simple rule that defines the style of the ID called masthead. For this exercise, the style is a white background-color.

3   Open your 06_index_work.html file.

4   The first step is to replace the existing <div> tag used for the header with one of the new HTML5 elements. Within your HTML, locate the following section of code:

```
<div id="masthead">
    <h1>The web's #1 resource for smoothie recipes</h1>
    <img src="images/smoothieworld_logo.jpg" width="200"
height="150" alt="smoothieworld_logo" />
</div>
```

The only content nested inside this div element is an image for the site logo and a heading 1 used for the tagline.

5   Delete the opening and closing div tags and replace them with the following:

```
<header id="masthead">
    <h1> The web's #1 resource for smoothie recipes </h1>
    <img src="images/smoothieworld_logo.jpg" width="200"
height="150" alt="smoothieworld_logo" />
</header>
```

The W3C specification explains that, "the header element represents a group of introductory or navigational aids." The specification also indicates that, "A header element is intended to usually contain the section's heading (an h1–h6 element or an hgroup element), but this is not required. The header element can also be used to wrap a section's table of contents, a search form, or any relevant logos."

In HTML5, you can use the <header> element multiple times on a page. Later in this lesson, you will learn more about when and where you could add additional headings.

An issue to consider about the <header> element, which is new to HTML5, is compatibility with web browsers not familiar with HTML5 tags. An explanation of this issue and how to resolve it is given in the next paragraphs.

6   Choose File > Save and preview your page in your current browser. If your browser supports the HTML5 `<header>` element, you will see no difference between this page and the page you previewed at the beginning of this lesson. If you use a browser that does **not** support the `<header>` element, the background color of the header will be orange.

The page as seen in a browser that supports the HTML5 `<header>` element.

Browsers that do not support the HTML5 `<header>` element will not recognize the style associated with it.

The difference in background colors occurs because a browser that does not support HTML5 will not render the style of the `<header>` element properly; the orange color you see is the background color of the surrounding div. Even though they are nested within the `<header>` element, the site logo and the site tagline remain visible because they use elements that the browser can recognize: `<img>` and `<h1>`.

This simple example demonstrates the dilemma concerning the new HTML5 elements: How can you use these tags if their styles are not recognized by older browsers? The next section shows two solutions for this problem.

The WHATWG defines the official use for HTML5 elements

A group called the WHATWG was formed to define and document the HTML5 specification. HTML5 is still under development, so we recommend using this group's website as your central resource for learning more about the new HTML5 elements and how to use them. You can find the WHATWG website at *http://developers.whatwg.org/*.

Adding support for HTML5 elements in browsers

To recap, when a web browser encounters an unknown element, and this element has associated CSS styles, this creates a problem. To be more specific, many older browsers treat the unknown `<header>` element as an inline (or text-level) element, not as a block element. Recall that inline elements are generally found within a block of text; for example, the `<strong>` element and the `<em>` element are inline. Block elements use blocks of space on the page and create new lines when added; for example, the `<p>` element and all the heading elements are block-level. When a browser treats a block element as inline, the result can often be problematic. To resolve this issue, you can add a line of CSS code to force the new HTML5 elements to display as block, not as inline.

1   If your reset.css style sheet is not currently open, open it now by choosing File > Open and navigate to your HTML5_06lessons folder. At the top of the page (after the first two lines of comment code), add the following block of code:

```
header, section, aside, nav, footer, figure, figcaption {
    display:block;
}
```

You listed all the selectors you'll use in this lesson. If needed, you can return to this section and add more new HTML5 selectors. The reason you put these rules within the reset.css document instead of the base.css document is so you can reuse this reset.css file for new HTML5 pages.

2   Save your CSS file and close it. Preview your page in your browser. If you happen to be using a browser that originally displayed orange in the header area, the background should be white again, demonstrating that the `<header>` style is being rendered properly.

The steps above will not work for Internet Explorer 6, 7, and 8 because these browsers completely ignore unfamiliar tags, rather than render them as inline, thus causing more significant problems. JavaScript is the best solution for supporting these older browsers, in particular the JavaScript library called Modernizr. This library is available for free download at www.modernizr.com.

If your browser still displays an orange header, you should refresh the page. Older versions of Safari, in particular, need to refresh the cache in order to use the most recent style sheet.

Because the various versions of Internet Explorer represent such a large proportion of web browsers, it would be a shame if there was no way to use HTML5 tags for these browsers. Luckily, there is a solution in the form of the Modernizr JavaScript library. The Modernizr library adds support for displaying HTML5 elements in older browsers and for enabling HTML5 elements in Internet Explorer 6, 7, and 8. The JavaScript within the library is designed to detect features within any browser, and then allows you to target styles as needed. There are rare occasions when a user's web browser does not support JavaScript, or JavaScript is turned off; in such cases, none of the fixes will be visible and the page will be broken. The majority of browsers do support JavaScript and it is rarely turned off by design. You'll now add a link to the Modernizr library.

3   In the head section of your HTML, locate the links to your two external stylesheets, and then add the following line:

```
<link rel="stylesheet" media="screen" href="reset.css" type="text/
css" />
<link  rel="stylesheet" media="screen"  href="base.css" type="text/
css" />
<script src="modernizr-1.7.js" type="text/javascript"></script>
```

This file is currently located in the HTML5_06lessons folder. Because Modernizr is an evolving JavaScript library, so you should visit *http://www.modernizr.com* and make certain you have the latest version.

4   Save your file and preview with Internet Explorer 6, 7, or 8. The header section now has its original background color, as intended.

 The web's #1 resource for smoothie recipes

An older browser, such as Internet Explorer 6, will display the HTML5 <header> element when using the Modernizr JavaScript library.

Continue using the new HTML5 elements now that you have provided support for virtually all popular browsers.

Adding the HTML5 <nav> elements

You'll now add the new HTML5 sectioning elements to divide your page into logical sections; the new sectioning elements are <section>, <article>, <aside>, and <nav>. You'll start by adding the <nav> element, since it's the most intuitive one.

1   Locate the following block of code in your HTML:

```
<div id="nav">
    <ul>
        <li><a  class="nav-home" href="08_layoutwork.html">Home
        </a></li>
        <li><a class="nav-about" href="08_aboutus.html">About Us
        </a></li>
        <li><a class="nav-recipe" href="recipes.html">Recipes
        </a></li>
        <li><a class="nav-submitrecipese"href="submitrecipe.html">
        Submit a Recipe</a></li>
        <li><a class="nav-forum"href="forum.html">Forum</a></li>
        <li><a class="nav-contact"href="contact.html">Contact Us
        </a></li>
    </ul>
</div>
```

This code uses a common list-based CSS navigation technique. The list in this code is unordered and nested within the div called nav. The new HTML5 <nav> element replaces the original div and ID.

2   Add the following code:

```
<nav>
    <ul>
        <li><a class="nav-home" href="08_layoutwork.html">Home</a>
        </li>
        <li><a class="nav-about" href="08_aboutus.html">About Us</a>
        </li>
        <li><a class="nav-recipe" href="recipes.html">Recipes</a>
        </li>
        <li><a class="nav-submitrecipese"href="submitrecipe.html">
        Submit a Recipe</a></li>
        <li><a class="nav-forum"href="forum.html">Forum</a></li>
        <li><a class="nav-contact"href="contact.html">Contact Us</
        a></li>
    </ul>
</nav>
```

3   You must now update the CSS selector used in your stylesheet. In your text editor, open your base.css stylesheet and locate the following code:

```
#nav {
    background-color:#60668B;
    height:35px;
    background-image:url(images/bg_nav.gif);
    background-repeat:repeat-x;
}
```

Remove the ID selector #nav and replace it with the nav selector, as instructed below.

3   Make the following change to your code:

```
nav {
    background-color:#60668B;
    height:35px;
    background-image:url(images/bg_nav.gif);
    background-repeat:repeat-x;
}
```

The styles are now connected to the nav element, not to the #nav ID. Choose File > Save to save your stylesheet. Preview your page in the browser. Notice that the navigation is still not working properly.

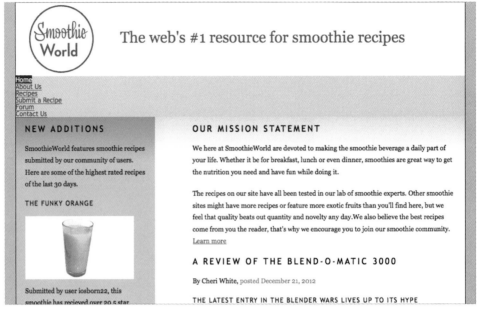

Your navigation appears broken because you need to update all styles associated with the #nav ID.

The navigation appears broken because there are other styles using the ID name #nav; you need to update them all.

Close your browser and return to your text editor.

4   In your base.css stylesheet, locate the rules below the nav rule. You need to update three different selectors: #nav li, #nav ul li a and #nav ul li a:hover. These selectors are called contextual selectors in CSS, and they target specific tags within the context of the parent style (in this case, the ID #nav.) For example, #nav li defines a style for list elements (li) inside the #nav div element.

Make the changes highlighted in red:

```
nav li {
    float:left; width:120px;
    height:35px;
    background-color:#7D83A4;
    text-align:center;
    border-left:1px black solid;
    border-right:1px black solid;
    line-height:35px;
}
```

```
nav ul li a {
    color:#ffffff;
    text-decoration:none;
    display:block;
}

nav ul li a:hover {
    background-color:#29336b;
    color:#F8F068;
}
```

5 Choose File > Save. Preview your page in the browser; your navigation should appear as it did originally.

If your navigation still appears broken, try refreshing your page in the browser. Some browsers hold onto the cache of the old page and need to be reloaded.

Your navigation now uses the HTML5 <nav> *element.*

Adding the other HTML5 sectioning elements

The other elements in the sectioning category are `<section>`, `<article>`, and `<aside>`. You'll add the `<section>` element first. The official definition of the section element is that it "represents a generic section of a document or application. A section, in this context, is a thematic grouping of content, typically with a heading." The definition also indicates that "The section element is not a generic container element. When an element is needed for styling purposes or as a convenience for scripting, authors are encouraged to use the div element instead. A general rule is that the section element is appropriate only if the element's contents would be listed explicitly in the document's outline."

You can find this definition at http://developers.whatwg.org/sections.html#sections.

This means that you can use a section when you need to divide important content, such as text and images, into logical areas. For example, the page you have been working on is a home page with content that is divided visually: the column on the left has some content and images; the second column to the right has content introducing users to the site, a product review, and images. The sidebar content is unrelated to the main content, and you will return to it later in the lesson. As you walk through the next steps, take note of the ID names, as they provide clues to the designer's intended use for these parts of the page.

1 Locate the opening `<div>` tag for the introduction section:

```
<div id="introduction-content">
```

Locate the closing `<div>` tag further down the page; you will change this tag shortly. The commenting code will help you identify it.

```
    <p><small>&copy; copyright 2038 SmoothieWorld.com.</small></p>
</div>
<!-- End of Introduction Content -->:
```

2 Scroll back to the opening `<div>` tag and replace it with the section tag as follows:

```
<section id="introduction-content">
```

3 Now scroll to the closing `</div>` tag and replace it with closing section tag:

```
    <p><small>&copy; copyright 2038 SmoothieWorld.com.</small></p>
</section>
<!-- End of Introduction Content -->:
```

The parent element of this new section is called `<div id="innerwrap">` and it is used for presentation purposes only, not for content. The style associated with this div gives it a background color and a tiled background image. Since this div is for presentation only, you can leave it as is.

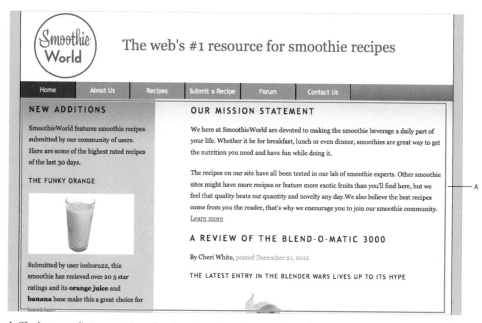

A. *The Innerwrap div is presentation only, not content, so it remains as a* `<div>` *element*

You can still use div elements in HTML5, but the best practice is to use them when there is no better choice within the new HTML5 elements.

4   Save your file and preview your page in the browser. Before continuing with the exercise, you need to understand the document outline model that HTML5 uses.

HTML5 document outlines

A weakness of the current HTML and XHTML specifications is the lack of a good document outline model. Consider the traditional outline you might create before writing a report or paper. Outlines illustrate the level of importance for your content as well as the relationships between this content. The HTML5 sectioning elements are designed to naturally create an outline structure from your web pages. Imagine if every web page had a "table of contents" that was automatically created from the structure of the tags being used. This is the intent of the HTML5 document outline.

The benefits of document outlines are not immediately apparent with current web browsers and mobile devices, but they can be useful for assistive devices, such as screen readers. For example, an HTML5-enabled screen reader might encounter a page with the `<nav>` element and choose to skip the nav, give the user the option to skip it, or read each item within the nav.

HTML and XHTML pages currently have document outlines based on the heading tags only, so they are very limited. The new HTML5 document outline model provides more detailed and meaningful outlines. For example, consider the following:

```
<body>
    <header>
        <h1>Welcome to our site</h1>
            <p>The best website in the world!</p>
    </header>
    <nav>
        <h1>Site Navigation</h1>
    </nav>
    <section>
        <h1>Breaking News</h1>
            <h2>Car overturns on highway</h2>
    </section>
</body>
```

This HTML has the following document outline:

1. Welcome to our site

    1. Site Navigation

    2. Breaking News

        1. Car Overturns on Highway

In this example, the `<nav>` and `<section>` elements create new sections within the outline, but their name comes from the nested heading. This makes headings a much more significant part of the document outline for HTML5 sites. The HTML5 model lets you add a new h1 element per section, so different sections of the page can have their own hierarchy, as shown in the example above.

A potential complication is that currently, the HTML5 specification states that sectioning elements must contain headings, or they appear listed as Untitled in the outline. For example, in the HTML example above, deleting the heading 1 element from the `<nav>` element makes the outline appear as follows:

1. Welcome to our site

    1. *Untitled* NAV

    2. Breaking News

        1. Car Overturns on Highway

Untitled sections in an outline might not seem important from a visual perspective, and this is an area of the HTML5 specification still being refined at the time of this writing. The rules dictating HTML5 outlines might change, but you should keep in mind that document outlines can help organize your HTML5 content and teach you more about sectioning. Creating a good document outline today will help ensure your site benefits when future browsers begin to use them. Designers and developers who prioritize the accessibility of their sites should pay particular attention to the role of the document outline.

h5o is a tool you can use to view the HTML5 outline in your browser. Access this tool at http://code.google.com/p/h5o/.

Deeper accessibility with WAI-ARIA roles

The Accessible Rich Internet Applications Suite (WAI-ARIA), whose goal is to organize and improve accessibility across the Web, is being developed alongside the HTML5 specification. A portion of the specification, called landmark roles, is specifically designed to be used with HTML and XHTML elements. A landmark role is a way of categorizing and identifying different parts of a web page. For example, a role called banner identifies the region that contains the primary heading of the page. You can add this role as an attribute for the HTML5 `<header>` element, for example:

```
<header role="banner">
```

Some of the landmark roles have direct equivalents to HTML elements. For example, the `role="form"` attribute is used for form elements and the `role="navigation"` is used for the HTML5 `<nav>` element. You can use landmark roles today, but you might need to review your code in the future to ensure that it is aligned with the specification when it is finalized.

You can learn more about WAI-ARIA and landmark roles at
http://www.w3.org/WAI/PF/aria/usage#usage_intro

You can find the W3C specification for WAI-ARIA 1.0 at
http://www.w3.org/WAI/PF/aria-practices/

The aria-practices page above also includes sample code and best practices for adding landmark roles into your web pages.

Adding the footer element

Keep in mind that the `<header>` element you added earlier is not a sectioning element and will not define a new section in a document outline. Similarly, the `<footer>` element is not categorized as a sectioning element; you can have more than one footer element per page. For example, you could have a site footer and a footer within a section. In this exercise, you will simply replace the original div named `footer` with the new HTML5 footer element.

1   In your HTML page, locate the `div` element with the ID attribute `footer` and make the following change:

```
<footer id="siteinfo">
    <p>Copyright SmoothieWorld 2011 </p> <p>Registration on or use of
this site constitutes acceptance of our <a href="useragreement
.html"> user agreement </a> and <a href="privacy.html">Privacy
Policy.</a></p>
</footer>
```

2   Open your base.css external stylesheet, locate the `#footer` ID, and change the selector as follows:

```
#siteinfo {
    clear:both;
    background-image:url(images/footer_background.jpg);
    background-repeat:no-repeat;
    width:960px;
    height:118px;
    padding-top:10px;
}
```

3   Below this rule, there is a contextual selector for paragraphs inside the footer that you need to update. Replace the `#footer p` selector as follows:

```
#siteinfo p {
    margin:10px 0 0 20px;
    width:280px;
    font-family:Verdana, Geneva, sans-serif;
    font-size:0.689em;
}
```

4   Save your HTML and CSS files, and then preview your page in the browser. Scroll to ensure the footer is displaying as expected. (If the image is not visible, try refreshing your browser page before checking your code for errors.) In a browser that supports the HTML5 tags, your page appears as it did when you previewed it earlier in this lesson.

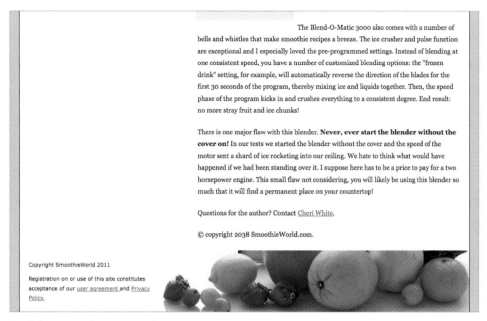

The Blend-O-Matic 3000 also comes with a number of bells and whistles that make smoothie recipes a breeze. The ice crusher and pulse function are exceptional and I especially loved the pre-programmed settings. Instead of blending at one consistent speed, you have a number of customized blending options: the "frozen drink" setting, for example, will automatically reverse the direction of the blades for the first 30 seconds of the program, thereby mixing ice and liquids together. Then, the speed phase of the program kicks in and crushes everything to a consistent degree. End result: no more stray fruit and ice chunks!

There is one major flaw with this blender. **Never, ever start the blender without the cover on!** In our tests we started the blender without the cover and the speed of the motor sent a shard of ice rocketing into our ceiling. We hate to think what would have happened if we had been standing over it. I suppose here has to be a price to pay for a two horsepower engine. This small flaw not considering, you will likely be using this blender so much that it will find a permanent place on your countertop!

Questions for the author? Contact Cheri White.

© copyright 2038 SmoothieWorld.com.

Copyright SmoothieWorld 2011

Registration on or use of this site constitutes acceptance of our user agreement and Privacy Policy.

Your design now uses the <footer> *element.*

In the next few exercises, you will group content using a combination of the tags you have learned, along with some new ones.

Adding the article and aside elements

In this section, you will learn about the <article> and <aside> elements, beginning with the article element. The W3C definition states that <article> is "a self-contained composition in a document, page, application, or site and that is, in principle, independently distributable or reusable, e.g. in syndication. This could be a forum post, a magazine or newspaper article, a blog entry, a user-submitted comment, an interactive widget or gadget, or any other independent item of content."

The key concept in the above definition is that it is self-contained. The <article> element was designed for content that can be extracted from its containing page; for example, the content referring to the Blender review in your current page.

You can nest the <article> *element within a* <section> *element, as in this exercise.*

1   About halfway down your page, locate the following heading 2 element: `<h2>A review of the Blend-o-Matic 3000</h2>` and add an opening `<article>` tag on the line above it:

```
<article>
    <h2>A review of the Blend-o-Matic 3000</h2>
```

2   Scroll to find the last paragraph of the review. Add the closing tag for the `<article>` element as indicated:

```
        <p><small>&copy; copyright 2038 SmoothieWorld.com.</small></p>
    </article>
</section>
<!-- End of Introduction Content -->
```

How will the article element be used?

The article element in HTML5 is optimal for content that might end up being published in different contexts or even on separate devices. For example, if you publish a weblog entry, visitors typically visit your website to read it. Nowadays, content can be redistributed in various ways and syndicated in formats, such as RSS feeds for newsreader applications, email, mobile applications, and more. In other words, the structure of published content needs to be flexible enough so reformatting is not required for different devices. The article element also contributes to accessibility by providing another level of logical structure within a document.

3   In HTML5, an `article` element can have a header, so you will add one now. Locate your opening `<article>` tag and immediately after, add a new header element within the article:

```
<header>
    <h2>A review of the Blend-o-Matic 3000</h2>
    <p>By Cheri White, <span class="posttime"> posted December 21,
2012</span></p>
    <h3>The latest entry in the Blender Wars lives up to its hype </h3>
</header>
```

Recall that in HTML5, you can have multiple headings per page as long as they are in different sections. In addition to the header, you can add a `<footer>` section within the article to help structure this section.

4   Locate the author contact and copyright section and add the following code:

```
<footer>
    <p>Questions for the author? Contact<a href="mailto:cheri@
    smoothieworld.com">Cheri White</a>.
    <p><small>&copy; copyright 2038 SmoothieWorld.com.
    </small></p>
</footer>
</article>
</section>
```

The rest of this exercise illustrates the use of the aside element. You can use the aside element in two ways. One is based on the traditional use of a sidebar for a website; the second is for an area of related content within a `<section>` element. You will start with the sidebar of the site.

5   In your HTML, locate the opening `<div>` tag with the ID name aside:

```
<div id="aside">
    <h2>New Additions</h2>
        <p>SmoothieWorld features smoothie recipes submitted by
        our community of users. Here are some of the highest rated
        recipes of the last 30 days.</p>
```

You will replace the `<div>` tag with the `<aside>` tag and change the ID name to make it more logical.

6   Change the opening `<div>` tag as follows:

```
<aside id="secondary-content">
    <h2>New Additions</h2>
        <p>SmoothieWorld features smoothie recipes submitted by our
community of users. Here are some of the highest rated recipes of
the last 30 days.</p>
```

This ID more accurately represents the role of this content. Make sure you close the `<aside>` tag.

7   Locate the original closing `<div>` tag and change it to a closing `<aside>` tag:

```
    <a href="#"><img src="images/learn_more.png" alt="Learn More"
width="235" height="187"></a>
</aside>
```

8   Open your base.css file and locate the original `#aside` selector; you need to change this to your new ID `#secondary-content`. Change the code as follows:

```
#secondary-content {
    float:left;
    width:300px;
    background-image:url(images/sidebar_bg.png);
    background-repeat:repeat-x;
    background-color:#EAB8C3;
}
```

There are related styles that used the original `#aside` selector, and you need to change all of them.

9   Change the selectors in the following three sets of style rules from `#aside` to `#secondary-content`:

```
#introduction-content p, #introduction-content h1,
#introduction-content h2, #introduction-content h3,
#secondary-content p, #secondary-content h2,
#secondary-content h3
```

and

```
#secondary-content img {
```

and

```
#introduction-content h2, #secondary-content h2, {
```

You'll now look at the alternative use for the `<aside>` element.

10 Locate the following code within the `<section>` element:

```
<div class="articleaside">
    <h3>Need more Data?</h3>
        <p> See how we put the Blend-O-Matic 300 to the test.
        <a href="#">Link.</a></p>
</div>
```

The `articleaside` class style for this div element is a small box floated to the left that allows the article content to flow around it. This is a common technique used to separate the continuous flow of text and lead the reader's eye towards other content. In some cases, this content might be a quote from the article itself (known as a pull quote), or a way to direct the reader to other related content, as is the case in this example.

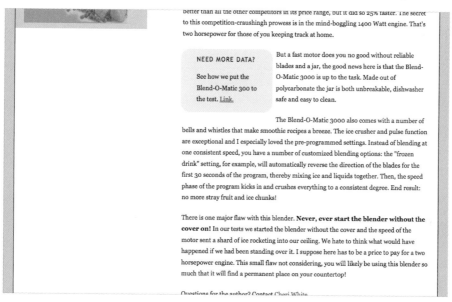

The `articleaside` *class represents a small, floated box within the article.*

To replace the div element with something more meaningful, use the aside element again.

11 Replace the div element as follows:

```
<aside="articleaside">
    <h3>Need more Data?</h3>
        <p>See how we put the Blend-O-Matic 300 to the test.
        <a href="#">Link.</a></p>
</aside>
```

When you use the `<aside>` element nested within a `<section>` element, as you did here, it represents content that is somewhat related to the section. When you use it as you did in the initial example, the `<aside>` element is a sidebar considered secondary content unrelated to the main content of the page.

12 Save your HTML and CSS files and preview your page in the browser.

Additional HTML5 elements

There are several new elements you can use to make the content of your pages more meaningful. For example, the `<figure>` and `<figurecaption>` elements help identify images and associated captions within your content. You'll also learn about the new `<time>` element, which lets you embed time and date information into your content.

1   Within the Blend-O-Matic article, locate the `<img>` tag linking to the blendomatic_3000.jpg image within your images folder, and add the following code:

```
<figure>
    <img src="images/blendomatic_3000.jpg" alt="Blend-O-Matic 3000
blender" />
    <p> The Blend-O-Matic 3000 retails for $199.99 </p>
</figure>
```

The `<figure>` element is designed for areas of your page, such as images, charts, and graphs. You can also use the `<figcaption>` element to provide further context.

2   Replace the paragraph tag with the figcaption tag using the following code:

```
<figure>
    <img src="images/blendomatic_3000.jpg" alt="Blend-O-Matic 3000
blender" />
    <figcaption> The Blend-O-Matic 3000 retails for $199.99
</figcaption>
</figure>
```

You can style the new elements as you would other elements. You'll now format the figure and the caption within the article.

3   Open your base.css file and add the following rule for the figure:

```
figure {
    float:right;
    border:1px solid gray;
    padding:0.25em;
    margin:0 1.5em 1.5em 0;
}
```

Save your CSS file and then preview your page in the browser. This style floats the image over to the right and applies borders, padding, and margin to set it off from the rest of the page.

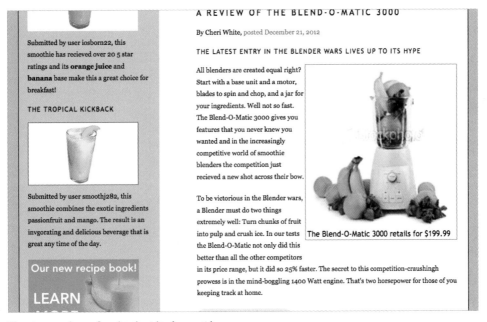

The <figure> element floated to the right of your article.

You will now style the caption. Return to your text editor.

4   Add the following style rule below your figure rule:

```
figcaption {
    text-align:center;
    font:italic 0.9em Georgia, "Times New Roman", Times, serif;
}
```

Save your HTML and CSS files and preview your page in the browser. This centers the caption and styles the text. You'll now add the new <time> element to help logically mark up your pages.

5   At the beginning of the article, locate the paragraph indicating the author's name and the date posted:

```
<p>By Cheri White, <span class="posttime"> posted December 21,
2012</span></p>
```

The problem with this format is that you can't indicate the time and date of the post in a format readable by a computer system. HTML5 adds the `<time>` element to help future web applications, such as calendars, make use of the data.

6   Add the following code:

```
<p>By Cheri White, <span class="posttime"> posted
<time datetime="2012-12-21">December 21, 2012</time>
</span></p>
```

The `datetime` attribute is formatted by year, month and day and is not required, but it addresses the problem of having computer-readable data on a web page. Additionally, if you publish the content, you can add a `pubdate` attribute.

7   Add the `pubdate` attribute, as shown here:

```
<p>By Cheri White, <span class="posttime"> posted
<time datetime="2012-12-21" pubdate > December 21, 2012</time>
</span></p>
```

If you use `pubdate`, a datetime attribute must also be present (as it is here). Save your HTML and CSS files and preview your page in the browser.

Revisiting familiar HTML elements

In addition to the new elements covered in this lesson, HTML5 redefines some of the existing HTML 4 elements to make them more useful. There are several elements that have been available for use in HTML for years, but are used infrequently. In some cases, the elements were not consistently styled in browsers and people did not use them. In other cases, the reason for using the tag changed over time. The best examples are the elements `<b>` and `<i>`. In the early days of HTML, `<b>` was used for bolding text and `<i>` was used to italicize text. With the advent and use of CSS, these tags were no longer used because they conflicted with the idea that HTML was intended for structure, not style. The preferred alternative for these tags are the `<strong>` tag instead of the `<b>`, and the `<em>` tag instead of `<i>`. These two elements are more flexible and structurally based. For example, you can use the `<strong>` tag not only to make font appear bold, but to make it uppercase, and the effect is the same.

HTML5 has redefined the `<b>` and `<i>` tags to make them consistent with the semantic intent of HTML.

1   In the first paragraph of the Blend-O-Matic article, locate the first instance of the product name Blend-O-Matic 3000 and add the following code:

```
<p> All blenders are created equal right? Start with a base unit and
a motor, blades to spin and chop, and a jar for your ingredients.
Well not so fast. The <b>Blend-O-Matic 3000</b> gives you
features...
```

The W3C specification states that the <b> element "represents a span of text to be stylistically offset from the normal prose without conveying any extra importance, such as key words in a document abstract, product names in a review, or other spans of text whose typical typographic presentation is boldened."

You can find more information at http://developers.whatwg.org/text-level-semantics.html#the-b-element.

2   Locate the last paragraph, find the phrase "Never, ever start the blender without the cover on!" and replace the <b> tags around the phrase:

```
<p>There is one major flaw with this blender. <strong> Never, ever
start the blender without the cover on! </strong> In our tests...
```

The W3C specification states that the strong element "represents strong importance for its contents." In this case, the content is a warning, so you can use this tag. The default styling for both tags is the same, so you will set a style for the <strong> tag to make it more conspicuous.

3   In your base.css file, add a new style at the bottom of your stylesheet as follows:

```
strong {
    font-weight:normal;
    color:red;
}
```

By setting the font-weight to normal, you override the default bolding, then you add the color red. All <strong> elements will now be styled the same way.

4   Save your HTML and your CSS file and preview in the browser.

The Blend-O-Matic 3000 also comes with a number of bells and whistles that make smoothie recipes a breeze. The ice crusher and pulse function are exceptional and I especially loved the pre-programmed settings. Instead of blending at one consistent speed, you have a number of customized blending options: the "frozen drink" setting, for example, will automatically reverse the direction of the blades for the first 30 seconds of the program, thereby mixing ice and liquids together. Then, the speed phase of the program kicks in and crushes everything to a consistent degree. End result: no more stray fruit and ice chunks!

There is one major flaw with this blender. Never, ever start the blender without the cover on! In our tests we started the blender without the cover and the speed of the motor sent a shard of ice rocketing into our ceiling. We hate to think what would have happened if we had been standing over it. I suppose here has to be a price to pay for a two horsepower engine. This small flaw not considering, you will likely be using this blender so much that it will find a permanent place on your countertop!

Questions for the author? Contact Cheri White.

© copyright 2038 SmoothieWorld.com.

Copyright SmoothieWorld 2011

Registration on or use of this site constitutes acceptance of our user agreement and Privacy Policy.

The <strong> element is used to signify importance for the content.

The `<i>` element has been redefined in much the same way. The W3C states that `<i>` represents "a span of text in an alternate voice or mood, or otherwise offset from the normal prose, such as a taxonomic designation, a technical term, an idiomatic phrase from another language, a thought, a ship name, or some other prose whose typical typographic presentation is italicized." This contrasts with the `<em>` tag, which "stress[es] emphasis of its contents." A simple way to distinguish the two is that the `<em>` element changes the meaning of the word, while the `<i>` element does not.

5   Save your HTML and CSS files. You are done with this lesson.

Self study

1   There are additional HTML5 elements not covered in this lesson. Recall that the HTML5 specification will be finalized in the year 2014. For up-to-date resources, see *www.thehtmldoctor.com*. For updates to the specification, see the primary sources for the HTML5 specification at *http://developers.whatwg.org/*.

2   You can also download the HTML5 outliner at *http://code.google.com/p/h5o/* and install one of the bookmarklets if it is supported by your primary browser. Save a copy of the page and add new sections, articles, and different levels of headings to see how the outline changes.

Review

Questions

1   True or false; HTML5 allows the use of only one `<header>` and one `<footer>` element per page.

2   What is sectioning content in HTML5? Name the four elements grouped within this category.

3   Define the `<aside>` element and give examples of the two main ways it can be used.

Answers

1   False. The `<header>` and `<footer>` elements can be used multiple times on a page. For example, you can have a site-wide header or footer and a section header or footer.

2   Sectioning elements in HTML5 define the scope of headers and footers, and are used to logically divide the areas of an HTML document. Sectioning elements also start new sections within a HTML5 document outline. The four sectioning elements are `<section>`, `<nav>`, `<aside>`, and `<article>`.

3   The `<aside>` element represents content, often called the sidebar, when it is separated from the content around it and used in the main context of a page. When used within a `<section>` element, the aside presents content vaguely related to the surrounding content, such as a pull quote.

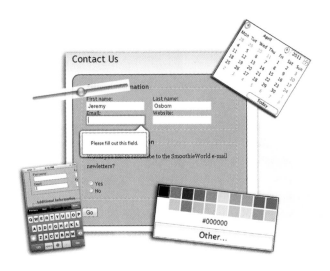

What you'll learn in this lesson:

- Backwards compatibility for HTML5 forms

- An overview of the new form elements in HTML5

- How to create a form using the new elements

Creating HTML5 Forms

In this lesson, you will learn how use the new HTML5 form elements in a way that is consistent and compatible with current web browsers.

Starting up

You will work with several files from the HTML5_07lessons folder in this lesson. Make sure you have loaded the HTML5lessons folder onto your hard drive from the supplied DVD. See "Loading lesson files" in the Starting Up section of this book.

 See Lesson 7 in action!

Use the accompanying video to gain a better understanding of how to use some of the capabilities shown in this lesson. The video tutorial for this lesson can be found on the included DVD.

To accurately preview the HTML5 content you will create in this lesson, you need a browser that supports the relevant HTML5 form features. See "Using web browsers that support HTML5 tags" in the Starting Up section of this book to determine whether you are using such a browser, or for instructions on downloading one.

The need for updated forms

Forms are one of the oldest and most familiar examples of interactivity on the Web. The FORM element was introduced to HTML in 1993, and the associated controls, such as check boxes, radio buttons, and the submit button, are a familiar part of the web user's environment. The functionality of forms has remained largely unchanged for many years. For this reason, the Web Hypertext Application Technology Working Group (WHATWG) began working on an update in the mid-2000s called the Web Forms 2.0 specification. The WHATWG integrated this specification into the current HTML5 specification.

The new components of HTML5 forms add functionality that web designers and developers traditionally incorporated through other means, such as JavaScript and Flash. For example, a common feature on many website forms is the required field, which prevents a user from submitting data until specific form fields have been filled. This functionality was not built into HTML 4.0.1, but it is now available in HTML5. Similarly, the limitations of the current library of form controls forced designers and developers who wanted sophisticated functionality, such as sliders and date pickers, to create JavaScript or other scripting language alternatives. HTML5 forms facilitate the creation of some of these types of features, thus reducing the amount of scripting knowledge needed to incorporate them.

Reviewing how forms work

Users interact with forms through *controls*, and HTML specifies a number of control types. For example, the following code creates a simple form that uses a *text input* control and a *submit input* control:

```
<form>
    First name:<input type="text" name="firstname" />
    <input type="submit" value="Go">
</form>
```

A simple form using standard control types is currently available in HTML and XHTML.

HTML5 introduces several new input types for varied information, such as email, telephone numbers, web addresses, and more. When rendered on the page, many of the new input types appear as traditional form fields, and a few appear as new controls. For example, the range input type is rendered as a slider in a browser that supports it.

```
<input type="range" min="0" max="100" value="50"/>
```

The range input type renders
as a slider on the page.

In addition to input types, the functionality of a form object can be dictated by its attribute. For example, a check box with no attribute specified will not appear selected; adding the checked attribute adds a check mark so the check box appears selected.

```
<input type="checkbox" checked />
```

An input type for a check
box with the checked attribute.

You can also style forms and form elements with CSS. In the next exercise, you will review the various components of a form and how to style them.

The components of a form

In this exercise, you will build a simple contact form and style it. The goal is for you to review standard forms as applicable to HTML 4.0 and XHTML 1.0 before adding the HTML5 features.

1 In your text editor, open 07_contactform.html located in the HTML5_07lessons folder. This page contains a very simple contact form that might be used to send a customer's name to a company.

```
<form id="contactform" action="" method="post">
    First name:<input type="text" name=" "> <br />
    Last name:<input type="text" name=" ">
    <input type="submit" value="Go">
</form>
```

Preview the page in your browser. Currently, the form has the two form fields and a submit button. Close your browser and return to your text editor.

A simple form currently exists with two text input fields and a submit button.

2   Notice that the opening form tag has three attributes: ID, action, and method.

The ID attribute lets you style the form with CSS. Currently, it sets the background color, width, and some padding.

The action attribute specifies the form-processing agent; in other words, the location to send the user's data. Typically, this value is a URL that points to a script hosted on a server. The script then takes the submitted data and processes it in a variety of different ways, such as placing it into a database; it could even format it into an email. When you leave the action value blank, as you did in this exercise, the form data is submitted to the URL the browser is currently on. There are other ways in which form data can be processed, but listing all such ways is beyond the scope of this lesson.

The method attribute for this exercise has a value of post; the other possible value is get. For the purposes of this exercise, the role of this attribute is not important. You can learn more about the method attribute at *http://www.w3schools.com/TAGS/att_form_method.asp.*

3 The second line is a text input control for the First name. As noted in the previous section, text is the default input type for forms. Note that the name attribute for this exercise is empty; you will now add it by typing the following code:

```
<form id="contactform" action="" method="post">
    First name:<input type="text" name="firstname"><br />
    Last name:<input type="text" name="lastname">
    <input type="submit" value="Go">
</form>
```

The name attribute you choose in a form control is important because it is used to refer to this control in the submitted data. For example, a name such as `textfield1` instead of `firstname` would not meaningfully represent the nature of the submitted data.

4 You'll now add a `<label>` element around the first line by typing the following code:

```
<label>First name:<input type="text" name="firstname"> </label> <br />
<label>Last name:<input type="text" name="lastname"> </label>
```

The `<label>` element is optional, but it makes your forms more accessible by letting the user click the text of the form field to select it; without a label, the user would have to click directly inside the form field. The addition of the `<label>` element is even more important for users who rely on assistive technology such as screen readers. When a form element has a label, additional cues and direction are present in the form, and these can be picked up by various devices. In short, adding labels to form elements helps make your form accessible by all users, and much more likely to be completed.

For more information about improving the accessibility of your forms, see http://webaim.org/techniques/forms/.

5 You'll now add a `<fieldset>` element to group the form elements on the page, and the `<legend>` element to add a caption to the top of the form. Add this code on the line below the opening form tag:

```
<fieldset>
    <legend> Personal Information </legend>
    <label>First name:<input type="text" name="firstname"> </label><br />
    <label>Last name:<input type="text" name="lastname"> </label>
</fieldset>
<input type="submit" value="Go">
```

The `<fieldset>` element groups relevant sections of a page. The first section of your form groups the fields for the user's personal information. You will add another fieldset to group form elements related to subscriptions for the site's newsletter.

6   After the closing `</fieldset>` tag, add the following code:

```
<fieldset>
   <legend>Additional Information</legend>
   <p>Would you like to subscribe to the SmoothieWorld e-mail
newsletter?</p>
<ol>
   <li> <input name="subscribe" type="radio"> <label>Yes</label> </li>
   <li> <input name="subscribe" type="radio"> <label>No</label> </li>
</ol>
</fieldset>
```

Make sure that you place this new `fieldset` element before the submit button code.

Note that you are using the `radioinput` type: one for Yes, the other for No. Both have the same name value. When radio buttons have the same name, users can only select one of them. Use check boxes to provide multiple options.

7   Choose File > Save and preview your page in the browser. Click the Last name text and note that the text field is activated as a result of the `<label>` element. Adding the `fieldset` and `legend` elements let you define the two sections on the page. Click the radio buttons and note that you can only select one button at a time.

Clicking the text for First name and Last name activates these fields because they have labels.

You can style form elements in CSS. You will now add some styles to this page.

8 Close your browser and return to your text editor. Open the base.css stylesheet located in your HTML5_07lessons folder. Scroll to the end of the stylesheet. For this lesson, all form styles are grouped into one section. Note the style rule that sets all margins and padding values of the form elements is zero. Also notice the style rule for the ID `#contactform` is empty.

```
form {
    margin:0 0 0 0;
    padding:0;
}

#contactform {

}
```

You will define a width for this ID and add some padding to override the default style of the form and to better position it within the page. You'll also add a background color, borders, and curved corners.

9 Add the following code:

```
#contactform {
    background: #9AB4D7;
    padding: 20px;
    width: 400px;
    border:solid #6E3E4D 2px;
    -webkit-border-radius: 18px;
    -moz-border-radius: 18px;
    border-radius: 18px;
}
```

The first four rules are basic properties that add background color, padding, width, and a border. The last three styles are varieties of the rule that modifies the corner radius of the form; you need all three styles to ensure cross-browser compatibility. Lesson 11 teaches you more about these CSS3 properties and how to use them.

10 Choose File > Save. Switch back to 07_contactform.html and preview your page in the browser. The padding and width styles create a narrower form and add space within the form.

Your contact form styled with CSS.

 If your browser does not support the `border-radius` *property, you will not see the rounded corners on your form.*

You will now add margins to the `fieldset` elements to increase the amount of space between the Required and Optional sections. Close your browser and return to your base.css stylesheet.

11 Add the following rule below the one for the contactform:

```
#contactform fieldset {
    margin-bottom:20px;
}
```

12 You can also add rules to style the legend. Add the following new rule to make the text bigger, bolder, and more colorful:

```
legend {
    color:#384313;
    font-size:1em;
    font-weight:bold;
    padding-bottom:10px;
}
```

You can also use positioning properties to control the location of your form objects. This is where the `<label>` element is useful.

13 Add the following rule to style the label elements inside the contact form:

```
#contactform label {
    float:left;
    font-size:13px;
    width:110px;
    margin-right:60px;
}
```

By floating the label elements to the left, you can place the first and last name fields on the same line. Defining the width and adding margins can also help you accomplish the same goal.

Save your file and preview it in the browser.

The label elements are now floated and have margins.

Notice that there are two problems with your page: the first and last name fields are not even because there is a break element used to place them on separate lines. In addition, the radio buttons are floated. You will fix these two problems now. Close your browser and return to your text editor.

14 In your HTML on the 07_contactform.html page, locate the `</br>` tag after the First name line and delete it. The first and last name fields are now aligned.

To fix the radio buttons, add additional information to your label and input tags as explained in the next steps.

15 Add the following code to your four label and input elements:

```
<label for="firstname">First name:<input id="firstname" type="text"
name="firstname"></label>
<label for="lastname">Last name:<input id="lastname" type="text"
name="lastname"> </label>
```

and further down in the second fieldset:

```
<li>
    <input name="subscribe" id="yes" type="radio">
    <label for="yes">Yes</label>
</li>

<li>
    <input name="subscribe" id="no" type="radio">
    <label for="no">No</label>
</li>
```

The for attribute defines a binding between each label and its new ID. Now that you have defined a specific connection in the HTML, you can create specific styles in the CSS. For this exercise, you will add two styles for the radio buttons to return them to their original position.

16 In your base.css stylesheet, add the following styles (be sure you type the following code carefully, an added or missing space may not result in the correct results):

```
#contactform label[for=yes],#contactform label[for=no] {
    float:none;
}
```

This completes the loop and assigns styles to the labels of the yes and no radio buttons.

Save your stylesheet and your HTML file and preview your page in the browser. Your form now has styles that are consistent, attractive, and useful.

Adding specific styles for the labels gives you precise control over their appearance.

This concludes the review of web form foundations and styling. Keep this file open, in the next exercise you will add some of the new HTML5 form input types and attributes to your contact form.

Adding new HTML5 input types and attributes

The first new input type you will add is the email input type, designed to identify a user's email address. Note that when a browser does not support this new HTML5 input type, the browser reverts to the default text input type. For this particular input type, the page looks and acts the same from the user's perspective.

1   In your 07_contactform.html file, locate the code for the Last name field and add the new email input type on the next line as follows:

```
<label for="lastname">Last name:<input id="lastname" type="text"
name="lastname"></label>
<label for="email">Email:<input id="email" type="email"
name="customeremail"></label>
```

2   Save your file and preview it in the browser.

```
Contact Us

  Personal Information
  First name:           Last name:
  [        ]            [          ]
  Email:
  [                  ]
```

Your email form field appears below the first two form fields.

The new email input type form field looks just as the first two text input type form fields. A new email classification in the HTML will eventually let designers easily sort the data from websites. Potentially, this means that the data could be sent automatically to a specific database. Additionally, future browsers could render all email input type fields differently from other type fields. For example, an email icon or another visual cue could be placed within the field.

Mobile devices take advantage of HTML input types

Web browsers designed for mobiles devices are taking advantage of the new HTML5 input types. For example, Apple's mobile Safari browser for iOS devices, such as the iPhone and iPad, render many of the new HTML5 input types differently than desktop browsers. Consider the email input type: when you tap the form field of the email input type on an iOS device, the onscreen keyboard changes automatically. The following figure shows the standard onscreen keyboard; note the size and placement of the spacebar.

Standard iPhone onscreen keyboard.

(continues)

Mobile devices take advantage of HTML input types (continued)

When the email form field is in focus, notice that the spacebar's width narrows, and the @ symbol and the period appear to the right.

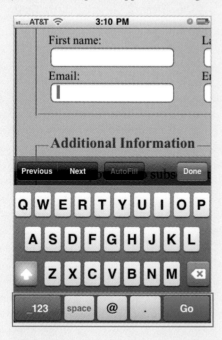

The iPhone onscreen keyboard changes when an email field is in focus.

The user needs the @ and period symbols to add a proper email address. Without the keyboard change, the user would need to manually change the keyboard layout to access the symbols. When the user taps a new field, the screen returns to the standard layout.

Other HTML5 input types also trigger changes to the iOS onscreen appearance; for example, the URL input for website addresses, and the tel input for telephone numbers are recognized by the browser.

Resources for determining browser support

Apple's iOS offers good support for the new HTML5 form features, but it is not full support. The following subsections describe two resources you can use to determine the range of support current browsers provide for the various form features in HTML5.

Looking up support for all browsers

The site *caniuse.com* features a table that lists the level of support for HTML5 form features in four categories: *Supported*, *Not Supported*, *Partially Supported*, and *Support Unknown* (this category is reserved for future browsers). You can then cross reference the level of support for past, current, and future versions of the most common web browsers.
http://caniuse.com/#feat=forms

(continues)

Mobile devices take advantage of HTML input types (continued)

Determining support for your own browser

Visiting *caniuse.com* doesn't tell you specifically which HTML5 inputs and attributes are supported in your current browser. Visiting the following website automatically identifies your browser, displays a table that lists the details of each new HTML5 type and attribute, and indicates whether a given type and attribute would work in your browser.
http://www.miketaylr.com/code/input-type-attr.html

Another new HTML5 input type is URL, designed for website addresses.

3   If your browser is still open, close it and go back to your 07_contactform.html file. Add the following code below the email field:

```
<label for="email">Email:<input id="email" type="email"
name="customeremail"></label>
<label for="website">Website:<input id="website" type="url"
name="customerwebsite"></label>
```

If you preview this page in a web browser you will see a new form field for the website. It will be helpful in the future to have this new input type to categorize website URLs for data.

You will now add a placeholder attribute for the First name and Last name fields. Placeholder text is a visual prompt within a form field that helps your users understand what to type in the field. Before HTML5, you could only add this feature with a scripting language, such as JavaScript.

4   Add the following code to the First name and Last name fields:

```
<label for="firstname">First name:<input id="firstname" type="text"
name="firstname" placeholder="Enter Your First Name" ></label>
<label for="lastname">Last name:<input id="lastname" type="text"
name="lastname" placeholder="Enter Your Last Name" ></label>
```

5   Save your file and preview it in the browser. The First name and Last name fields now have placeholder text within them. If your browser does not support the placeholder text, you will only see a blank field.

Close your browser. You will now add a required attribute to the First name, Last name, and Email fields. A required attribute in a field forces the user to enter information into the field before submitting the form. As is the case with placeholder text, required fields could only be added with a scripting language before HTML5.

6   Add the following code for the First name, Last name, and Email fields:

```
<label for="firstname">First name:<input id="firstname" type="text"
name="firstname" placeholder="Enter Your First Name" required></label>

<label for="lastname">Last name:<input id="lastname" type="text"
name="lastname" placeholder="Enter Your Last Name" required></label>

<label for="email">Email:<input id="email" type="email"
name="customeremail" placeholder="Required Field" required></label>
```

Save your file and preview in the browser. Type your first name and last name, but do not type an email address. Click the Go button. If your browser supports the required attribute, you might see a visual alert. If your browser does not support the attribute, your data will be submitted and disappear. The following figure illustrates the behavior of Firefox 5.0, which triggers a popup on the first field and outlines all required fields in red.

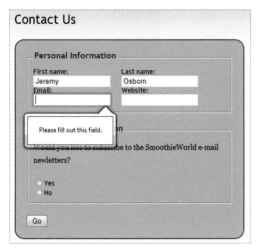

The required field alert in the Firefox 5.0 browser.

Remember that you can obtain up-to-date information regarding the support different browsers offer for form validation at http://caniuse.com/#feat=form-validation.

Autofocus is another HTML5 attribute you can now use. The `autofocus` attribute lets you predetermine the form field where you want the user to start. The result is a useful lead for the user.

7   Add the following code to the First name field:

```
<label for="firstname">First name:<input id="firstname" type="text"
name="firstname" placeholder="Enter Your First Name" required
autofocus></label>
```

Save your page and then preview it in the browser. If your browser supports the autofocus attribute, the First Name field will be focused with your cursor in the field. Begin to type your first name. In the previous step, you typed your first name in full, so the form should auto complete the name. This is the default behavior of HTML5 form fields. You might want to disable this behavior, particularly when the fields are used to enter potentially sensitive data, such as credit card information. You can use the autocomplete attribute to make this feature unavailable.

8   In your text editor, locate the first name field and add the `autocomplete` attribute and value as follows:

```
<label for="firstname">First name:<input id="firstname" type="text"
name="firstname" placeholder="Enter Your First Name" required
autofocus autocomplete="off"></label>
```

Save your page and then preview it in the browser. Begin typing your first name in the field; it should not be auto completed. Typing the Last name field should still trigger the autocomplete.

To make the autocomplete attribute unavailable for an entire form, add `autocomplete="off"` *to the opening form tag.*

You can easily add the new HTML5 types and attributes described in this subsection to new and existing forms. Browsers that do not support the features don't negatively impact your site because their behavior to these new features is similar to browsers that do support the features. If your site must have functionality, such as required fields and auto-complete for all browsers, you will need to add scripting solutions; different options are explained at the end of this lesson.

Save and close 07_contactform.html as well as base.css.

Creating an order form with new HTML5 input types and attributes

In this next exercise, you will build a basic form using the new `list`, `datalist`, `min`, and `max` attributes. The `list` attribute and `datalist` input types let you create a menu of choices for a user to choose from. The `min` and `max` attributes help define a range of numbers. All four of these attributes replace and address current reliances on JavaScript.

Important: The `datalist` *element used in this exercise has very limited support in browsers. As of this writing, Firefox and Opera are the only two browsers to support it. If you do not have a version of these browsers on your current system, you can still follow the exercise. Later in this lesson, you will learn techniques that let you add support for older browsers.*

1   Choose File > Open, navigate to your HTML5_07lessons folder, and open the 07_orderform.html document. The initial form element and fieldset have already been created for this exercise; you will add the datalist element.

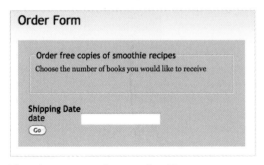

This is the empty contact form you will modify.

2   In the line below the `<legend>` element, add the following line:

```
<form id="orderform" action="" method="post">
    <fieldset>
        <legend> Order free copies of smoothie recipes </legend>
        <input type="text" list="smoothierecipes">
        <p>Choose the number of books you would like to receive</p>
    </fieldset>
```

The `input type` is the common `text` type, and the `list` attribute defines a meaningful name for the group of smoothie recipes you will add. The list attribute requires a `<datalist>` element to be useful.

3   Add the datalist element as follows:

```
<form id="orderform" action="" method="post">
    <fieldset>
        <legend> Order free copies of smoothie recipes </legend>
        <input type="text" list="smoothierecipes">
        <datalist id="smoothierecipes">

        </datalist>
        <p>Choose the number of books you would like to receive</p>
    </fieldset>
```

Be sure to press the Return key a few times between the opening and closing `<datalist>` tags because you need to add three option elements. The datalist element requires an option element for every choice you want the user to have. For this exercise, you will add three options for different smoothie recipes.

4   Add the three following option elements within the `<datalist>` element:

```
<datalist id="smoothierecipes">
    <option value="Mango Smoothie">Mango Smoothie</option>
    <option value="Strawberry Smoothie">Strawberry Smoothie</option>
    <option value="Banana Smoothie">Banana Smoothie</option>
</datalist>
```

Save your file and preview it in your browser. If you have a browser that supports the datalist element, press the down arrow on your keyboard to see the choices appear.

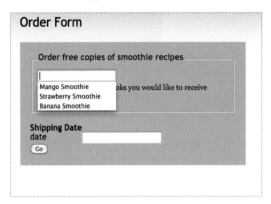

The datalist *element lets the user type a custom value or choose from a pre-defined list.*

For an up-to-date list detailing the support of the datalist element in different browsers, visit:
http://caniuse.com/#feat=datalist

5   You'll now focus on the next section of the form, the section labeled "Choose the number of recipe books you would like to receive". How could you add a form field that prevented the user from adding any number above 3? In HTML5, there is a new input type called `number` you can use; you can also specify the minimum and maximum numbers allowed for a form field.

6   Close your browser; in your text editor, locate the paragraph, "Choose the number of books you would like to receive," and add the following code:

```
<p>Choose the number of books you would like to receive</p>
<input type="number" value="1">
```

The number state creates a field with a default value of 1. You need to add the min and max attributes to set number limits.

7 Add the following min and max attributes and their values:

```
<input type="number" min="1" max="3" value="1">
```

In a browser that supports these attributes, such as Safari 5, a new control appears; for this exercise, the new control is a vertical double-arrow, often referred to as a spin box control. A user with a browser that supports the number input type and the min and max attributes can click the arrows and cycle through the 3 options.

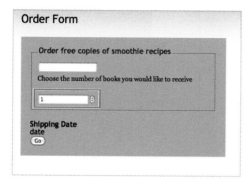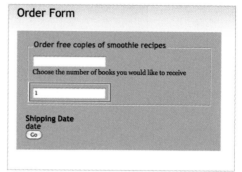

A browser that supports the min *and* max *attributes displays a control, as the figure on the left shows. A browser that does not support the* min *and* max *attributes reverts to a plain text field, as the figure on the right shows.*

You can convert this spin box control into a slider bar by changing the input type value from number to range.

8 Close your browser and in your text editor change the input type value as follows:

```
<input type="range" min="1" max="3" value="1">
```

Save your file; if you are using a supported browser, you should see a slider with a thumbnail you can drag along the path.

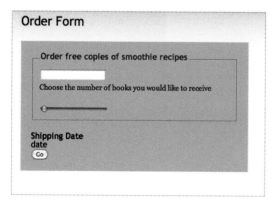

A slider bar control lets the user click and drag a thumbnail along a path, thus affecting the page.

You can perform other actions with the slider. For example, you could increase the max value and add the step attribute to force the slider to move along specific intervals. You could also have the thumbnail first appear in the middle of the bar by changing the value attribute. Both of these examples are illustrated in the next step.

9   Close your browser and in your text editor modify the max and value attributes, and add the new step attribute as follows:

```
<input type="range" min="1" max="100" value="50" step="10" >
```

Save your page and preview in the browser. The thumbnail should appear in the center of the slider; when you drag it, it should move in increments of 10.

Note that in this example, the slider has no effect on the page. You could connect the value of the slider to an object through JavaScript. The following example demonstrates the effect.

10 In the head section of your HTML page, locate the `<script>` element that links to the modernizr library; on the line below, add the following new `<script>` tag and JavaScript code:

```
<script src="modernizr-1.7.js"></script>
<script type="text/javascript"> function showValue(newValue) {
    document.getElementById("range").innerHTML=newValue; }
</script>
```

You'll now need to add the necessary JavaScript and a number for the JavaScript to control.

11 Add the following JavaScript event to your slider code and the span element:

```
<input type="range" min="1" max="100" value="50" step="10"
onchange="showValue(value)" >
<span id="range"></span>
```

Save your file and preview the page in your browser. When you click and drag the thumbnail, the number value changes.

Using JavaScript, you can view the value of the slider as you drag it.

Keep in mind that the slider control, and the ability to style it, still has limited and inconsistent browser support. Currently, there is no simple way to style this control using CSS; browser manufacturers will likely add this ability in the future.

The elements discussed thus far represent the limit of what today's web browsers can render. The next section provides a brief description of form controls that are currently under development. Close your HTML file as you will not need in in the next exercise.

HTML5 form features under development

Many of the new HTML5 form features replace JavaScript solutions used today. HTML5 also provides other sophisticated controls for forms; for example, the date picker and the color picker. Native browser support for these features, particularly without help from JavaScript, is extremely limited.

Date picker

You can see an example of a date picker control when you click the calendar icon on an airline website. The current implementation for these controls is most often based on JavaScript. HTML5 forms can add a date picker natively now, but browser support is virtually non-existent, with the exception of the Opera web browser. The basic code for this control is very simple:

```
<input type="date">
```

Version 11.0 of the Opera web browser will use the control illustrated in the following figure when the page is rendered.

A date picker as rendered in the Opera web browser.

You can use other values for the date picker control, including `time`, `week`, `datetime`, and `datetime-local`. When these input types are fully supported, it will make many designers' and developers' jobs easier.

Color picker

You can't find color pickers on websites as often as you can date pickers, but a color picker control is also part of the HTML5 form specification. Color pickers are more often used in web applications as components that let the user indicate a color for a specific purpose; for example, to change a background or color scheme. Currently, the primary solution for developers and designers who want to add a color picker to their web applications is to use a JavaScript plug-in, such as Jpicker. The HTML5 code for a color picker is very simple:

```
<input type="color">
```

Version 11.0 of the Opera web browser will use the control illustrated in the following figure when the page is rendered:

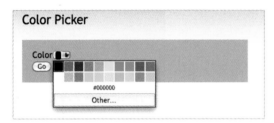

A color picker as rendered in Opera 11.

Providing fallbacks for browsers that don't support HTML5 features

As indicated in the previous section, the more advanced HTML5 form elements, such as the Date and Color pickers, are currently under development and you should not currently use them as part of your website design. In the case of the more stable features, such as the `required` and `placeholder` attributes, only the browsers that support the features will display the content. The following figure shows an example of a browser that supports the placeholder attribute and a browser that does not. In this case, the First and Last name fields are empty in the browser that does not support the attribute.

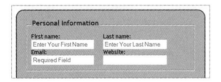 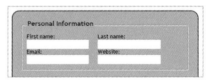

A browser that supports the HTML5 `placeholder` attribute is shown on the left; a browser that does not is shown on the right.

If you want placeholder text to appear for browsers that do not support HTML5 form features, you will need to provide a JavaScript fallback. The fallback needs to do two things: detect if the browser supports HTML5, and then substitute a JavaScript placeholder in the form. The Modernizr JavaScript library (used at the beginning of Lesson 6 to provide support for HTML5 elements in Internet Explorer 6, 7, and 8) is a good choice for this.

The Modernizr library is unique because it detects if a specific HTML5 form feature is supported in the browser; when the form feature is not supported, Modernizr calls the JavaScript required for the feature. This technique is relatively new in web design, and it is sometimes referred to as *regressive enhancement* or a *polyfill*.

This section explains how to use three different JavaScript libraries, Modernizr.js, yepnope.js, and hf5.js, to ensure that your HTML5 form features are active in the browsers that support them, and that a backup JavaScript option is used for browsers that don't support them.

1   Open the HTML5_07lessons folder. Locate these two files: modernizr.custom.03287. js and h5f.js. The first file is a custom version of the Modernizr JavaScript library that combines the standard Modernizr code with the code from a script loader called Yepnope. For more information about the role of script loaders and how to generate custom code, be sure to read the "Creating Custom Modernizr Code" section later in this exercise.

The second file, h5f.js, is an example of JavaScript that adds features, such as placeholder text or required fields, to web pages.

2   In your text editor, choose File > Open, navigate to your HTML5_07lessons folder, and open the 07_contactform.html document you worked on earlier in the lesson. Note that within your head section and below the links to the stylesheets, there is a link to the custom Modernizr code:

```
<script src="modernizr.custom.03287.js"></script>
```

You will now add a new script element below this line, and then add a JavaScript function.

3   Type the following code:

```
<script src="modernizr.custom.03287.js"></script>

<script>
    yepnope({
        test:Modernizr.input.placeholder,
        nope:'h5f.js'
        });
</script>
```

This JavaScript function uses the Modernizr detection code to test whether the user's browser supports the HTML5 placeholder attribute. If it does, the browser uses it. If the browser does not support the attribute, it uses the h5f.js library to provide the feature. This is an elegant solution because the h5f JavaScript code is downloaded only when the user needs it.

You need more code to complete the process.

4   Add the following code and pay careful attention to all of the syntax:

```
yepnope({
    test:Modernizr.input.placeholder,
    nope:'h5f.js',
    callback:function(url, result, key) {
    H5F.setup(document.getElementById(" "));
    } });
```

This code is a callback function that ensures the h5f.js code will not be used until the page downloads it. Note the empty quotation marks on the fifth line: you need to add the name of the ID you are targeting to make the link between this new JavaScript and your HTML.

5   Scroll to locate the opening form tag in your HTML and note that it has the ID name, contactform; this is the value you need to add in your function.

```
<form id="contactform" action="" method="post">
```

6   Scroll back to your function and add the ID value:

```
yepnope({
    test:Modernizr.input.placeholder,
    nope:'h5f.js',
    callback:function(url, result, key) {
    H5F.setup(document.getElementById("contactform"));
} });
```

This completes the necessary code: browsers that support the HTML5 `placeholder` attribute will use it; browsers that don't support it will load the JavaScript `placeholder` alternative.

Save your file. In order to test this page, you would need access to a browser that does **not** support the HTML5 placeholder attribute.

For example, the following figure compares the form as seen in Firefox 5.0 (which supports the HTML5 `placeholder` attribute) and Internet Explorer 8 (which does not support the `placeholder` attribute and is using the JavaScript fallback).

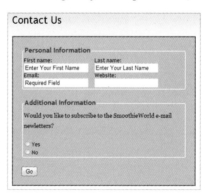

A browser that supports the HTML5 placeholder attribute is shown on the left; a browser that uses the JavaScript option is shown on the right.

Creating custom Modernizr code

The Modernizr JavaScript library is primarily a browser detection script with additional features, such as adding support for HTML5 elements. You do not always need to access all the code within the library; Best Practices is to not download scripts when you only need a small percentage of the functions within. For such cases, you can use the Modernizr 2 library, which lets you generate custom code using only those features you want to support.

1. Go to the following address: *http://modernizr.github.com/Modernizr/2.0-beta/* (Note: Modernizr 2.0 is a beta version at the time of publication.) A list of check boxes to detect CSS3, HTML, and Miscellaneous properties appears.

CSS3   **HTML5**   **MISC.**
                          toggle   toggle   toggle
- [ ] @font-face   - [ ] applicationCache   - [ ] Geolocation API
- [ ] flexible box model   - [ ] Canvas   - [ ] Inline SVG
(flexbox)   - [ ] Canvas Text   - [ ] SVG
- [ ] text-shadow   - [ ] Drag 'n Drop   - [ ] SMIL
- [ ] rgba()   - [ ] hashchange   - [ ] SVG clip paths
- [ ] hsla()   - [ ] History (pushState)   - [ ] Touch Events
- [ ] border-image   - [ ] HTML5 Audio   - [ ] WebGL
- [ ] border-radius   - [ ] HTML5 Video
- [ ] box-shadow   - [ ] IndexedDB
- [ ] opacity   - [x] Input Types   **OTHER**
- [ ] background-size   - [x] Input Attributes   toggle
- [ ] multiple backgrounds   - [ ] localStorage   - [x] HTML5 Shim/IEPP
- [ ] CSS Animations   - [ ] postMessage   - [x] Modernizr.load
- [ ] CSS Columns   - [ ] sessionStorage   (yepnope.js)
- [ ] CSS Gradients   - [ ] Web Workers
- [ ] CSS Reflections   - [ ] Web Sockets
- [ ] CSS 2D Transforms   - [ ] Web SQL Database   **GENERATE IT!**
- [ ] CSS 3D Transforms
- [ ] CSS Transitions   After generating, copy the
                                                                 source below or hit the
                                                                 download button

`// MINIFIED SOURCE`

Select checkboxes to add the desired tests and features to your custom Modernizr code.

2. To generate the custom code used in the last exercise to detect whether HTML5 form features are present, select the Input Types and Input Attributes options. In the Other section, note that the yepnope.js library you used in the previous exercise is included by default.

3. Click the Generate button to create the custom code, and then click the Download button to download the external JavaScript file. You can save this file in your root folder, and then link to it from any HTML page that needs it.

7. Choose File > Save All and then close your lesson files.

Congratulations! You have completed this lesson.

Self study

The best way to experiment with the new HTML5 forms is to use them within a project. Save a copy of your 07_contactform.html document and name it **07_addprofileform.html**. Create a new form that would be used to build the user profile for a SmoothieWorld profile page. Be sure to add fields for email, URL, and any required fields you might think necessary.

Review

Questions

1 What is the `<label>` element and how can it be used in a form?

2 What is the `placeholder` attribute and why would you use it in a form?

3 Todd is designing a hotel website and is considering using the date input type in order to add a date picker control, allowing users a way to access a popup calendar to make reservations. What factors should go into his decision to use the HTML5 date input type?

Answers

1 The `<label>` element associates a label (typically invisible) for a specific input element. Labels can be clicked on by the user resulting in better usability. Additionally, labels can be bound to an ID element allowing for custom styling by the designer.

2 The `placeholder` attribute is the initial text that appears within a form field. You can use placeholder text to give your users additional guidance for what to enter in any given field.

3 The date input type has very little browser support at this time. If Todd uses it without a fallback option, the hotel users will not see a datepicker control. A better option would be to provide a JavaScript fallback for users whose browsers do not support the input type.

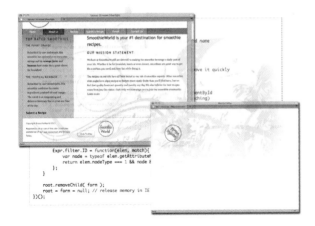

What you'll learn in this lesson:

- An overview of how to use JavaScript
- How to use the jQuery JavaScript library

Introduction to JavaScript and jQuery

In this lesson, you'll learn the fundamentals of adding interactivity to your pages with JavaScript and the jQuery JavaScript library.

Starting up

You will work with several files from the HTML5_08lessons folder in this lesson. Make sure you have loaded the HTML5lessons folder onto your hard drive from the supplied DVD. See "Loading lesson files" in the Starting Up section of this book.

See Lesson 8 in action!

Use the accompanying video to gain a better understanding of how to use some of the capabilities shown in this lesson. The video tutorial for this lesson can be found on the included DVD.

This lesson uses the TextWrangler text editor to create the markup, but you can use any text editor and achieve the same results.

Interactivity on the Web

The Web is an interactive medium by nature, and hyperlinks are good examples of this. Even the most basic website requires user interaction, and the decisions made by the designer can affect the user's perception of the site as well as their experience. HTML offers very few possibilities for interaction, but by adding CSS, you have options such as CSS rollovers and the ability to style hyperlinks. CSS does have certain limitations, which you can overcome by using the JavaScript scripting language and interactive media such as Flash.

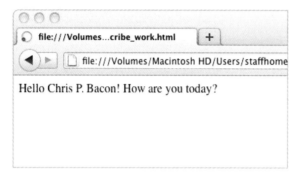

A form button with no JavaScript attached will do nothing when the user clicks on it.

Adobe Flash

Flash was designed in the early days of the Web to perform interactive tasks. It began as a way to create and share animations on the Web, and quickly grew to include sophisticated interactivity and the ability to display and control video. In recent years, alternative technologies, such as Microsoft Silverlight and the HTML5 family, have emerged as an alternative to Flash and share many of its benefits and disadvantages. The functionality and role of Flash and Silverlight often overlap with HTML, CSS, and JavaScript and sometimes even replace them.

JavaScript

JavaScript lets you extend the functionality and appearance of a website through a range of interactive tasks that vary from the simple, such as validating a form, to the complex, such as animated slide shows. JavaScript is a scripting language that is more complicated to learn and use than HTML and CSS. The availability of JavaScript libraries has made it easier to add interactive elements, which has resulted in an increase in the number of developers using JavaScript. JavaScript libraries provide interactive functions, largely hidden from view from the designer, that can be added to a page with little effort. Later in this lesson, you will learn about jQuery, one of the JavaScript libraries.

The next part of this lesson provides an overview of working with JavaScript technology, and you will create an interactive photo gallery.

JavaScript basics

JavaScript is a scripting language that has its own syntax and structure. A full description of JavaScript and how to use it is beyond the scope of this book. This lesson provides a brief introduction, but there are several books and training courses where you can learn about JavaScript. Some references are listed below.

JavaScript References

These are a few resources we recommend for learning JavaScript.

Eloquent JavaScript: A Modern Introduction to Programming

Eloquent JavaScript provides an introduction to the JavaScript programming language and programming basics that you can apply to other languages. This HTML version includes interactive examples and a way to use interactive code.

http://eloquentjavascript.net/

JavaScript Bible

This book is a JavaScript reference guide written for designers who want to improve their programming skill-set.

DOM Scripting: Web Design with JavaScript and the Document Object Model

This book by Jeremy Keith was written with a designer audience in mind and focuses on how to add enhancements to your web pages.

In this lesson, you will gain a basic understanding of how JavaScript interacts with HTML, which will serve as a foundation you can apply to more advanced scripting languages, such as PHP. In the following steps, you will work with a simple form to understand some of the basic concepts of JavaScript.

1   In your text editor, choose File > Open and navigate to your HTML5_08lessons folder. Choose the 08_subscribe.html file, and then click Open. To ensure you have a backup copy of this file, you'll save the document with a new name.

2   Choose File > Save As and name this file **08_subscribe_work.html**. Be sure to save this file in the HTML5_08lessons folder.

Take a moment to examine the HTML code; note that it is completely created with HTML and as such, lacks functional interactivity.

3   Preview the page, and then click the Submit button. Nothing happens, except for the default behavior of the button, which is a non-functional element on your web page.

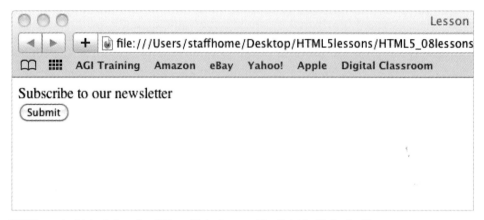

HTML cannot validate whether a form field was filled out; you need JavaScript for this functionality.

You need JavaScript to make this button interactive. HTML lets you perform activities, such as control the text that appears on the button, but offers no interactivity control. You will add JavaScript code to trigger a window to appear in your browser and prompt you to type your name. When you type your name and click OK, your JavaScript code will write your name on the page.

4   Close your browser and in your text editor below the `<title>` tag in your page, type the following code:

```
<script type="text/javascript">

</script>
```

You need to indicate in your HTML that you want to use JavaScript, just as you do with CSS. You can place these instructions anywhere in the HTML code, but best practice is to add them to the `<head>` section of your page.

5   Add the following code:

```
<script type="text/javascript">
function show_prompt()
</script>
```

A function in JavaScript is code that will be executed by an event on the page. In this case, the code is called `show_prompt()`, and it is unique code that tells your web browser to open a small pop-up window. The event that triggers this function is the user clicking the Submit button.

The `show_prompt()` function needs more information to work.

6   Add the following code below the function:

```
<script type="text/javascript">
function show_prompt()

{
  var name=prompt();
}

</script>
```

In this line of code, you have declared a variable and its value. This variable, called `name`, obtains its value from the `prompt` function. One line of code is the minimum amount of information you need to make something happen in your JavaScript.

To trigger the JavaScript code, you need to add an instruction to your HTML button that describes how to trigger the code and what function to use.

7   Add this code to the HTML for your button:

```
<input type="button" onclick="show_prompt()" value="Submit" />
```

The `onclick` code is known as a JavaScript event and the value `"show_prompt()"` is the JavaScript function that you declared in step 5 in your `<script>` tag. Now, you have completed a logical chain that essentially says: "When a user clicks on this Submit button, call the `show_prompt` function. When the `show_prompt` function runs, it will call another function named `prompt`."

8   Save your file and preview the page in your browser. Click the button and you see a pop-up window appear in your browser. The appearance of this window is different depending on which browser you are using.

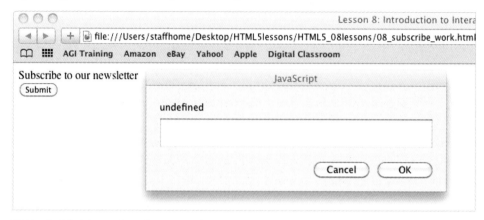

Clicking the Submit button triggers the pop-up window.

Now that you have created the pop-up window, you will add more code to populate your prompt window with information, as instructed in the next step.

9   Close your browser and add the following code to your JavaScript variable declaration (added in step 6):

```
var name=prompt("Please enter your name","Chris P. Bacon");
```

Save your file and preview it in your browser. Test the page again by pressing Submit. The new values you just added are now visible within the window. You will now add code to your JavaScript to take the value of the text box and write it out onto a new HTML page.

10   Close your browser and add the following code to your JavaScript code:

```
<script type="text/javascript">
function show_prompt()
{
  var name=prompt("Please enter your name","Chris P. Bacon");
  if (name!=null && name!="")
    {
    document.write("Hello " + name + "! How are you today?");
    }
}
</script>
```

This code is composed of two parts: an `if` statement and a `then` statement. The `if` statement looks for a value in the text field; if there is a value, the `document.write` line is run, and the name value is displayed.

The characters `!=` *and* `&&` *contained in the code (*`name!=null && name!=""`*) are known as operators in JavaScript and they help build the logic of any given function.*

The `document.write` code is a statement that instructs your web browser to write data on a web page. In this case, the statement writes the text "Hello" plus the content of the prompt window text field, followed by "How are you today?"

11 Save your page, and then preview it in your browser. Leave the default name value in for now and click OK. A new page is built based on the code you added in the previous step. Click the Back button in your web browser, click the Submit button again, and then type your name. Click OK; a new page with the new value is created.

In some browsers (such as Safari) you may be seeing just a blank page. This is due to the way that different browsers handle document.write. If this is case for you, move on to the next step.

The value from the text field is written on the page.

This is a relatively simple JavaScript function, but it should give you a basic understanding of how JavaScript communicates with the HTML elements on a page, as well as the basic logic of a JavaScript function. In the next exercise, you'll learn about JavaScript events.

JavaScript events

The JavaScript event you worked with in the previous exercise was an `onclick` event that triggered the code when you clicked the Submit button. There are other events you can use, and to better understand how these events work, you will modify the current example.

1   In your HTML code, change your `onclick` event to the `onmouseover` event (highlighted in red):

```
<input type="button" onmouseover="show_prompt()" value="Submit" />
```

2   Save your file and preview it in your browser. Now, place your cursor over the button without clicking; the prompt window appears. The `onmouseover` event triggers the JavaScript as soon as the cursor enters the area of the button.

Events are often based on user interaction, such as moving the mouse cursor over an object.

The onmouseout *event is closely related to* onmouseover *except that it triggers the JavaScript when the cursor leaves the area of the button.*

Currently, this event is tied to your button, but you can move the event from the button to the actual page.

3   Select the `onmouseover` event and its value, and then press Ctrl + X (PC) or Command + X (Mac OS) to cut the code. Locate the opening body tag and press Ctrl +V (PC) or Command +V (Mac OS) to paste the code, as shown here:

```
<body onmouseover="show_prompt()">
```

A mouseover event on the actual page will work, but best practice is to use the `onload` event, which triggers your JavaScript as soon as the page is opened:

```
<body onload="show_prompt()">
```

4   After changing the event to onload, save your page and preview it in your browser. As soon as your page opens, you trigger the prompt window. You could enter the text here, but as the event is currently structured, it would write the text to the page, so click Cancel.

The onload event can be useful, but for this example, it would be distracting for the user.

With this exercise, you learned that JavaScript lets you choose where and how you call it. In both cases, user interaction triggers the code, but the onload event gives the user little choice as to when to trigger the code, whereas the onclick event (attached to the button), gives the user more of a choice.

Placing your JavaScript into an external document

You can save JavaScript in an external file that is linked from your HTML pages in much the same way you do with external style sheets. The benefits are the same: to easily update code that's located in a single file.

1   In your text editor, choose File > New, and then choose File > Save. In the dialog box that appears, save this file in your HTML5_08lessons folder as **promptwindow.js**. The extension .js is for external JavaScript files. Keep in mind that your text editor may have a separate menu command for creating JavaScript files, in this case, you should choose that option. Additionally, if any text was automatically generated, you should delete it.

2   Return to 08_subscribe_work.html and select the code within the two `<script>` tags. Do not select the script tags themselves.

3   Press Ctrl + X (PC) or Command + X (Mac OS) to cut this code out of your document. Switch to the promptwindow.js document and press Ctrl + V (PC) or Command + V (Mac OS). Save this file.

4   Switch back to your HTML page, and add the following code (highlighted in red) to your opening `<script>` tag:

```
<script type="text/javascript" src="promptwindow.js">

</script>
```

5   Save your page and then preview it in your browser. The script works as it did before.

6   Close your browser, and then close your HTML and JavaScript documents since you will be working with new files in the next exercise.

If your script is not working, check to make sure you spelled the name of the JavaScript file correctly. Also, check to make sure that the JavaScript file is on the same level as your HTML file within your root folder.

There are multiple benefits to saving your JavaScript in an external file. Some of these benefits are:

- The ability to place multiple functions within a single document (although inline JavaScript has this benefit as well).

- Having a single reference for your JavaScript makes it easier for debugging purposes.

- The external JavaScript file can be cached by the web browser, thus preventing the need to reload the script on new pages.

The Document Object Model

JavaScript has access to objects within a browser; this is how the pop-up window from your previous exercise appeared on screen. This access takes advantage of the Document Object Model (DOM), which is a convention for accessing data within HTML pages. This model describes how all elements in an HTML page, such as forms and images, are related to the topmost structure, known as the *document*.

JavaScript has access to the document and the related elements on your page in a way that HTML does not. This access allows JavaScript to:

- Validate form fields
- Detect the browser being used
- Respond to user events
- Store and retrieve information on a user's computer

Recall the first exercise and the section of code you added labeled `document.write` (the seventh line from the top).

```
<script type="text/javascript">
function show_prompt()
{
  var name=prompt("Please enter your name","Chris P. Bacon");
  if (name!=null && name!="")
    {
    document.write("Hello " + name + "! How are you today?");
    }
}
</script>
```

This section of code is referred to as a function. The behavior demonstrated on your page is one of the simplest examples in JavaScript because there are very few objects in the document. Most HTML documents have multiple objects, and it is possible to pass a text value to another part of the page, or to submit it via a form.

JavaScript frameworks

Imagine the following scenario: A designer is starting a new project and her client is interested in adding an interactive photo gallery to the site. The designer also needs to create a form that requires JavaScript validation. Since the designer is new to JavaScript, she finds code she can use for the photo gallery and the form validation, and adds it to her page. The designer later gets another job similar to the first, and she decides to reuse the code from her first project, so she saves the JavaScript code into an external file.

The designer now has a reusable library of code she can add to future projects, but there are some potential problems with this approach:

- The designer needs to organize, maintain, and update her library.
- The code the designer found could be poorly written.
- Poorly written JavaScript can slow down the performance of a website and/or cause security issues. Unless the designer is an expert at optimizing code, she may be unknowingly distributing bad code.

JavaScript frameworks are a better solution. There are several professionally written libraries available for use by designers. These libraries are large collections of functions built and tested by other designers and developers to form a common library. These collections of functions are available for immediate use, so if a designer needs to add an accordion menu (a menu that collapses and expands based on user events), he or she might readily find the code they need.

You will now use jQuery, one of the most popular and accessible JavaScript frameworks for designers. jQuery is useful for designers because it uses CSS syntax to search and access the page, thereby decreasing the amount of scripting language you need to learn.

Hiding an element with jQuery

In this exercise, you'll create an expandable container the user can toggle open and closed. The figures below show jQuery's animation features. The first image contains a box in its initial view; readers interested in the calorie content of the smoothie can click the *See calories* link to expand this section. The second image shows the expanded box after the user has clicked the button.

An example of the collapsible box you will create.

As you will see, jQuery lets you experiment with different methods of expanding the box and with the timing. The collapsible box will take two exercises to complete; in this first exercise, you will hide the section.

1   Perform this step to see the code of the jQuery framework. If you'd prefer to not see this, move on to step 2. Choose File > Open. In the dialog box that appears, navigate to your HTML5_08lessons and open the jquery.js file. Scroll to see the functions contained within the file. This file is well commented, so you can get a sense of what the functions do. When you are finished, close the file without saving it.

```
// Check to see if the browser returns elements by name when
// querying by getElementById (and provide a workaround)
(function(){
    // We're going to inject a fake input element with a specified name
    var form = document.createElement("div"),
        id = "script" + (new Date).getTime();
    form.innerHTML = "<a name='" + id + "'/>";

    // Inject it into the root element, check its status, and remove it quickly
    var root = document.documentElement;
    root.insertBefore( form, root.firstChild );

    // The workaround has to do additional checks after a getElementById
    // Which slows things down for other browsers (hence the branching)
    if ( document.getElementById( id ) ) {
        Expr.find.ID = function(match, context, isXML){
            if ( typeof context.getElementById !== "undefined" && !isXML ) {
                var m = context.getElementById(match[1]);
                return m ? m.id === match[1] || typeof m.getAttributeNode !== "undefined" && m.getAt
            }
        };

        Expr.filter.ID = function(elem, match){
            var node = typeof elem.getAttributeNode !== "undefined" && elem.getAttributeNode("id");
            return elem.nodeType === 1 && node && node.nodeValue === match;
        };
    }

    root.removeChild( form );
    root = form = null; // release memory in IE
})();
```

You can reference the functions in the jQuery document in your web page, but you rarely need to modify them.

2   Open the document jquerytoggle.html located in your HTML5_08lessons folder. Preview this page in your browser. The section of the page you will hide is the list below the heading *Calories per serving*. Close your browser and return to your document. Scroll to locate the HTML for this section; the list is wrapped in a `div` tag with the ID `CalorieBox`. This is the div you will hide.

3   In the jquerytoggle.html page, add the link to the jQuery JavaScript file, which is located in your HTML5_08lessons folder.

In the head section, immediately below the closing `</style>` tag, add the following code:

`<script type="text/javascript" src="jquery.js"></script>`

Choose File > Save. Your document can now access the functionality within the library. Note that this link to the jQuery library should go on every page that might reference code within it. Now you will add another script tag to add code that hides your Calories box.

4 Immediately below the `<script>` tag you just added, type the following code to add an empty `<script>` element:

```
<script type="text/javascript" src="jquery.js"></script>
<script>

</script>
```

You will now add a line of code that is included in almost every project that uses jQuery.

5 Add the following code into your empty `<script>` element:

```
<script>
  $(document).ready(function() {

  });
</script>
```

In this code, the `$` symbol is a reference to the jQuery object and `ready` is the event to respond to (in this case, the document being ready). In addition, you are defining a new function with `function`. This section of code is referred to as a ready function and prevents your code from searching the DOM until the document is fully loaded.

For example, in the following code, you will hide text on your page, so you want this code to be hidden when the page first loads.

6 Scroll to locate the HTML code close to the bottom of the page that begins with the line `<div id="CalorieBox">`. This is the element on the page that you will hide; it contains a definition list that has the calorie values. jQuery allows objects in the DOM to be selected by several criteria. Since you want to select one specific element, you will search for that specific ID.

7 Scroll back up the page and add the following code immediately below your `document.ready` function:

```
$(document).ready(function() {
  $('#CalorieBox').hide();
});
```

The hash tag (#) tells jQuery to search for an element with the ID `'CalorieBox'` (using the CSS selector syntax). Once found, jQuery will run the selected element's hide function, which is also a jQuery function.

8 Save your page, and then preview it in your browser. Your Calories section has disappeared from the page. Note that all the functionality for this effect is condensed in the line you added in the last step. This line works because the jQuery library is referenced in your HTML page.

The `CalorieBox` *before hiding it with jQuery*   The `CalorieBox` *after hiding it with jQuery*

This page lacks a trigger to cause the box to appear. You will now add this trigger by adding a link to the *Calories per serving* heading, as well as more jQuery code.

Adding an event to trigger the show effect

The effect you want to create is to expand the list currently hidden when the user clicks the *Calories per serving* heading. To do this, you will make the heading a link and give it an ID.

1 Locate the Calories per serving heading and add the following attributes:

```
<h4><a id="triggerCalorieBox" href="#">Calories per serving</a></h4>
```

You are giving this heading an ID so you can target it with another line of jQuery. The href attribute is a dummy link that makes the heading a hyperlink, but is only there to serve as a trigger.

2 Scroll to your JavaScript code and add these four lines:

```
$(document).ready(function() {
  $('#CalorieBox').hide();
  $('a#triggerCalorieBox').click(function() {
    $('#CalorieBox').show();
    e.preventDefault()
  });
});
```

The first line identifies the hyperlinked ID you created in step 1 and attaches it to a click event. The second line is the instruction to show the `CalorieBox` ID. The third line is needed to override the default behavior of the hyperlink. (As previously noted, this hyperlink doesn't go to another page, so this line is necessary.) The fourth line is the closing bracket for the new function. (The opening bracket for this function is on the `.click(function()` line.)

3 Save your page and then preview it in your browser. Click the *Calories per serving* link; the box expands. The style for this box has been defined as 450 pixels wide with a black border on all sides.

Clicking the link triggers the box to expand.

4 To enable the box to close again upon clicking, you need to add a line of code to hide the box after it has been expanded. The effect you want is for the user to toggle the box open and close by clicking the link. jQuery has a toggle effect you can use. You simply need to replace the show effect you have with the toggle. Replace the show effect with the following code:

```
$('a#triggerCalorieBox').click(function() {
  $('#CalorieBox').toggle();
  e.preventDefault();
```

5 Save your page and preview it in your browser. The CalorieBox is still hidden when the page loads. When you click it, it expands, and when you click again, it collapses. Close your browser and return to your text editor.

Using the toggle effect, the user can now open and close the box.

To make the show-and-hide effect more interesting, you will use the animation capabilities of jQuery.

6 In the lines of code you have already written, you can add control for the speed of the show-and-hide effect. Add the following code:

```
$('#CalorieBox').toggle('slow');
```

Save your page and then preview it in your browser. Clicking the link now results in a slow expansion of the box. If you want more precise control of the speed of the effect, jQuery allows you to control the speed using millisecond number values.

7 Return to your text editor and replace the 'slow' value with a millisecond value (be sure to remove the single quotation marks, which are used for keywords such as 'slow' or 'fast'):

```
$('#CalorieBox').toggle(1200);
```

The 1200 milliseconds value is equivalent to 1.2 seconds. Save your page and then preview it in your browser. Clicking the link now results in a much slower expansion of the box. You'll now increase the speed of this effect.

8   Return to your text editor and replace the 1200 value with **500**, the equivalent of one-half second:

```
$('#CalorieBox').toggle(500);
```

You also have options to change the behavior of the box: in addition to `.show`, `.hide`, and `.toggle`, there are effects such as `.slideDown`, `.fadeIn`, and `.fadeOut`. You'll change your toggle effect to the slideToggle effect.

9   Add the following code:

```
$('#CalorieBox').slideToggle(500);
```

Save your page and preview it in your browser. When satisfied, close your browser and your file since you will be working with a new document in the next exercise.

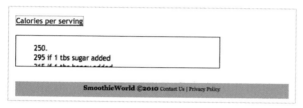

The `slideToggle` *effect changes the behavior of the animation.*

As you can see, jQuery allows different options for your designs. The ability to show and hide animated elements is just one thing you can do with this library. The best way to learn more about jQuery is to go online to the source at *jQuery.com*, or to explore other online resources.

More advanced jQuery

jQuery and other similar JavaScript libraries are now used with increasing frequency on modern websites. User interface elements, such as drop-down or accordion menus, are two examples of these effects. You will also find jQuery used in slide shows, forms, multimedia, and much more.

As you explore jQuery, you will see that it supports plug-ins, which are sets of additional code that rely on some functionality in jQuery, and then build upon it. For example, in the previous exercise, the ability to control the speed of the box was limited. You could choose to start expanding the box slowly, and then speed up the expansion as it reached the end. In animation, this is referred to as easing, and several jQuery plugins have been created that give designers access to these effects.

Adding plug-ins involves adding another external JavaScript file to your site, and then linking to it. This adds new functions that you can then refer to in your HTML. For more information on plugins as well as documentation and examples, go to *http://plugins.jquery.com*.

Self study

1 Experiment with different effects for your jQuery calorie box. For example, replace the `.slideToggle` effect in the jquerytoggle.html page with the `.fadeIn` effect.

2 Experiment with the speed values in your code (currently set to 500 milliseconds) to see how they affect the behavior of the element.

3 Browse jquery.com, use the online interactive tutorials, and choose an example to integrate into your page.

Review

Questions

1 What is an event as it relates to JavaScript and HTML?

2 What is a JavaScript library, and what are the advantages of using one?

3 In this line of code, what does the number 500 stand for?

```
$('#CalorieBox').toggle(500);
```

Answers

1 An event on an HTML page often originates from a user interaction, such as clicking a button or loading a page. These events can then trigger specific JavaScript code that runs in the user's browser.

2 A JavaScript library, such as jQuery, is a collection of JavaScript code that lives inside an external JavaScript file. You can easily reference a library to add functionality, such as animated menus or user interface elements. Using a library is advantageous for designers because they can add relatively sophisticated behavior without writing complex JavaScript code.

3 Milliseconds.

What you'll learn in this lesson:

- Adding video with the `<video>` element
- Adding audio with the `<audio>` element
- Providing fallbacks for browsers
- Controlling a video with JavaScript

Working with Video and Audio Elements

Adding video and sound to a web page makes a website more engaging. Media provides a way to grab the attention of your visitors, and it also provides a way to reach audiences that would otherwise bypass long lengths of text. HTML5 directly addresses the need to deliver video and audio.

Starting up

You will work with several files from the HTML5_09lessons folder in this lesson. Make sure you have loaded the HTML5lessons folder onto your hard drive from the supplied DVD. See "Loading lesson files" in the Starting Up section of this book.

See Lesson 9 in action!

Use the accompanying video to gain a better understanding of how to use some of the capabilities shown in this lesson. The video tutorial for this lesson can be found on the included DVD.

To accurately preview the HTML5 content you will create in this lesson, you need a browser that supports HTML5 tags. See "Using web browsers that support HTML5 tags" in the Starting Up section of this book to determine whether you are using such a browser, or for instructions on downloading one.

Adding video

Before the advent of HTML5, you needed third party plug-ins, such as Flash, QuickTime, or Silverlight, to show video. HTML5 has replaced this need by specifying an HTML video element that runs natively in the browser and integrates with JavaScript.

In this section, you will learn to add video to your web page such that the video begins automatically when the page loads, and takes advantage of the native browser player controls.

1   From the HTML5_09lessons folder, open the index.html page. On line 8 inside the body element, add the following line of code.

```
<video src='videos/BigBuck.ogg' autoplay></video>
```

As is the case with the `image` element, the `video` element has an `src` attribute where the value points to the location of the video file you want to play. The `autoplay` attribute tells the browser to begin playing the video as soon as the page loads.

Save the file and preview the Web page in the latest versions of Chrome, Firefox, or Opera. You should see a page similar to the figure below; the video should begin playing automatically.

The video element displayed in Firefox.

If you do not see video playing, it is possible you need to update your browser. For more information on the importance of this, be sure to read the "Starting Up" section of the book.

Since there is a standard way to declare a video in HTML, browser developers have the responsibility of ensuring the browser follows the standard and displays the video properly. As a web developer, your job is to focus on your content and customizations.

2   To provide more control over the video playback, remove the `autoplay` attribute and add a `controls` attribute so your line of code appears as follows:

```
<video src='videos/BigBuck.ogg' controls ></video>
```

Save your work, then move to your web browser. If the page is open, refresh the page in your web browser; if the page is closed, re-open the work file you are using for this lesson. The figures below show the native browser controls for Chrome, Firefox, and Opera.

Native browser controls in Chrome, Firefox, and Opera.

Click the play button and the video should begin. Drag the slider bar and the current position of the video should change accordingly.

Just by adding the `controls` attribute to the video element, each browser adds interactive playback controls, including a play/pause button, time codes, volume control, and position slider.

With the `autoplay` attribute removed, the first frame, or black rectangle, appears on the screen until the video begins playing. If you want to display a custom preview image instead of the first frame or black rectangle, use the `poster` attribute.

3   Add the `poster` attribute after the `controls` attribute and set the value to **"poster854.jpg"** as follows:

```
<video src='videos/BigBuck.ogg' controls poster='poster854.jpg'></video>
```

Setting the `poster` attribute tells the browser to load an image and place it above the `video` element. Once the video begins, the image disappears and the video is displayed.

Save your file and refresh your browser. You will see the poster image now instead of a black screen.

A preview image is now shown when the page loads.

By default, the `video` element is resized to fit the encoded media file. To control the size of the `video` element, use the `width` and `height` attributes.

4   Add the following `width` and `height` attributes:

```
<video src='videos/BigBuck.ogg' controls poster='poster854.jpg'
width='320' height='180'></video>
```

This resizes the video but you should also substitute a small poster image as well. Change the value of the poster as follows:

```
poster='poster320.jpg'
```

5   Save the file and refresh your browser; the web page should appear similar to the following figure.

The video element resized to 320 × 180.

Additional attributes

In additon to the autoplay, controls, and poster attributes, the video element has a few other attributes for use:

audio: This attribute allows you to mute the volume of your video. Currently, the only supported value is `'muted'`.

loop: This attribute will trigger your video to automatically begin playing again when it reaches the end.

preload: This attribute will allow you to begin loading the video as soon as the page loads and can reduce the amount of time it takes to load when the user clicks play.

Adding support for more browsers

There are many formats and codec for video, and not all are supported equally across the different HTML5-enabled web browsers. Each video file acts as a container for multiple files that contain the audio and video. The Ogg format is open standard, open source–friendly, and is supported natively by the latest versions of Chrome, Firefox, and Opera.

Another popular web video format is MP4, specifically, an MP4-containing video that uses the H.264 codec and audio that uses the AAC codec. Both H.264 and AAC codecs also support multiple levels of profiles, which are used to provide different levels of compression and quality. To reach the widest array of devices and browsers, you should use the baseline profile for H.264 video and the "low complexity" profile AAC.

MP4 files encoded, as explained in the previous paragraph, are supported by the latest versions of Internet Explorer, Safari, iOS, and Android. Making your videos available in both Ogg and MP4 formats lets you to reach the most users with modern browsers and devices. In this section, you will learn to add multiple source files to a video element, which allows the browser to select the file based on the format it supports.

1   Remove the `src` attribute from the video element.

2   Add a `source` element as a child of the `video` element and set the `src` attribute of the source element to **`'videos/BigBuck.ogg'`** as follows:

```
<video controls poster='poster320.jpg' width='320' height='180'>
    <source src='videos/BigBuck.ogg' />
</video>
```

3   Add another child `source` element below the one from the previous step and set the `src` attribute to **`videos/BigBuck.mp4`**. as follows:

```
<video controls poster='poster320.jpg' width='320' height='180'>
    <source src='videos/BigBuck.ogg' />
    <source src='videos/BigBuck.mp4' />
</video>
```

4   Save your file and refresh the web page in a browser. When you open your HTML code in Chrome, Firefox, or Opera, the first source file is used because the browsers support the Ogg file format. When you open your HTML code in Internet Explorer or Safari, the second source file is used because the MP4 format is supported.

The web browser checks source files for compatibility in the order they appear in the video element. In this scenario, Internet Explorer and Safari download enough of the Ogg formatted file to attempt to load the file. When the file cannot be loaded, the browser moves from the current source file to the next source file. The browser continues to attempt to load each source file until a compatible file is found or there are no more files to try.

To assist the browsers in determining compatible files and prevent the user from downloading unsupported files, you can use the `type` attribute of the `source` element. The value of the `type` attribute describes the file format, video codec, and audio codec of the source file.

5   Add a `type` attribute to the first `source` element to describe the Ogg file format using the following syntax:

```
<source src='videos/BigBuck.ogg' type='video/ogg; codecs="theora,
vorbis"'>
```

This tells the browser that the BigBuck.ogg file is saved in the Ogg file format, and that the video was with the Theora codec, and that the audio is encoded with the Vorbis codec.

For the MP4 file, add the following value for the `type` attribute to the second `source` element:

```
<source src='videos/BigBuck.mp4' type='video/mp4; codecs="avc1.42E01E,
mp4a.40.2"'>
```

This tells the browser that the BigBuck.mp4 file is saved in the MP4 format, the video is encoded with H.264 using the baseline profile, and the audio is encoded with the AAC codec using the "low complexity" profile.

When the browser loads your HTML code, it checks for compatibility based on the `type` attribute and saves time and bandwidth by not downloading every file.

Once you set up support for a variety of modern browsers, you can add additional code for older browsers that do not support HTML5: when your page is loaded in an older browser that does not support the `video` element, it will ignore it and use the alternative.

Adding fallback support for older browsers

1   Add an `h1` element with a link to the BigBuck.mp4 file after the second source element as follows:

```
<video controls poster='poster320.jpg' width='320' height='180'>
    <source src='videos/BigBuck.ogg' type='video/ogg; codecs="theora,
    vorbis"'>
    <source src='videos/BigBuck.mp4' type='video/mp4;
    codecs="avc1.42E01E, mp4a.40.2"'>
    <h1><a href="videos/BigBuck.mp4">Download the video</a></h1>
</video>
```

If you save the file and load the web page in an older browser that does not support HTML5, you would see the message to download the video.

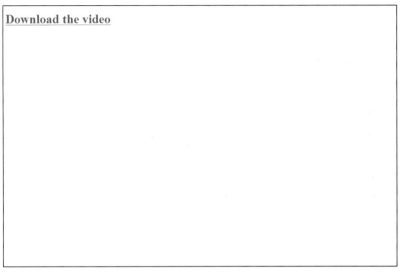

The fallback message displayed in a browser with no HTML5 support.

If you load the same HTML code in a modern browser, the `h1` element and the download link will be ignored because the `video` element is supported.

To provide an even better alternative for older browsers, you can use Flash as a backup to play the video on the web page. Using the same technique as the last step to provide alternate HTML for unsupported elements, you can use an `object` element that references a Flash file as the last child of the `source` elements.

FlowPlayer is an open source Flash-based video player released under a GPL license. A Flash-based fallback video player is useful because Flash supports the MP4 video format and is installed on the majority of computers connected to the Internet. The FlowPlayer files are included within the lesson folder in the player folder. For more information on FlowPlayer, visit their site at flowplayer.org.

2   Remove the fallback h1 element from the previous step and insert an object element with the following properties and child elements.

```
<video controls poster='poster320.jpg' width='320' height='180'>
    <source src='videos/BigBuck.ogg' type='video/ogg; codecs="theora,
    vorbis"'>
    <source src='videos/BigBuck.mp4' type='video/mp4;
    codecs="avc1.42E01E, mp4a.40.2"'>
    <object width="320" height="180" type="application/x-shockwave-
    flash" data="player/flowplayer-3.2.5.swf">
        <param name="movie" value="player/flowplayer-3.2.5.swf" />
        <param name="allowfullscreen" value="true" />
        <param name="flashvars" value='config={"clip": {"url": "videos/
        BigBuck.mp4", "autoPlay":false, "autoBuffering":true}}' />
    </object>
</video>
```

A complete description of this code is beyond the scope of this lesson. The following is an overview of what the code means.

The object element tells the browser to load the Flash player plug-in and run the flowplayer-3.2.5.swf file of the same size as the video element. The path to the MP4 file is then passed using the flashvars parameter.

3   If you save this file and load the page in an older browser that does not support HTML5, the browser bypasses the source and video elements and loads the object element. If the Flash player is installed, the page should appear similar to the following figure.

A Flash player loaded as a fallback for browsers with no HTML5 support.

To ensure the best performance, you should make sure the latest version of the Flash Player is installed on your system. In older versions of the Flash Player, you may see video but no fullscreen option. Visit http://get.adobe.com/flashplayer/ *to install the latest version.*

4   As a final fallback measure, add the `h1` element from the previous step as a child element of the `object` element after the third `param` element:

```
<object width="320" height="180" type="application/x-shockwave-flash"
data="player/flowplayer-3.2.5.swf">
    <param name="movie" value="player/flowplayer-3.2.5.swf" />
    <param name="allowfullscreen" value="true" />
    <param name="flashvars" value='config={"clip": {"url": "videos/
    BigBuck.mp4", "autoPlay":false, "autoBuffering":true}}' />
    <h1><a href="videos/BigBuck.mp4">Download the video</a></h1>
</object>
```

To review, the following scenarios are now supported:

- If the browser supports the `video` element, the `source` elements are analyzed and a supported format is selected.

- If the `video` element is not supported and the Flash player plug-in is installed, the MP4 file is used in the flash-based video player.

- If the `video` element is not supported and the Flash player plug-in is not installed, the `h1` element is displayed and the MP4 file is made available for download.

The WebM video format

In the Spring of 2010, Google announced the WebM video codec, an alternative to OGG and H.264. In the winter of 2011, it was announced that Google's Chrome browser would only support OGG video and the WebM format, but not H.264.

Although the adoption of WebM video is currently small, there is no doubt it will grow in the near future. Mozilla Firefox recently added support for WebM in Firefox 4, and Microsoft has also released a component plugin that allows WebM to run in Internet Explorer 9 (and presumably 10).

Of course this leaves out Apple's Safari, both for desktop and mobile. Apple has not announced any support for the WebM format at this time, preferring to focus on H.264. The addition of the WebM format can add to the confusing landscape for those not familiar with web video. The key point is to remember that there is no single video format that will work across all browsers and devices, and it will be necessary to provide fallbacks to users for quite some time.

Controlling a video with JavaScript

In some scenarios, such as adding custom graphics or integrating media playback with other elements of the page, you might not want to use the native browser controls for the `video` element. To facilitate these types of situations, the `video` element exposes a JavaScript-based API to control media playback and retrieve properties of the video.

In this exercise, you will learn to add a button that stretches to the natural width of the video and controls whether the video is playing or paused.

1   From the HTML5_09lessons folder, open the controlling.html page. You will find a simple video tag that uses the Ogg file from the previous lesson as its source.

In this exercise, you should use either the latest version of Google Chrome or Mozilla Firefox. Other browsers (or older versions of Chrome/Firefox) may not display the video or the Play button may not appear as indicated.

The video element loaded on the page.

Note that the element resizes to the natural width and height of the encoded video because there is no explicit width or height set on the `video` element.

2   Add a `break` element after the `video` element to position the upcoming button below the `video` element. After the `break` element, add an `input` element with the `type` attribute set to `button` and the `value` attribute set to `Play`. Additionally, add an `id` attribute with a value of `playPause` as follows:

```
<video src="videos/BigBuck.ogg"></video>
<br />
<input type="button" value="Play" id="playPause" />
```

Save your file and preview the web page in Chrome; the page should appear similar to the following figure.

The video *element and the input button.*

3   To change the width of the button to match the width of the video, you must capture the video width once the metadata of the file has loaded, and then set the button width accordingly.

To capture the width of the video, add an event handler to the `onloadedmetadata` event of the `video` element and set the value to `setButtonWidth()` as follows:

```
<video src="videos/BigBuck.ogg" onloadedmetadata="setButtonWidth()">
</video>
```

Next, you need to define variables in JavaScript that reference the `video` element and the input element.

4   Between the open and close script elements, add the following lines:

```
var video = document.getElementsByTagName('video')[0];
var playPause = document.getElementById('playPause');
```

The first line reads a reference to the first `video` element on the page and saves it in a variable called `video`. The next line finds the `input` element by ID and saves a reference to it in a variable called `playPause`. On the next line, add the `setButtonWidth` function as follows:

```
function setButtonWidth(e){
    playPause.style.width = video.videoWidth + 'px';
}
```

Save your file and preview the web page in Chrome; the page should appear as follows:

The width of the input button dynamically set to the same width of the video.

To control the playback of the video with the click of the button, however, you must add event handlers for the play and pause events. You can use the same function to handle both events by first checking the paused property of the video element.

5   Add event handlers to the video element for play and pause, and set the value to setPlayPause() as follows:

```
<video src="videos/BigBuck.ogg" onloadedmetadata="setButtonWidth()"
onplay="setPlayPause()" onpause="setPlayPause()"></video>
```

6   Next, add an event handler to the click event of the button that instructs the video to play. You can define this code inline as follows:

```
<input type="button" value="Play" id="playPause"
onclick="video.play()" />
```

7   The last step is to define the setPlayPause function that toggles the button click event and text values between play and pause. Add this code within your <script> element as follows:

```
<script type="text/javascript">
    var video = document.getElementsByTagName('video')[0];
    var playPause = document.getElementById('playPause');
    function setButtonWidth(e){
        playPause.style.width = video.videoWidth + 'px';
    }
function setPlayPause(e){
    if(video.paused) {
        playPause.value = 'Play';
        playPause.onclick = function(e) { video.play(); }
    } else {
        playPause.value = 'Pause';
        playPause.onclick = function(e) { video.pause(); }
    }
}
```

Save your file and preview the web page in Chrome. When the button is pressed, the text should change to "Pause" and the video should begin playing. Pressing the button a second time should pause the video and the text should change to "Play".

There are many more properties and events exposed by the video element that allow you to completely recreate the native browser controls that can be found on the W3C website.

Adding audio

In some scenarios, such as podcasts and sound effects, you do not need to play both video and audio, and only need to play sound files. For such cases, the `audio` element comes in. The behavior, properties, and events of the `audio` element closely mirror the `video` element.

In this section, you will learn to add audio to your web page that takes advantage of the native browser player controls.

1   From the HTML5_09lessons folder, open the audio.html page. On line 8 inside the body element, add the following line of code:

```
<audio src='videos/BigBuck.ogg' controls></audio>
```

Save the file and preview the web page in Chrome, Firefox or Opera (you are using the Ogg format). Your browser's native player will appear:

An audio element using the native browser controls.

Recall that there is no visual component to the media file; there are other supported file formats, such as MP3 and WAV. Additional media files, without the video component, hold less data and are much smaller in size.

2   Close your browser and return to your text editor. Remove the `src` attribute from the `audio` element and add a `source` element with `src` attribute set to `videos/BigBuck.ogg`. And a second source element after the first with a source attribute set to `videos/BigBuck.mp3`.

```
<audio controls>
    <source src='videos/BigBuck.ogg' />
    <source src='videos/BigBuck.mp3' />
</audio>
```

Save the file and preview your web page in either Internet Explorer or Safari; the MP3 file should play when clicked.

Self study

The audio element is simple to use. Practice repeating the "Controlling video with JavaScript" exercise using audio instead of video. When practicing the exercise, be sure to replace the video element with the audio element in the source code.

Review

Questions

1   Name two attributes that you can add to the `<video>` element that can affect how video appears or works on your page.

2   What is a poster file and how would you use it?

3   Describe the role of a fallback as it relates to web video and name at least one example of one.

Answers

1   The controls attribute allows you to specify whether or not you want controls visible on your page. The autoplay attribute allows you to specify whether or not the video should be playing upon launch of the page. There are additional attributes as well. Such as width, height, loop, poster, preload and audio.

2   A poster file is an image file that you can specify as the introductory image for your video. Often, the poster file will be a representative frame or image from your movie.

3   A fallback in web video is related to the need to provide more than one video source for users visiting your website. Because there is no single video format that is supported across all browsers/devices, fallbacks, such as Flash video that play if the user's browser does not support H.264, are needed.

Lesson 10

What you'll learn in this lesson:

- Understanding the Canvas element
- Drawing shapes and paths
- Applying colors and gradient brushes
- Animating compositions

Working with Canvas

Canvas is a two-dimensional drawing API that is part of the HTML5 specification. The inclusion of a native drawing API enables developers to create drawings dynamically on a web page, often based on retrieved data or user interaction. Unlike the familiar formats for images such JPGs and PNGs, drawings created with Canvas can be updated in real-time.

Starting up

You will work with several files from the HTML5_10lessons folder in this lesson. Make sure you have loaded the HTML5lessons folder onto your hard drive from the supplied DVD. See "Loading lesson files" in the Starting Up section of this book.

See Lesson 10 in action!

Use the accompanying video to gain a better understanding of how to use some of the capabilities shown in this lesson. The video tutorial for this lesson can be found on the included DVD.

To accurately preview the HTML5 content you will create in this lesson, you need a browser that supports HTML5 tags. See "Using web browsers that support HTML5 tags" in the Starting Up section of this book to determine whether you are using such a browser, or for instructions on downloading one.

You can use the Canvas HTML element to define the drawing surface, but you must define the drawing instructions and the resulting lines, shapes, and colors in JavaScript. In this lesson, you will learn the fundamentals of the Canvas API, which include drawing shapes, paths, text and using colors and gradients. Afterwards, you will progress to more advanced concepts of drawing images, shadows, using transforms, and creating an animated drawing.

Understanding the Canvas element

The Canvas element is a little different than most other elements in HTML5. It is more complex in that it requires the help of JavaScript to work. Your first step is to add (or define) a canvas element in your HTML. Once you have defined the element, you must store a reference to the drawing context for that element as a variable in JavaScript. You can then use the context itself to write the drawing instructions.

1   Open the canvastemplate.html file in the HTML5_10lessons folder to find the template you will use for the upcoming exercises. This template defines a Canvas HTML element set to a width and height of 300, which declares the drawing surface. After the body of the page opens, the `<setup()>` JavaScript function is called. The function locates the Canvas HTML element by name and sets a variable to the drawing context of the Canvas. Once a reference to the drawing context is available, you can draw dynamic graphics. The HTML for your canvas template looks like this:

```
<body onload="setup();">
    <canvas id="lessonCanvas" width="300" height="300"style="margin:
    100px;"></canvas>
</body>
```

The code for your JavaScript looks like this:

```
<script type="text/javascript">
    function setup() {
        var canvas = document.getElementById('lessonCanvas');
        if (canvas.getContext) {
            var ctx = canvas.getContext('2d');

            <!--drawing instructions here -->

        }
    }
</script>
```

You will not be making any modifications to this file, but once you are ready to create canvas-based work on your own, you may use this as a starting point.

2   Choose File > Close without making any change to this file.

The benefits of the Canvas element

If you are a designer and begin to go through the following exercises, you may find the amount of scripting involved a bit unexpected. The `canvas` element allows you to create graphics that might otherwise be created in a program such as Photoshop, Illustrator, or, if they are animated graphics, created in Flash. The difference is that instead of using those program's drawing tools, you will be creating the shapes, gradients, text, and other objects in code.

The goal of this lesson is not to convert you to a programmer, but to expose the fundamentals of how the Canvas element works. Undoubtedly, there will be future applications that will allow you to create canvas based objects and animations without the need for writing the code by hand. In fact, we discuss a few of these developments at the end of the chapter. For now, though, building these objects from the ground up is the best way to understand the logic of working with the Canvas element.

The Canvas element has had reasonably good browser support over the years, and we can imagine that it will be used as a substitute for the sort of experiences you associate with Flash: games, animations, charts, graphs, data visualizations, and for creating vector user interfaces, among other uses.

One benefit of using Canvas for these scenarios is the lack of requirement for a browser plugin. There are additional benefits: user interface icons are one example of the type of graphics you could create with Canvas elements. Images created with Canvas elements can be saved out of a page as png files, so you could imagine a version of a web application that allows you to export images. Additionally, using a feature of Canvas output called data uri, you can embed images created in Canvas directly into CSS. As with many of the HTML5 features, it will fall upon designers and developers to begin creating unique implementations of the Canvas element. In the following exercises, you can begin the process yourself.

Drawing paths

Paths and basic shapes are the building blocks of drawing graphics with the canvas element. After you gain an understanding of the basic functions, you can draw more complex visuals, such as graphs based on data, animated game sprites, and other interesting visuals. The first few functions in this chapter also provide a high-level overview of how the Canvas element works.

Drawing rectangles

A rectangle is the simplest path to draw. The `<fillRect(x, y, width, height)>` function, which you must call within the `context` object, creates a rectangular path positioned and sized based on the parameters, and fills the rectangle based on the current `fillStyle`. The parallel function of `strokeRect` creates the same path and draws an outline based on the current `strokeStyle`, in place of a fill. The `clearRect` function uses the same parameters, but it clears all pixels on the canvas in the given rectangle.

1   Open the drawingrectangles.html file and save a copy of the file as
     drawingrectangles_work.html. In the code, you will find a Canvas element already
     defined, and a JavaScript function called `setup` that runs when the page opens. In the
     `setup` function, a reference to the 2D context of the Canvas element has been saved to a
     variable that you will use to draw.

2   In the if statement, after the `ctx` variable is set, add the following code to draw a
     rectangle that outlines the Canvas:

```
function setup() {
    var canvas = document.getElementById('lessonCanvas');
    if (canvas.getContext) {
        var ctx = canvas.getContext('2d');

        ctx.strokeRect(0, 0, 300, 300);

    }
}
```

Notice that the x and y coordinates are set to 0, which starts the rectangle path in the
upper left corner; the width and height are set to 300, thus matching the size of the
Canvas element.

3   After the line from the previous step, add the following two lines, which change the
     current stroke color from the default black to red, and draw a smaller rectangle outline:

```
ctx.strokeStyle = 'rgb(255, 0, 0)';
ctx.strokeRect(0.5, 0.5, 100, 100);
```

4   Save your drawingrectangle_work.html file and open the file in your browser. You should see
     a drawing similar to the following figure. As in many examples of HTML5, if you see nothing
     in your browser, you will need to make sure it supports the `canvas` element. For a list of past,
     current and future browsers that support this element, visit *http://caniuse.com/#feat=canvas*.

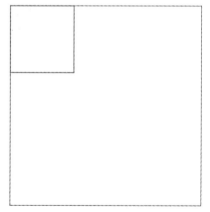

Black and red outlined rectangles.

Notice the Canvas element has a margin defined in CSS added as a visual aid only. This also
illustrates that you can style the Canvas element with CSS, as with other HTML elements.

5   Return to your text editor, and after the lines from the previous step, add the following line of code to draw a filled rectangle:

```
ctx.fillRect(20, 20, 100, 100);
```

6   Add two more lines of code to change the current fill color from the default black to green and draw another filled rectangle using the new color:

```
ctx.fillStyle = 'rgb(0, 255, 0)';
ctx.fillRect(50, 50, 100, 100);
```

7   Choose File > Save, then switch to your web browser. If the page is still open, refresh the page in your web browser, or re-open the work file you are using for this lesson. Your browser should display the following figure:

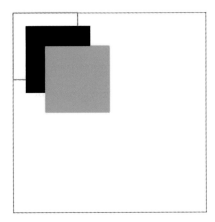

Black and red outlined rectangles with black and green filled rectangles created using HTML 5.

You can use `fillRect` to create the same path and fill it, rather than add an outline.

8   Keep the browser page open, and switch back to your text editor. In your text editor, after the lines from step five, add the following line of code to clear the pixels within the given rectangle:

```
ctx.clearRect(80, 80, 30, 30);
```

9   Save the document in your text editor, then move to your web browser and refresh the page; you should see a drawing similar to the figure below. The `clearRect` function resets the pixels to transparent, partially removing the color changes made by the previous calls to `strokeRect` and `fillRect`.

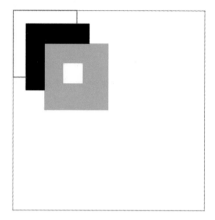

Black and red outlined rectangles with black and green filled rectangles and a rectangular hole.

Saving a canvas object as a .png file

Objects created in the canvas element can be saved as image files in some browsers. For example, if you have a copy of Firefox 3.6 or above, try right-clicking on the rectangles from the last exercise and choosing View Image. The image will appear in a separate tab. Right-click on this image and choose Save Image and you will be able to save a 300 × 300 pixel PNG file that could then be opened in an image editor, inserted into another web page, or anything else you can do with PNG files.

Drawing lines and circles

The rectangle functions from the previous section are basic drawing functions combined for ease of use. Imagine you wanted to recreate this same rectangle using more basic functions. Look at the rectangle function code again:

```
ctx.strokeRect(0, 0, 300, 300);
```

You could draw this rectangle with the following series of basic functions:

```
ctx.moveTo(0, 0);
ctx.lineTo(300, 0);
ctx.lineTo(300, 300);
ctx.lineTo(0, 300);
ctx.lineTo(0, 0);
ctx.stroke();
```

The moveTo(x, y) function creates a new sub path at the given coordinates. The lineTo(x, y) function adds a new point to the current sub path, connecting the previous one with a straight line. Finally, the stroke function draws the lines without filling the area within. It makes more sense to use the rectangle function because it is only a single line of code, however, understanding how the basic functions work is important because you can use them to create custom paths of any shape.

1   Open the drawinglinesandcircles.html file and save a copy of the file as **drawingcircles_work.html**. This file already has the drawing context enabled with the setup function. You will now add a rectangle and a series of zigzagging lines.

2   Within the setup function, after the line var ctx = canvas.getContext('2d');, add the following code:

```
ctx.strokeRect(0, 0, 300, 300);
ctx.moveTo(20, 20);
ctx.lineTo(100, 100);
ctx.lineTo(80, 200);
ctx.lineTo(200, 80);
ctx.lineTo(200, 200);
ctx.lineTo(280, 280);
ctx.stroke();
```

3   Save your work in your text editor, then switch to your browser. Refresh your browser page to review the HTML in your browser. The resulting page should be similar to the figure below:

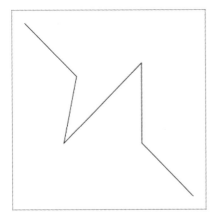

A black outline and a zigzag across the canvas.

You can see that the lineTo function is useful for drawing lines or rectangles. You will now change the fill color of the zigzag lines and add a red circle onto the path.

4   Switch to your text editor and add the following lines of code after the lines from step 2:

```
ctx.fillStyle = 'rgb(255,0,0)';
ctx.arc(100, 100, 16, 0, Math.PI * 2, false);
ctx.fill();
```

The first line changes the current fill color from the default black to red. The second line draws a full circle with a center point at the coordinates of (100, 100) and a radius of 16. The last three parameters of the arc function determine the length of the arc. startAngle and endAngle, measured in radians, define the start and end points; the direction the line is drawn between the two points is determined by the final anticlockwise parameter. The code above defines an arc that starts at 0 (the rightmost vertically centered point of a circle) and continues clockwise until it reaches the point of 2π radians, or a full 360 degree rotation, thus forming a circle. Finally, the fill function colors the path.

5   Choose File > Save, and then switch to your browser and preview the HTML page. As you can see, the circle was added to the current sub path of lines. Since the lines and the circle were part of the same sub path, the whole area was colored, not just the circle.

A black outline and a filled zig-zag.

6   To draw separate paths, you must use the beginPath function, which clears the current sub path and provides a fresh start. Return to your text editor and between the fillStyle and the arc function, insert the following lines as follows:

```
ctx.fillStyle = 'rgb(255,0,0)';
ctx.beginPath();
ctx.arc(100, 100, 16, 0, Math.PI * 2, false);
ctx.fill();
ctx.stroke();
```

The second line you added, ctx.stroke();, adds a separate stroke to the circle.

7   Save your work in your text editor and switch to your browser to preview the HTML page. Your drawing will appear as follows:

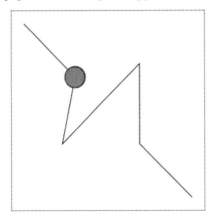

A black outline, zigzag, and a red circle.

8   With the circle created, you will now add a new object, in this case a semi-circle. Add the following lines of code:

```
ctx.beginPath();
ctx.arc(170, 170, 16, 0, Math.PI, true);
ctx.fill();
```

The code above starts a new path, keeping this arc independent of the previous circle. The values 170 and 170 define the center point, the value `16` defines the radius. The value 0 represents the `startAngle` and the `endAngle` is set to π, which will only draw a half circle, or 180 degrees, starting from 0. The value "true" is for the `anticlockwise` parameter, which means an arc will be drawn upwards.

9   Choose File > Save, and then preview the HTML page in your browser; you will see the following figure:

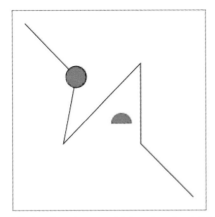

A black outline, zigzag, a red circle, and a red semi-circle.

If you set the `anticlockwise` parameter to false, the arc would trace clockwise, resulting in a half circle that curves downward.

Drawing with curves

The canvas element provides two drawing functions to help create curves: quadraticCurveTo(cpx, cpy, x, y) and bezierCurveTo(cp1x, cp1y, cp2x, cp2y, x, y). Both functions use control points to determine the curve of the path when drawing from one point to the next.

1   In the HTML5_10lessons folder, open the drawingcurves.html file and save a copy of the file as drawingcurves_work.html. The code is identical to the initial exercise for setting up a canvas element and saving the 2D context to a variable for reuse. In this exercise, you will draw several shapes to create a flower composition.

2   In the if statement after the ctx variable is set, add the following code to draw a rectangle that outlines the canvas.

```
ctx.strokeRect(0, 0, 300, 300);
```

This is the same outline rectangle as the last section, providing a visual reference for the borders of the canvas element.

3   Add the following lines after the line from the previous step to draw the stem of the flower:

```
ctx.fillStyle = 'rgb(0,173,104)';
ctx.moveTo(145, 150);
ctx.quadraticCurveTo(120, 200, 170, 280);
ctx.lineTo(190, 280);
ctx.quadraticCurveTo(125, 190, 155, 150);
ctx.fill();
```

The first line of code changes the fill to green. The remaining lines of code define the starting points, curves, and lines of the stem shape.

4   Choose File > Save. Switch to your browser, and then preview the HTML page. You will see the following figure:

The green flower stem shape.

You will now create a flower petal using the `bezierCurveTo` function, which uses two control points, unlike the single control point used with the `quadraticCurveTo` function from the last step. In addition, you will draw a number of guidelines using the same points to help visualize how the `bezierCurveTo` function works.

Since you will use a number of the same points to draw the petal and the guidelines, you can store the point values in variables for reuse.

5 Switch back to your text editor, then add the following of code after the lines from step 3.

```
var pt1 = { x: 155, y: 145 };
var pt2 = { x: 93, y: 106 };
var cp1 = { x: 111, y: 154 };
var cp2 = { x: 66, y: 131 };
```

6 Add the lines indicated below after the code from the previous step. This code changes the stroke and fill colors, and draws the first petal of the flower.

```
ctx.fillStyle = 'rgb(115,206,226)';
ctx.strokeStyle = 'rgb(0,111,174)';
ctx.beginPath();
ctx.moveTo(pt1.x, pt1.y);
ctx.bezierCurveTo(cp1.x, cp1.y, cp2.x, cp2.y, pt2.x, pt2.y);
ctx.bezierCurveTo(89, 65, 159, 118, 155, 145);
ctx.fill();
ctx.stroke();
```

The first two lines of code change the stroke to a dark blue color and the fill to a light blue color. The next four lines create a new path using the `bezierCurveTo` function to create smooth curves. The path is then filled and outlined.

7 Save the HTML file, then switch to your browser and preview the HTML page, reflecting your changes:

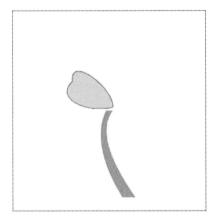

The stem shape with a single flower petal.

8   Switch back to your text editor and add the following lines of code after the lines from the previous step; these lines change the stroke and fill colors and draw the center of the flower, tying the illustration of the flower together:

```
ctx.fillStyle = 'rgb(243,237,99)';
ctx.strokeStyle = 'rgb(253,183,58)';
ctx.beginPath();
ctx.arc(155, 145, 10, 0, Math.PI * 2, false);
ctx.fill();
ctx.stroke();
```

9   To visualize how the `bezierCurveTo` function makes use of control points to define a curve, you will add a guideline using the same points as the first curve of the flower petal. Create the guidelines by adding the following lines of code after the lines from the previous step:

```
ctx.strokeStyle = 'rgb(255,0,0)';
ctx.beginPath();
ctx.arc(pt1.x, pt1.y, 2, 0, Math.PI * 2, false);
ctx.arc(cp1.x, cp1.y, 2, 0, Math.PI * 2, false);
ctx.arc(cp2.x, cp2.y, 2, 0, Math.PI * 2, false);
ctx.arc(pt2.x, pt2.y, 2, 0, Math.PI * 2, false);
ctx.stroke();
```

The first line changes the stroke to a bright red, which stands out from the flower drawing. The next six lines create a connected path of small circles at each point used by the first Bezier curve.

10 Save the HTML file, then switch to your browser and preview the HTML page, reflecting your changes.

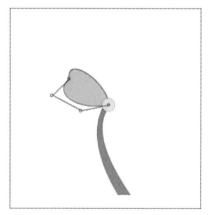

The flower with a single petal and visualization lines.

Shifting control points

More practice

After completing the Drawing Curves section, and to better explore how the `bezierCurveTo` function uses control points, modify the point values stored in step 4 of the lesson. As you change the values, you will notice that the guidelines continue to represent the points in use and the curve is drawn towards the control points.

As an example, change the x property of the `cp2` variable from `66` to `4`. The bottom curve of the flower petal is drawn towards the leftmost side of the canvas, where the second control point is placed.

Adding text

You can draw text, in addition to lines and shapes, on a canvas. Font family, size, and text-weight are set in a manner similar to CSS, and follow the same rules according to the fonts, sizes, and text weight values that are available. Unlike CSS, there is no concept of margins or padding, rather, text is positioned absolutely according to coordinates given in a XY format. In this section, you will create a greeter's name badge to explore drawing text on the canvas.

1 Open the addingtext.html file located in the HTML5_10lessons folder and save a copy of the file as **addingtext_work.html**. The file uses the same template you have been using, with the exception of two rectangles placed to make the background of the greeter's name badge.

2 Locate the second `strokeRect` function, add the following code to draw the header text:

```
ctx.fillText('HELLO MY NAME IS', 12, 40);
```

This line of code draws the text value of the first parameter at the coordinates of the second (x) and third (y) parameters. The default font is used and the color of the text is white, based on the fillStyle value set previously in the code.

3 Save the HTML file, then switch to your browser and preview the HTML page, reflecting your changes:

The greeter's name badge with a small header.

4   To increase the size and weight of the header text, insert the following line of code before the line from the previous step:

```
ctx.font = "bold 1.8em sans-serif";
ctx.fillText('HELLO MY NAME IS', 12, 40);
```

Notice that as with CSS, you can set font size using relative values. In this case, the header text will be 1.8 times the size of the canvas HTML element's font size, which is inherited from the body of the HTML page, unless you set it explicitly.

5   Save the HTML file, then switch to your browser and preview the HTML page, reflecting your changes:

The greeter's name badge with a more fitting header.

6   To add the name of the greeter to the badge, add another call to `fillText`. To make the text stand out and appear handwritten, you will use a different font at a larger size. After the code from step 2, add the follow lines.

```
ctx.fillStyle = 'rgb(0, 0, 0)';
ctx.font = 'bold 84px Comic Sans MS';
ctx.textAlign = 'center';
ctx.fillText('Dianne', 150, 150);
```

The first line sets the color of the text to black. The second line sets the font to an absolute height of `84` pixels and the default font family to `Comic Sans MS`, which is a script font. The next sets the horizontal alignment of the text in relation to the position coordinate to `center`. Other possible options for horizontal alignment are `right` or the default value, `left`.

7 Save the HTML file, then switch to your browser and preview the HTML page, reflecting your changes:

The greeter's name badge with a nice header and the greeter's name.

Using colors, styles, and gradients

You have used solid colors so far, but most objects transition smoothly from one color to another. This type of transition in Canvas is called a gradient, which is available as a linear or radial brush. Additionally, in this section, you will learn different ways to define colors, including areas of transparency.

1 Open the colorsstylesandgradients.html file located in the HTML5_10lessons folder and save a copy of the file as **colorsstylesandgradients_work.html**. The file makes use of a few paths that were included to make the shape of a soda glass.

2 Open your browser and preview the HTML page to see the empty soda glass.

An empty soda glass with a hard shadow.

3 Return to your text editor and after the `strokeRect` function, change the `fillStyle` color from black to gray, as shown here:

```
ctx.fillStyle = 'gray';
```

Previous sections of this lesson have all used `rgb` to define colors, but there are reserved keywords available for ease of use. Other keywords include basic colors, such as red, blue, orange, and purple.

4 Save the HTML file, then switch to your browser and preview the HTML page, reflecting your changes.

An empty soda glass with a softer shadow.

5 You can also fill up the glass with soda using a linear gradient. After the section commented as the "cup inline" and before the section commented as "cup outline", insert the following lines of code:

```
var lineGrad = ctx.createLinearGradient(150, 81, 150, 268);
lineGrad.addColorStop(0, '#fff');
lineGrad.addColorStop(0.05, '#450c0c');
lineGrad.addColorStop(0.6, '#874040');
lineGrad.addColorStop(1, 'rgba(202, 147, 147, 0.6)');
ctx.fillStyle = lineGrad;
```

The first line defines a new linear gradient brush where the first two parameters determine the start point of the gradient, and the next two parameters determine the end point of the gradient. The locations use x and y coordinates, as if you were positioning a rectangle or a circle.

The next four lines define the different color stops in the gradient. The first parameter determines the position of the color stop relative to the start and end point of the gradient (0 representing the start point and 1 representing the end point). The second parameter defines the color of the color stop.

The hexadecimal format is used to define the first three colors. The last color is defined using the `rgba` function, which extends the `rgb` function by adding another parameter used as the alpha or opacity of the color. Opacity is set on a scale from 0 to 1, where 0 represents a fully transparent color and 1 represents a fully opaque color.

We cover the concepts of RGBA in more detail in Lesson 11, Styling with CSS3.

The last line changes the `fillStyle` to the new linear gradient brush.

6   With the `fillStyle` set to the new linear gradient, your last step is to fill the cup outline. In the cup outline commented section, add the following line after the `stroke` function.

```
ctx.fill();
```

7   Save the HTML file, then switch to your browser and preview the HTML page, reflecting your changes:

A full soda glass.

8   Return to your text editor, using multiple radial gradients, you will add a few bubbles to the soda glass. After the `ctx.fill` line of code you added in step 6, add the following lines:

```
ctx.strokeStyle = 'rgba(255, 255, 255, 0.5)';
ctx.lineWidth = 2;
```

The first line changes the strokeStyle from the default black to a semi-transparent white. The second line changes the width of the stroke from the default 1 pixel to 2 pixels.

9   After the lines from the previous step, add the following lines:

```
var radGrad = ctx.createRadialGradient(116, 107, 1, 120, 110, 10);
radGrad.addColorStop(0, 'white');
radGrad.addColorStop(0.9, 'rgba(255, 255, 255, 0)');
```

The first line defines a radial gradient in a manner similar to the linear gradient. Start and end points for the gradient are set (first and second parameters for the start point, fourth and fifth for the end point). The main difference is the third and sixth parameters, which are used as the radius of the respective points.

In this example, the start point is defined at an x position of 116 and a y position of 107 with a radius of 1. The end point is defined at an x position of 120 and a y position of 110 with a radius of 10.

10 With the radial gradient appearance defined, you can use it to fill a circle to represent a bubble. After the lines from the previous step, add the following lines.

```
ctx.fillStyle = radGrad;
ctx.beginPath();
ctx.arc(120, 110, 10, 0, Math.PI * 2, false);
ctx.fill();
ctx.stroke();
```

11 Save the HTML file, then switch to your browser and preview the HTML page, reflecting your changes:

A full soda glass with a bubble.

12 To add another bubble, you must define a new brush because the coordinates are set to an absolute position. If you move or change the size of a bubble, you must move the brush as well. After the code from step 10, add the following lines.

```
radGrad = ctx.createRadialGradient(164, 140, 1, 168, 143, 8);
radGrad.addColorStop(0, 'white');
radGrad.addColorStop(0.9, 'rgba(255, 255, 255, 0)');
ctx.fillStyle = radGrad;
ctx.beginPath();
ctx.arc(168, 143, 8, 0, Math.PI * 2, false);
ctx.fill();
ctx.stroke();
```

13 Save the HTML file, then switch to your browser and preview the HTML page, reflecting your changes:

A full soda glass with two bubbles.

14 Add one more bubble to finish the composition: after the code from the previous step, add the following lines:

```
radGrad = ctx.createRadialGradient(127, 185, 1, 130, 188, 6);
radGrad.addColorStop(0, 'white');
radGrad.addColorStop(0.9, 'rgba(255, 255, 255, 0)');
ctx.fillStyle = radGrad;
ctx.beginPath();
ctx.arc(130, 188, 6, 0, Math.PI * 2, false);
ctx.fill();
ctx.stroke();
```

15 Save the HTML file, then switch to your browser and preview the HTML page, reflecting your changes:

A full soda glass with three bubbles.

Adding images

You can use a simple, single function called drawImage to draw an image to a canvas. The most difficult part is to ensure that when you call the function, the external image file has enough time to open. Once the image is available, the drawImage function provides you with great flexibility to decide the size and section of the image to show.

1   In the HTML5_10lessons folder, open the addingimages.html file and save a copy of the file as **addingimages_work.html**. The file is set up as a copy of the original canvas template introduced in the first section of this lesson.

2   Preview the fishlake.jpg found in the images folder to see the image that you will use in this section.

3   In the if statement, after the ctx variable is set, add the following code:

```
var img = new Image();
img.onload = function(){


}
img.src = 'images/fishlake.jpg';
```

The first line declares a new Image object and the second line defines a function for the onload event of the image. The last line sets the source file for the image; after that file is downloaded by the browser, the function from the second line is called.

4   Within the curly brackets ({, }) of the onload function, add the following code as follows:

```
img.onload = function(){
    ctx.drawImage(img, 0, 0);
}
```

This tells the canvas to draw the image at the XY position of 0,0.

5   Save the HTML file, then switch to your browser and preview the HTML page, reflecting your changes:

The fishlake image cropped.

The image opened, but it was also cropped because the original size of the image file is larger than the canvas element.

6   To resize the image to fit within the space, add the destination width of 300 and the destination height of 200 to the `drawImage` function. Modify the line from step 4 to the following:

```
ctx.drawImage(img, 0, 0, 300, 200);
```

This tells the canvas to draw the image at the XY position of 0,0, and then resize it to a width of 300 pixels and a height of 200 pixels.

7   Save the HTML file, then switch to your browser and preview the HTML page, reflecting your changes:

The fishlake image resized to fit within the available space.

8   As a final variant of the `drawImage` function, you can define the source position, width, and height along with the destination position, width, and height. Modify the line from step 4 to the following:

```
ctx.drawImage(img, 287, 132, 100, 100, 0, 0, 300, 300);
```

This tells the canvas to draw the image at the XY position of 0,0 at a width and height of 300, using a rectangular slice of the source image beginning at the position of 287,132 at a width and height of 100.

9 Save the HTML file, then switch to your browser and preview the HTML page, reflecting your changes.

Typically, this technique is not ideal, as it will tend to pixelate your images. In this case, it is for demonstration purposes.

The fishlake image zoomed in on a specific spot.

Using transforms

Transformations combined with Canvas drawing states enable the creation of complex and dynamic drawings. As discussed earlier in the lesson, global changes, such as `strokeStyle`, `fillStyle`, and `lineWidth`, are all stored in different layers of state change that you can save and restore. The three types of transformations (scaling, rotating, and translating) are also stored in the global state change layers and are easy to use once you understand how to use them in conjunction with the `save` and `restore` functions.

1 In the HTML5_10lessons folder, open the usingtransforms.html file and save a copy of the file as **usingtransforms_work.html**. The file has five rectangles drawn across the canvas.

2   Open your browser and preview the HTML page to see the rectangles.

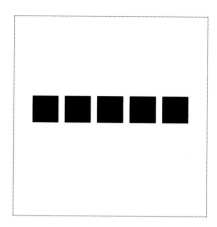

Five rectangles.

3   After the rectangle1 commented section and before rectangle2, add the following line of code as seen here:

```
//rectangle1
    ctx.fillRect(30, 120, 40, 40);

ctx.translate(0, 20);

//rectangle2
    ctx.fillRect(80, 120, 40, 40);
```

The translate transform offsets any subsequent drawing instructions based on the first parameter, which is the x offset value, and the second parameter, which is the y offset value.

4   Save the HTML file, then switch to your browser and preview the HTML page, reflecting your changes.

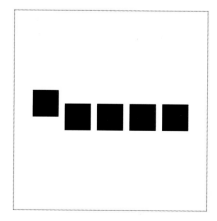

The last four rectangles pushed further down the y-axis.

5   You can see that once set, the translate transform applies to every drawing instruction following it. After the rectangle1 commented section and before the code from step 3, add the following line as follows:

```
//rectangle1
    ctx.fillRect(30, 120, 40, 40);
    ctx.save();
    ctx.translate(0, 20);
```

6   After the rectangle 4 commented section and before rectangle5, add the following line as follows:

```
//rectangle4
    ctx.fillRect(180, 120, 40, 40);

ctx.restore();

//rectangle5
    ctx.fillRect(230, 120, 40, 40);
```

Before you add the translate transform, you save a snapshot of the global canvas state. Once the fourth rectangle is drawn, you restore the global canvas state to its condition before the translate transform was applied.

7   Save the HTML file, then switch to your browser and preview the HTML page, reflecting your changes.

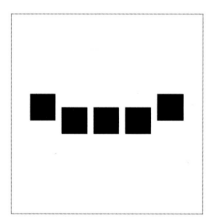

Only the middle three rectangles are pushed further down the y-axis.

8   Return to your text editor, after the rectangle 2 commented section and before rectangle3, add the following lines:

```
ctx.save();
ctx.rotate(0.19);
```

The first line saves another snapshot of the global canvas state. The second line adds a rotate transform where the parameter is equal to the angle of rotation measured in radians.

9   Save the HTML file, then switch to your browser and preview the HTML page, reflecting your changes.

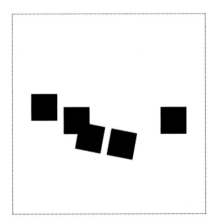

The last four rectangles are pushed down and the middle two are rotated.

Since you call the `save` function twice and the `restore` function once, the last rectangle is affected by the translate transform, but not the rotate transform.

10   After the rectangle 3 commented section and before rectangle4, add the following line:

```
ctx.restore();
```

11   Save the HTML file, then switch to your browser and preview the HTML page, reflecting your changes.

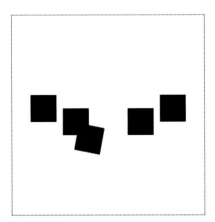

Three rectangles are pushed down and one is rotated.

12   After the `restore` function from step 5 and before rectangle5, add the following line:

```
ctx.scale(0.5, 0.7);
```

13 Save the HTML file, then switch to your browser and preview the HTML page, reflecting your changes:

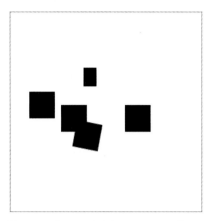

Three rectangles are pushed down, one is rotated, and one is scaled.

Creating a drawing loop

With a fundamental understanding of drawing, you can learn about the dynamic aspect of Canvas. JavaScript functions, such as `setInterval`, enable you to repeatedly call a drawing function. During each repetition, you can slightly modify your drawing, thus creating the illusion of an animation.

1 In the HTML5_10lessons folder, open the drawingloop.html file and save a copy of the file as **drawingloop_work.html**. The file is set up to draw a night sky with a UFO image.

2 Open your browser and preview the HTML page to see the night sky scene.

A night sky and a UFO.

3   Examine the JavaScript that creates the drawing loop.

As with previous sections, the onload event of the body calls the setup function that opens the image object and downloads the ufo.png file. You should note that both the `ctx` and `img` variables are initially declared outside the `setup` function. This enables the variables to be used in other functions, in this case, the `draw` and `drawbackground` functions.

After the image opens, you can use the `setInterval` function to call the `draw` function every 36 milliseconds.

The `draw` function then calls the `drawbackground` function, which draws the sky and stars. Then the "ufo" comment is reached, which is where the image of the UFO is drawn.

4   After the `img` variable is defined and before the `setup` function, add the following lines of code as follows:

```
<script type="text/javascript">
    var ctx;
    var img;
    var x = 0;
    var y = 40;
```

These variables are used to update the position of the UFO, but you then need to modify the `draw` function in order to make use of these new variables.

5   In the `draw` function, modify the `drawImage` to use the new variables and update the x variable as follows:

```
function draw() {
    drawBackground();

    <!--ufo-->
        ctx.drawImage(img, x, y);
        x += 1;
}
```

6   Save the HTML file, then switch to your browser and preview the HTML page, reflecting your changes. The UFO will slowly move horizontally across the canvas.

The UFO flying across the night sky.

7   To repeat the loop so the UFO returns after leaving the viewable area, reset the x variable when it becomes larger than the width of the Canvas. Additionally, increase the speed by adding more to the x variable, as follows:

```
x += 3;
if(x > 300){
    x = -50;
}
```

The value of the x variable is reset to -50 rather than 0 to account for the width of the UFO image.

8   Save the HTML file, then switch to your browser and preview the HTML page, reflecting your changes. When the UFO hits the right edge of the canvas, it will reappear at the left edge.

The UFO flying across the night sky and returning.

9   To create dynamic images, you can also use the `Math.random` function in JavaScript. For example, change the y variable randomly, so the UFO returns at an unknown level. In the if statement used to reset the x variable, insert the following line as follows:

```
x += 3;
if(x > 300){
    x = -50;
    y = Math.random() * 300;
}
```

`Math.random` returns a number between 0 and 1 that is multiplied by the maximum number you want returned. In this case, 300 is used to match the height of the Canvas.

10 Save the HTML file, then switch to your browser and preview the HTML page, reflecting your changes. When the UFO hits the right edge of the screen, it will reappear at a random position on the left edge.

The UFO flying across the night sky and returning randomly.

Additional canvas resources

The capabilities of the Canvas element has stirred great interest within the web design and development community. Here are a few resources to help you explore this area of HTML5.

Ai->Canvas
This is a plugin for Illustrator that allows you to export artwork from the application and use the resulting canvas code in your pages. There is even built-in support for animation.
http://visitmix.com/work/ai2canvas/

Lucidchart
This web application is very similar to flowchart applications such as Visio and was entirely built using the Canvas element. As a bonus, you can export artwork created in the application.
http://www.lucidchart.com/documents/demo

Explorercanvas
Add support for the Canvas element in Internet Explorer by adding this JavaScript to your pages.
http://code.google.com/p/explorercanvas/

Self study

Continue experimenting with the Drawing Loop exercise by changing the animated image and the composition of the background scene. To add an extra level of interaction, change the position of the animated image based on the position of the user's mouse. Try adding transforms to the composition, as well, to review how the effects of multiple transforms are applied.

Review

Questions

1   What are the basic requirements to draw with Canvas in HTML5?

2   How do you draw a circle in Canvas?

3   How do you define a semi-transparent color?

Answers

1   A Canvas element must be defined and added to the body of the page. Drawing instructions are then applied using a reference to the 2D Context of the Canvas element.

2   Using the `arc` function, a full circle can be drawn when the `startAngle` and `endAngle` are set to 0 and `Math.PI*2`. Angles are measured in radians and the `Math.PI` function is equal to 180 degrees.

3   The `rgba` function has four parameters. The first three, representing red, green and blue, are set to a value between 0 and 255, which determines the strength of the respective color. The final parameter is set to a value between 0 and 1, determining the opacity of the color.

What you'll learn in this lesson:

- Working with the `border-radius` and `border-image` properties
- Using vendor-specific prefixes
- Adding multiple background images
- Creating CSS gradients
- Creating CSS animations targeted for WebKit browsers, such as Mobile Safari for the iPhone and iPad

Styling with CSS3

In this lesson, you will learn to use CSS3 properties that enhance web pages with styling, such as rounded corners, border images, gradients, transparent colors, and animation.

Starting up

You will work with several files from the HTML5_11lessons folder in this lesson. Make sure you have loaded the HTML5lessons folder onto your hard drive from the supplied DVD. See "Loading lesson files" in the Starting Up section of this book.

See Lesson 11 in action!

Use the accompanying video to gain a better understanding of how to use some of the capabilities shown in this lesson. The video tutorial for this lesson can be found on the included DVD.

To accurately preview the HTML5 content you will create in this lesson, you need a browser that supports HTML5 tags. See "Using web browsers that support HTML5 tags" in the Starting Up section of this book to determine whether you are using such a browser, or for instructions on downloading one.

Understanding the role of CSS3

Cascading Style Sheets is a separate language from HTML, and the W3C specification that details the features and rules of CSS has its own timeline. The original CSS1 specification became a W3C recommendation in 1996; the CSS2 specification became a W3C recommendation in 1998; and an updated version, named CSS2.1, is in the final stages of becoming a final recommendation.

The details of the evolution of CSS are not as important as what it signifies: browser support. Designers and developers need to know which features they can use in their stylesheets and whether they will be supported by web browsers. CSS specifications can help evaluate whether the features are supported, but they cannot indicate whether individual browsers support a specific feature. For example, parts of the CSS2.1 specification (introduced in 2004) have incomplete support in some modern browsers. Consider the following HTML example:

```
<p>Big <strong>sale</strong> today on <em>all smoothies</em> in the
<a href="tropical/index.html ">Tropical</a> </p>
```

The CSS2.1 specification defines a concept called adjacent selectors that let you define a rule for all <em> elements that follow <strong> elements. For example, suppose you want the <em> element to be purple. The CSS for this rule is:

```
strong + em {
    color:purple;
}
```

This is an easy way to define styles for specific situations; in the preceding example, your current styles might define the <em> element as the color grey, but whenever an <em> element follows a <strong> element, it appears purple.

You could apply this technique to many other situations to simplify styles, but the technique is not widespread due to lack of browser support, specifically Internet Explorer 6 and 7.

The new CSS3 features face a similar dilemma, so to make it easier for developers and designers to sort through the complexities of browser support, the W3C has separated the new CSS3 features into modules, rather than release an entire update. Some examples of these modules are Backgrounds and Borders, Animations, Media Queries, and many more. Each module has different features with varying levels of browser support.

The following exercises highlight the browser support available for various CSS3 features, and provide guidance for how you can best use them. The first exercise explains the CSS Backgrounds and Borders module.

Using CSS3 `border-radius` and `border-image`

When CSS first became available, the addition of borders and background styling was a key feature. The border property lets you style any or all sides of a CSS box with a colored border. You can also adjust the thickness of the borders and choose from a few styles, such as dotted, dashed, and others.

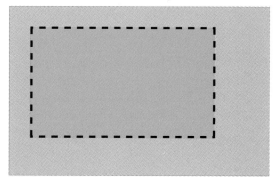

A box with a dashed border.

These features provide excellent tools for designers, but the ability to provide certain features is still missing. For example, you cannot create rounded corners using CSS2.1 and it is not part of its specification, but you can do it with CSS3 using the `border-radius` property. Other additions include the border-image property that lets you add an image to a border. In this exercise, you will use the `border-radius` and `border-image` properties.

1 Open the 11_borders.html file from the HTML5_11lessons folder. Preview this page in your browser. The Upcoming Sale box has a basic border and a background-color you will modify with the new CSS3 properties.

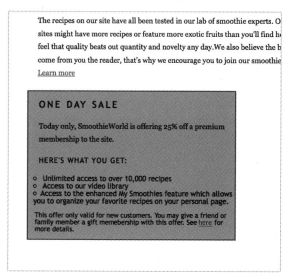

You will apply rounded corners to this box using the `border-radius` *property.*

Return to your text editor.

2 The style for this box is an internal style; locate the rules for the `.specialsale` class in the style section of your page:

```css
.specialsale {
    width: 400px;
    background-color:#D67E5C;
    border: 2px #773636 solid;
}
```

These properties define the appearance of this box. Your first task is to add a `border-radius` to create four curved corners.

3 Add the following `border-radius` property:

```css
.specialsale {
    width: 400px;
    background-color:#D67E5C;
    border: 2px #773636 solid;
    border-radius: 24px;
}
```

The `border-radius` property is part of the CSS3 specification and is widely supported by modern browsers (Safari 5.0+, Firefox 4.0+, Internet Explorer 9.0+, Google Chrome 10.0+, and Opera 11.0). Previous versions of these browsers are still in use; to support these older versions, you will add two additional properties with a vendor-specific prefix.

4 Add the following properties:

```css
.specialsale {
    width: 400px;
    background-color:#D67E5C;
    border: 2px #773636 solid;
    -webkit-border-radius: 24px;
    -moz-border-radius: 24px;
    border-radius: 24px;
}
```

The prefixes -webkit and -moz are vendor-specific, which means the properties only work in browsers that recognize and render these prefixes. Even though it means adding extra code, it increases the number of web browsers that can use the radius.

The curious case of vendor-specific prefixes

Vendor-specific prefixes first appeared after the year 2007. Browser manufacturers, such as Firefox, Safari, and Chrome, adopted this method to add features to their browsers in a way that was obvious to developers and designers reading the code. Vendor-prefixes allowed browser manufacturers to experiment and test new CSS properties with the intent of eventually dropping the prefixes and keeping the final CSS3 property. This is what has happened with properties such as `border-radius`. Browsers that work with a code base called Webkit, such as Apple Safari and Google Chrome, use the `-webkit` prefix; browsers that work with the Gecko code base, such as Mozilla Firefox, use the `-moz` prefix. The official CSS3 specification has adopted the `border-radius` property, and now the latest versions of Safari, Chrome, and Firefox support this property with no prefix needed. You should use these vendor-specific prefixes to provide maximum support for older Gecko-based and Webkit-based browsers.

5   Choose File > Save and preview your page in the browser. If your browser supports the `border-radius` property, you should see the rounded corners. If your browser does not support it, the standard square corners appear.

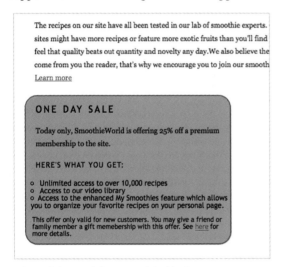

A box with four rounded corners, as defined by the `border-radius` *property.*

There are more options available to style your box. For example, you can define only some of the corners as rounded, as explained in the next step.

6   Return to your text editor and add the following values to all three of your `border-radius` declarations:

```
-webkit-border-radius: 24px 0 0 0;

-moz-border-radius: 24px 0 0 0;

border-radius: 24px 0 0 0;
```

This is a CSS shortcut that assigns values to the top-left, top-right, bottom-right, and bottom-left sides, respectively. In this example, the top-left corner is rounded while the rest are set to no radius, making them square.

A box with only the top-left radius property set.

To apply the same radius to the bottom-right corner, change the third value, as shown in the next step.

7 Add the 24px value to the third value:

```
-webkit-border-radius: 24px 0 24px 0;
-moz-border-radius: 24px 0 24px 0;
border-radius: 24px 0 24px 0;
```

Use CSS shorthand to simplify the value as follows: border-radius: 24px 0. *Using this notation, the* 24px *value refers to the top-left and bottom-right corners, and the* 0px *value refers to the top-right and bottom-left corners.*

You can create other effects with the border-radius: the radius at each corner has two components, vertical and horizontal. Adding a forward slash between a set of values lets you create different effects, as shown in the next step.

8 Replace the current radius values with the following:

```
-webkit-border-radius: 48px / 24px;
-moz-border-radius: 48px / 24px;
border-radius: 48px / 24px;
```

Save your file, and then preview your page in the browser.

> The recipes on our site have all been tested in our lab of smoothie experts. C
> sites might have more recipes or feature more exotic fruits than you'll find h
> feel that quality beats out quantity and novelty any day. We also believe the l
> come from you the reader, that's why we encourage you to join our smoothi
>
> Learn more
>
> **ONE DAY SALE**
>
> Today only, SmoothieWorld is offering 25% off a premium
> membership to the site.
>
> **HERE'S WHAT YOU GET:**
>
> o Unlimited access to over 10,000 recipes
> o Access to our video library
> o Access to the enhanced My Smoothies feature which allows
>   you to organize your favorite recipes on your personal page.
>
> This offer only valid for new customers. You may give a friend or
> family member a gift memebership with this offer. See here for
> more details.

A box with horizontal radii set to 48px and the vertical radii set to 24px.

If your box is square again, it is possible you have an older browser that supports the border-radius *property but does not have support for the horizontal and verticall radii syntax.*

In this example, the value 48px applies to the two horizontal radii (on the top and bottom) and the 24px applies to the two vertical radii (on the right and the left).

Another new CSS3 property is the border-image property, which lets you replace an existing border with an image, so you can create unique border effects not available with the border-style property. The range of options for the border-image property is extensive and the property is not fully supported, so this lesson only explains the basic application of the property.

9   The border-image property is easier to understand if you have no border-radius applied, so you will add a CSS comment to prevent the browser from displaying the radius styles. Add the following commenting code to your border-radius rules:

```
/*-webkit-border-radius: 48px / 24px;
-moz-border-radius: 48px / 24px;
border-radius: 48px / 24px;*/
```

Increase the width of the border to help you understand the effects, as explained in the next step.

10 To change the width of the border, increase the value from 2 to 20:

```
border: 20px #773636 solid;
```

Add the border-image properties, as shown in the next step. Note that you need to add rules for Webkit and Gecko to maintain maximum compatibility among browsers.

11 Add the `border-image` properties and the link to the image file as follows:

```
/*-webkit-border-radius: 48px / 24px;
-moz-border-radius: 48px / 24px;
border-radius: 48px / 24px;*/

-webkit-border-image: url("images/border-bg.png") 33%;
-moz-border-image: url("images/border-bg.png") 33%;
border-image: url("images/border-bg.png") 33%;
```

The image file border-bg.png has been configured to help you understand how the `border-image` property works. The graphic file represents the four corners and four sides of the border and the background of the element. This graphic file is segmented into nine parts; each part is applied to a box. The figure below, on the left, shows the initial image. The figure on the right shows how the image is segmented into nine parts when you use the `border-image` property.

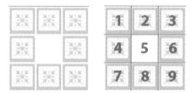

The original image (left). An overlay showing how the image is segmented into nine parts (right).

Parts 1, 3, 7, and 9 are used for the corners; parts 2, 4, 6, and 8 are used for the sides; part 5 is used for the center or background of the element (empty for this example). Specifying a value of 33% indicates where the image should be cut relative to the height and width of the image. Because of the way this graphic was made, cutting by 33% maintains the individual squares and circles.

12 Save your file, and then preview it in the browser.

ONE DAY SALE

Today only, SmoothieWorld is offering 25% off a premium membership to the site.

HERE'S WHAT YOU GET:

o Unlimited access to over 10,000 recipes
o Access to our video library
o Access to the enhanced My Smoothies feature which allows you to organize your favorite recipes on your personal page.

This offer only valid for new customers. You may give a friend or family member a gift memebership with this offer. See here for more details.

The default appearance of a border image segmented by 33%.

As the figure on the right shows, the four squares (parts 1, 3, 7, 9) are applied to the corners. The four circles (parts 2, 4, 6, 8) are applied to the sides and are stretched to fit. Part five is also stretched, but you cannot see it because it is white. Stretching is the default behavior of the border-image, but you have options to create different effects.

13 Return to your text editor and add the following attribute to your `border-image` value:

```
-webkit-border-image: url("images/border-bg.png") 33% repeat;
-moz-border-image: url("images/border-bg.png") 33% repeat;
border-image: url("images/border-bg.png") 33% repeat;
```

Save your file and preview in the browser; the border-image now repeats parts 2, 4, 6, and 8 along the sides of the box.

The border-image after repeating parts 2, 4, 6, and 8.

The `border-image` property will become a powerful tool for designers who want to create more complex and interesting borders. Browser support for this property is still inconsistent; browsers that do not support it will display the standard border style.

For a list of browsers that support the border-image property and for more examples, visit: http://www.css3files.com/border/#borderimage

Adding multiple background images

The `background-image` property has always been an essential tool for designers using CSS because of the ability to add a background image to any box, tile the image horizontally or vertically, and position the image. Note that CSS2.1 only allows one background image per container. CSS3 provides support for multiple background images, thus letting designers create more complex styles.

In this exercise, you will create a striped background for your page using a combination of three background images. If you have an image editor installed, you can open the images used: bg1.png, bg2.png, and bg3.png. Each image is a simple colored gradient that fades to transparency; the transparency provides the bulk of the layered effect.

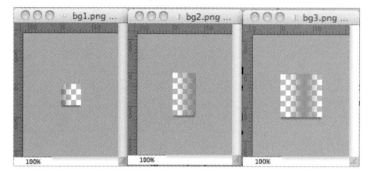

The three image files used are vertical gradients that fade from the color to transparency.

1   Open the 11_backgrounds.html file, located in the HTML5_11lessons folder, and then open the base.css stylesheet. Preview the page in your browser.

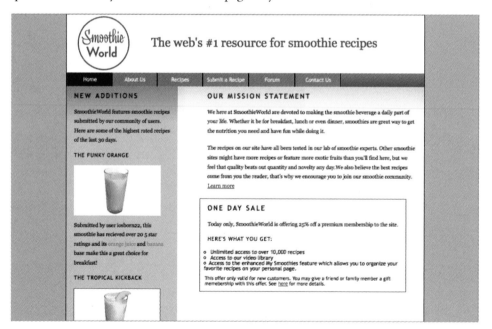

The initial appearance of your page.

You will now add a background image to the body of the page.

2 Open the base.css file in the HTML5_11lessons folder and scroll to the body rule. Currently, there is a property for the `background-color`; add the declaration for your first `background-image` as follows:

```
body {
    font-family: "Trebuchet MS", Tahoma, Arial, sans-serif;
    font-size:100%;
    background-color: #B3BBCA;
    background-image: url(images/bg1.png);
}
```

Save your HTML page, and then preview it in the browser. This is the standard tiling effect of a background image; the bg1.png is semi-transparent, so the blue background color is visible beneath the background image.

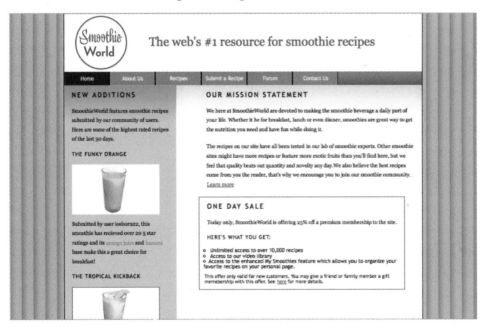

The body of your page with a single (semi-transparent) background image tiled horizontally and vertically.

Since the effect is repetitious, it could be distracting to the user. You will now layer another semi-transparent background image above the current one.

3   Return to your text editor and add the URL link to the next background image; ensure you add the comma between the two images:

```
body {
    font-family: "Trebuchet MS", Tahoma, Arial, sans-serif;
    font-size:100%;
    background-color: #B3BBCA;
    background-image: url(images/bg1.png), url(images/bg2.png);
}
```

Save your stylesheet and preview your page in the browser. The bg2.png image has a transparent gradient and a smaller width and height. Both background images are automatically tiled, but the smaller graphic is tiled at shorter intervals, thus interacting with the graphic underneath it in unique ways, including blending colors. You will further increase the variety and complexity of bars and colors by adding a third layer.

4   Add another URL link for the third background image as follows:

```
background-image: url(images/bg1.png), url(images/bg2.png),
url(images/bg3.png);
```

Save your stylesheet and preview your page in the browser. Now you have three layered, semi-transparent background images interacting with each other to create a complex and layered background for your page. Extend the width of your browser and note that the background is automatically visible.

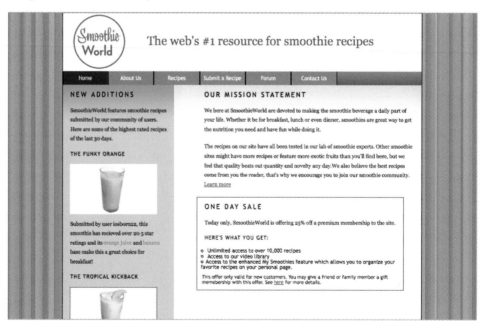

The body of your page with three (semi-transparent) background images tiled horizontally and vertically.

CSS3 multiple background images are supported in modern browsers; browsers that do not support the feature will default to the first background image (for this example, bg1.png). For this reason, we recommend making this image an acceptable and logical fallback for users with non-supported browsers.

You can use multiple background images in other ways. For example, a common technique for background images is to position them using keywords such as top and right.

5   In your 11_backgrounds.html file, scroll to the .specialsale class in the internal stylesheet. Add the following code to include an image of blueberries in the top right corner of the container:

```
.specialsale {
    width: 450px;
    border: 2px #773636 solid;
    background-image: url(images/blueberry.jpg);
    background-repeat: no-repeat;
    background-position: top right;
}
```

By setting the background-repeat value to no-repeat, only a single instance of the image appears. The background-position value of top right places the image at the top right corner of the container. You can currently achieve this effect in CSS2.1, but you cannot add and position another image within the same container, as you will do in the next step.

6   Using your text editor, enter the following code to add an image of an orange at the top left corner:

```
background-image: url(images/blueberry.jpg), url(images/orange.png);
background-repeat: no-repeat;
background-position: top right, top left;
```

Save your file and preview the page in the browser.

CSS3 allows you to position multiple background images within a container.

The previous step demonstrates the ability to add another background image; the next step shows how you can control the placement of the orange graphic. Instead of using simple keywords, you can specify a position with pixels or other values.

Depending on the level of support, you may find your browser supports the multiple background images but not the positioning.

7   Add the following code to position the orange graphic below the heading One Day Sale:

```
background-position: top right, 0 -45px;
```

The first value is the horizontal position and the second value is the vertical position. The negative value of -45px lets you move the graphic beyond the top border of the container. Save your file and preview it in the browser. The orange graphic has moved up and it is located below the One Day Sale heading.

Multiple background images allow this type of independent control. You can also gain more flexibility when you make changes to the surrounding container. Increase the width of your container to see this effect, as explained in the following step.

8   In your .specialsale class style, change the width value to create a wider box:

```
.specialsale {
    width: 550px;
    border: 2px #773636 solid;
    background-image: url(images/blueberry.jpg), url(images/orange.png);
    background-repeat: no-repeat;
    background-position: top right, 0 -45px;
}
```

Save your file and preview in the browser.

The blueberry image shifts when the container is widened, but the separate orange image is unaffected.

Even though the container is wider, the blueberry image remains aligned to the top right corner, and the orange image is positioned using the precise pixel values you assigned to it.

Working with CSS3 transparency and opacity

CSS3 lets you create complex styles using transparency and opacity, but you should understand the vocabulary and differences between the syntax and application of the properties. CSS3 adds a new level of control when adding color as RGBA values. In the CSS2.1 specification, you can use the common hexadecimal colors and color keywords, or create a specific color by assigning values between 0 and 255 for Red, Green, and Blue. CSS3 lets you control a fourth value called alpha, which allows you to change the opacity of a color value. In this exercise, you will learn to use the RGBA color values and the opacity property, which is easily confused with RGBA.

1   Open the 11_rgba.html file in your text editor located in the HTML5_11lessons folder. Preview this page in the browser. There are three boxes on the page with the text "A Colorful Heading". The top box has no background color; the second and third boxes have background color of white.

2   Return to your text editor and locate the `<style>` section at the top of the page; each box has two classes assigned to it: one for the box and another for the heading inside the box. You will work with the top container first, the two styles are as follows:

```
.rgba {
    width: 450px;
    height: 100px;
    border: #000 4px solid;
}

.rgba h1 {
    text-align:center;
    font-weight:bold;
    font-size:48px;
    color:rgb(200,30,35);
}
```

The current color property uses three RGB values to create the dark red color for the heading. The first value (200) represents the red value, the second value (30) represents the green value, and the third value (35) represents the blue value. The fourth value you can now use in CSS3, a (or alpha), controls the opacity of a color. By default, the alpha value is 1.0 or 100% opacity. You need to specify the value to use it.

3   Change the rgb value to rgba as follows:

```
.rgba h1 {
    font-weight:bold;
    font-size:48px;
    color:rgba(200,30,35);
}
```

If you do not specify an alpha value, 100% opacity is automatically used. For this example, the heading would not appear different.

4   To change the opacity, add a new value in decimal form:

```
color:rgba(200,30,35,0.5);
```

Save your file and preview your page in the browser.

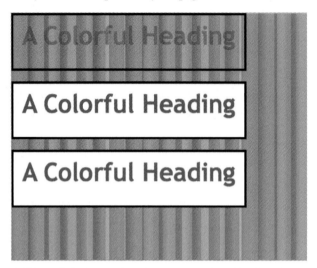

A heading with the RGBA values of 200, 30, 35, and 0.5 (the alpha value is 0.5).

The `rgba` property is relatively well supported in modern browsers; if your browser supports it, the background of the page should appear behind the semi-transparent heading.

 For a list of browser support for the `rgba` *property, visit:* http://caniuse.com/#feat=css3-colors.

Browsers that do not support RGBA use the RGB value, so the user does not see the transparency effect. Remember that RGBA only applies to colors. To affect the transparency of a container and its contents, use the opacity property, as explained in the next step.

5   In your text editor, locate the .opacity class and add the following property:

```
.opacity {
    width: 450px;
    height: 100px;
    border: #000 4px solid;
    background-color:#FFF;
    opacity: 0.5;
}
```

Save your file and preview it in the browser. Setting the opacity value set to 0.5 (or 50%) causes the entire container and its contents to appear semi-transparent.

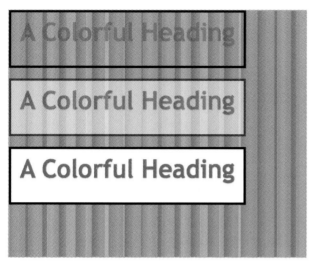

The entire container and the heading within are now at 50% opacity.

You can make further use of the new `rgba` and `opacity` properties with another new CSS3 property, `box-shadow`.

6   Return to your text editor and add the following property to your `.opacity` class:

```
.opacity {
    width: 450px;
    height: 100px;
    border: #000 4px solid;
    background-color:#FFF;
    opacity: 0.5;
    box-shadow: 15px 10px;
}
```

The first value (`15px`) is the horizontal offset of the shadow to the right; the second value (`10px`) is the vertical offset to the bottom.

You can offset a shadow horizontally to the left by using a negative value. Likewise, a negative value for the vertical offset places the shadow to the top.

The horizontal and vertical offset values are required, but you can add a third, optional value to change the blur distance of the shadow, as shown in the next step.

7   Add the following value to your `box-shadow` declaration:

```
box-shadow: 15px 10px 10px;
```

The box-shadow property benefits from vendor-specific prefixes to be compatible with as many browsers as possible. Add support for Webkit and Moz now, as explained in the next step.

8   Add the following two properties to increase support for Webkit and Moz browsers:

```
-webkit-box-shadow: 15px 10px 10px;
-moz-box-shadow: 15px 10px 10px;
box-shadow: 15px 10px 10px;
```

Save your file and preview in the browser. Your second container now has a drop shadow. Since the container has an opacity value of 0.5, the drop shadow is subject to the same transparency effect. If you are still not seeing the shadow, it may still be a matter of browser support. Webkit browsers appear to need a color value to reliably display the shadow. You will be adding this color value in a few steps.

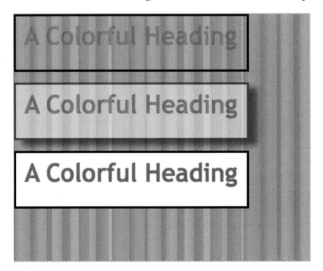

The box-shadow *property applies a drop shadow to your container.*

You will now add a drop shadow to the third box and control the color and opacity of just the drop shadow using RGBA values.

9   In your style section, locate the `.dropshadow` class. This style is the same as the final
`.opacity` class from the last step, but opacity is at the default value of 100%. Add the
following `box-shadow` declaration:

```
.dropshadow {
    width: 450px;
    height: 100px;
    border: #000 4px solid;
    background-color:#FFF;
    -webkit-box-shadow: 15px 10px 10px;
    -moz-box-shadow: 15px 10px 10px;
    box-shadow: 15px 10px 10px;
}
```

These style rules as similar to the ones you applied in the last step, but now you can see
the default black color of the drop shadow. Save your file and preview in the browser.

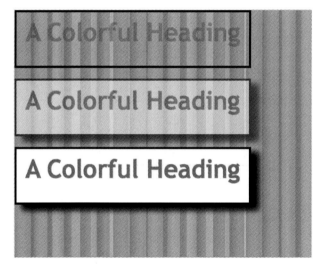

The default color of box shadows is black.

Use RGBA values when you need to control the color and opacity of the drop shadow.

10   Return to your text editor and add the following RGBA value to your three `box-shadow` properties:

```
-webkit-box-shadow: 15px 10px 10px rgba(0,0,0,0.5);
-moz-box-shadow: 15px 10px 10px rgba(0,0,0,0.5);
box-shadow: 15px 10px 10px rgba(0,0,0,0.5);
```

When the first three RBGA values are 0, as in this example, the resulting color is pure black. Recall that the fourth value represents the opacity value; for this example, the opacity is set at 0.5 (50%). Save your file and then preview in the browser.

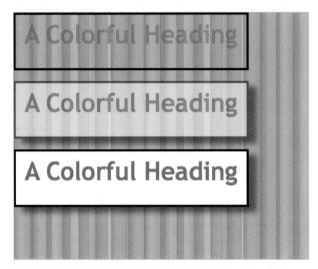

Use the RGBA value to reduce the opacity of a box-shadow without affecting the opacity of the surrounding container.

Box-shadows and RGBA values have the same level of support among browsers. For browsers that do not support these values, such as Internet Explorer 6, 7 and 8, no box-shadow appears.

Internet Explorer 9 supports box-shadow, but if you need the equivalent effects in earlier versions of IE, use the Internet Explorer-only filter property. For more information, visit: http://hedgerwow.appspot.com/demo/shadow.

Using CSS3 gradients

Gradients are a common design element on many web pages, but prior to CSS3, designers had to create a gradient in an image editor, such as Photoshop, and then export it as a web graphic. Since gradients are decorative, designers often use the CSS `background-image` property to apply the gradient image to a container or to the body of the page. With image-based gradients, you cannot easily update or modify the gradient colors. In the CSS3 images module, native gradients are available using new properties, including `linear-gradient` and `radial-gradient`. Native gradients let you update and experiment easily and efficiently.

Gradients in CSS are similar to gradients in programs such as Illustrator or Photoshop. All gradient images have at least two color stops, which represent absolute color values. For example, the figure below shows a color stop of blue on the left and a color stop of green on the right. The transition point between the two stops is where one color makes the transition to the other, and it is often located in the middle of the two stops, but you can change the location.

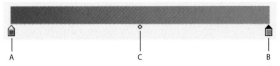

A simple blue-green gradient with a transition point exactly in the middle.
A. *blue color stop* **B.** *green color stop* **C.** *transition point*

You can create more complex gradients by adding more color stops or by moving the transition point. In the next exercise, you will apply a gradient to the background of a container and learn about some of the available options.

Note that there are no current versions of Internet Explorer that support CSS3 gradients (previews of Internet Explorer 10 have announced support). Gecko and Webkit-based browsers require vendor-specific prefixes, and the syntax for creating gradients is different for each type of browser. CSS gradients are fairly recent in the timeline of CSS3 technology, but fortunately, different browser manufacturers are settling on a standard syntax. In the following exercise, you will learn about browser compatibility issues, but you can obtain more information about browser support for CSS gradients at *http://caniuse.com/#feat=css-gradients*.

1   Open the 11_gradients.html file from the HTML5_11lessons folder. This file has a simple container with a white background and a headline. You will add a basic horizontal gradient with a white and a black color stop with the Gecko syntax, and then you will add the same property using the Webkit syntax.

2   Add the following code to your gradient class:

```
.gradient {
    width: 450px;
    border: #000 4px solid;
    background-color:#FFF;
    background-image: -moz-linear-gradient(white, black);
}
```

The gradient in this example starts at the top and ends at the bottom. To reproduce this in Webkit browsers, add the same declaration with the `-webkit` prefix.

3   Add the following code:

```
.gradient {
    width: 450px;
    border: #000 4px solid;
    background-color:#FFF;
    background-image: -moz-linear-gradient(white, black);
    background-image: -webkit-linear-gradient(white, black);
}
```

The browser support in the example above is still incomplete: recent versions of Google Chrome (a Webkit-based browser) would display the gradient, but Apple Safari (also a Webkit browser) would not because Apple Safari uses a different syntax. The next step shows this syntax, but keep in mind that Safari has announced they will discontinue their syntax and use the one shown above.

4   Add the following code between your two existing background-image declarations. You cannot add the new background-image last because it would override the other Webkit background-image.

```
.gradient {
    width: 450px;
    border: #000 4px solid;
    background-color:#FFF;
    background-image: -moz-linear-gradient(white, black);
    background-image: -webkit-gradient(linear, 0 0, 0 100%,
        from(white),
        to(black)
        );
    background-image: -webkit-linear-gradient(white, black);
}
```

The Safari syntax is more complex: the first line describes the category of gradient (linear), the starting position (0, 0), and the ending position (0, 100%). The next two lines, from(white) and to(black), define the two color stops.

If you have Firefox 3.6+, Safari 4.0+, or Chrome 8.0+, save the file and preview it in the browser. You should see a linear gradient stretching from top to bottom.

A linear gradient stretching from top to bottom.

CSS gradients potential for the future

Currently, there is a lack of standardization among current browsers, but the future timeline of support for browsers addresses this. The following subsections describe other aspects and potential uses of CSS gradients.

Angles and Multiple stops

The ability to change the angle of a gradient and to add multiple stops will provide fine control over the gradient appearance.

```
background-image: -moz-linear-gradient(45deg, white, green, black);
```

This code creates a gradient with a 45 degree angle and a green color stop between the white and black stops, as shown in the following figure.

A 45 degree gradient with multiple color stops.

Radial Gradients

Radial gradients are easy to add and have a few additional values.

```
background-image: -moz-radial-gradient(60% 60%, circle closest-
corner, white, black);
```

A radial gradient with a circle shape and a positioned center point.

The first two values (60% 60%) define the center point of the radius; for this example, the center point is 60% from the top and 60% from the left of the container. You can also designate a circle shape instead of an ellipse, and specify a size (for this example, closest-corner).

Repeating Gradients

Currently, to achieve a repeating gradient effect, you need to use a background-image and then tile it horizontally or vertically. In CSS3, you can repeat linear and radial gradients.

```
background-image: -moz-repeating-linear-gradient(left, white 80%,
black, white);
```

A repeating gradient.

The result of the code above is a white-to-black-to-white gradient repeated horizontally. By starting and ending with the same color stop (`white`), you can achieve a smooth repeating pattern.

Using RGBA colors

You can use RGBA colors to add transparency to any gradient, thus providing depth. A possible use is to add a layer of depth to an image or a button. In the following example, a transparent gradient is applied to the H1 style, thus allowing the background image of the container to show through.

```
.gradient h1 {
    margin:0;
    font-weight:bold;
    font-size:48px;
    color:#C33;
    text-align:center;
    background-image: -moz-linear-gradient(rgba(174, 185, 196, 0.9),
    rgba(110, 124, 140, 0.9));
}
```

A semi-transparent gradient applied to the background of a heading allows the image below to show through.

CSS3 transforms, transitions, and animation

A CSS transform lets you rotate, scale, or skew an element on your page. For example, with a simple transform you can rotate an image on the page slightly to one side for aesthetic effect. You can also animate transforms; for example, animating the scale property lets you create an enlarging or minimizing effect on an image or other element. The perspective property lets you simulate an object positioned or animated in 3D space.

You can use a CSS transition to change one or more CSS property values over time. For example, when a user clicks a button, a transition would let you create an animated effect from the default color of the button to another color.

CSS animations can appear similar to transitions because you can use both to create the illusion of motion onscreen, but CSS animations use keyframes that allow you to specify how often to repeat the illusion of movement.

The following exercise will help you understand the difference between transitions and animations, and learn more about all three features.

Targeting the iPhone and Webkit browsers

As mentioned before, CSS3 has been divided into several modules, such as the Backgrounds and Borders module, the Images module, and many others. As a result, different browser manufacturers can focus on different modules; the most significant example is the CSS Transform and Animation modules, for which Apple Safari has had support for years. In fact, Apple's Mobile Safari has had longtime support for these features, and this is one of the reasons behind the success of the iPhone and the iPad. These devices use Apple's operating system, iOS, which does not support Flash. CSS animations were supported on the iPhone as early as 2007 to provide an alternative for the type of animation traditionally associated with Flash.

Creating CSS3 transforms and transitions

In the following exercise, you will only use the CSS properties associated with Webkit; some of the transform and transition features covered in this lesson are supported in other browsers, but not to the same degree as Webkit browsers such as Safari (desktop and mobile) and Chrome. This will change with future releases of Firefox and Internet Explorer 10; for now, these properties are used mostly by designers and developers who need to target Webkit.

For most of this exercise, you must have a Webkit browser such as Safari or Google Chrome.

1   Open the 11_transitions.html document from the HTML5_11lessons folder. Preview this page in your browser. You should see a basic page with an image centered in the middle. You will begin the exercise by applying the transform property to the image to rotate it.

You will rotate the image on this page using the CSS3 transform *property.*

2   Return to your text editor; notice that the `<img>` element is contained within a `div` element with the class name "transform" .

```
<div class="transform">
<img src="images/learn_more.png">

</div>
```

3   Locate the `.transform` class in the internal stylesheet at the top of your page. Add three `transform` properties as follows:

```
.transform {
    margin-top:2em;
    -webkit-transform: rotate(45deg);
    -moz-transform: rotate(-45deg);
    transform: rotate(-45deg);
}
```

Notice that you have added the supported `transform` properties for Gecko browsers. The `transform` property has a higher level of support than the animation properties you will use in this exercise. If a browser does not support the `transform` property, the object is displayed in the non-transformed state.

Choose File > Save, and then preview in the browser. If your browser supports the transform property, you should see the image rotated 45 degrees.

To determine whether your browser supports the transform *property, and for a list of browsers that support it, visit* http://caniuse.com/#feat=transforms2d.

An image transformed by 45 degrees with the transform *property.*

The example above is a simple example of a 2D transform. Next, you will see an example of a CSS transition that uses a hyperlink.

4   Use your text editor to locate the div container that holds the hyperlink:

```
<div class="fade">
    <a href="#">Fade</a>
</div>
```

The class called fade is a style that adds a top margin to the container, thereby placing it below the image.

5   Add a new class to the hyperlink as follows:

```
<div class="fade">
    <a href="#" class="transition">Fade</a>
</div>
```

You now need to create a class for this hyperlink.

6 In your internal stylesheet, add the following two rules:

```
.fade {
   margin-top: 6em;
}

a.transition {
   padding: 5px 0px;
   background: #C9C;
}

a.transition:hover {
   background: #F6C;
}
```

The first rule, a.transition, adds padding and a background color of light pink to the hyperlink. The second rule, a.transition:hover, specifies the appearance of background color of a bright pink when the user places the mouse cursor over the link.

Save your file and preview in the browser. Place your mouse cursor over the link; the background color should change color from a muted pink to a bright pink. This behavior is possible because hyperlinks are pseudo-classes and have four properties: link, visited, hover, and active. For this example, you are defining a style for the hover pseudo-class. You will now add a CSS3 transition that will fade between the default background color and the hover style.

7 Add the following Webkit-only properties to your a.transition class:

```
a.transition {
   padding: 5px 0px;
   background: #C9C;
   -webkit-transition-property: background;
   -webkit-transition-duration: 1s;
}
```

The -webkit-transition-property defines the property to transition; for this example, you are choosing the background property. The -webkit-transition-duration defines the length of time for the transition; for this example, you have chosen one second (1s).

Save your file and preview the page in the browser. Place your mouse cursor over the hyperlink; it should fade to a bright pink. When you move your cursor away from the link, it should fade to the original color.

The transition is triggered when the user places the mouse cursor on and off the hyperlink.

8   Return to your text editor. Add a property to smooth out the animation further:

```
a.transition {
    padding: 5px 0px;
    background: #C9C;
    -webkit-transition-property: background;
    -webkit-transition-duration: 1s;
    -webkit-transition-timing-function: ease-out;
}
```

Easing is a technique commonly used in all animations that lets you define the speed of the transition. This property is different from the duration, which is still 1 second; the value `ease-out` starts your transition quickly and then slows it toward the end. The value `ease-in` starts the transition slowly and then speeds it. The value `linear` provides a constant rate of acceleration.

There are two other values you could potentially use here: `ease-in-out` *and* `cubic-bezier`. *For a more in-depth explanation and demonstration of easing, visit* http://www.the-art-of-web.com/css/timing-function/

Save your file and place your mouse cursor over the hyperlink. There is a difference in speed that you might not notice immediately; easing differences are more noticeable with longer durations.

9   You can write the transition properties in shorthand, as is the case with many CSS properties. Replace the three lines you have written with the following line:

```
a.transition {
    padding: 5px 0px;
    background: #C9C;
    -webkit-transition: background 1s ease-out;
}
```

You can also animate multiple properties; for example, you could change the color of the hyperlink text when the user clicks it, as explained in the following steps.

10   First, you must add a new class for the state of the hyperlink you want to target; for this example, the `active` pseudoclass (active is the appearance of the link when the user clicks it). Add the following rule:

```
a.transition:hover {
    background: #F6C;
}

a.transition:active {
    color: yellow;
}
```

Now you have to add this new `color` property to the original transition code.

11   In your `a.transition` class, add the following values, making sure to include the comma after the ease-out value to separate the two properties you are targeting:

```
a.transition {
    padding: 5px 40px;
    background: #C9C;
    -webkit-transition: background 1s ease-out, color 0.1s linear;
}
```

In this example, you are defining the property to be transitioned (color), the duration (0.1 seconds), and the easing to be used (linear). Save your file and preview in the browser.

A color transition for the hyperlink has been added.

When you place your mouse cursor over the hyperlink, it should fade as demonstrated before; when you click the hyperlink, it should briefly flash yellow (the transition has a very short duration).

You cannot target every CSS property as a transition, but you can target a large number of them. For example, you could create a transition for a gradient background image or the borders of a button. For a complete list of the CSS properties you can target with the transition property, visit *http://www.w3.org/TR/css3-transitions/#properties-from-css-*.

Working with CSS animation

The difference between CSS animation and CSS transitions is not immediately apparent because both properties create an illusion of motion. For example, the simple fading effect you created in the previous exercise responds to user interaction (it fades when you place your mouse cursor over it and fades again when you move your mouse cursor away), but you cannot specify the number of times it should fade. If you want the hyperlink button to flash three times when the user places the cursor over it, you would not use a transition, but the CSS animation property. You will achieve a similar effect in this exercise using the smoothie image.

1 Open the 11_animation.html document from your HTML5_11lessons folder. Preview this page in your browser. This is the same file you used in the last exercise, but with a different file name. You will now add the Webkit-specific animation properties.

We recommend using the latest version of Apple's Safari browser for this lesson although other Webkit browsers, such as Google Chrome, may also support these new features.

2   Locate the .spin class in your internal stylesheet and add the `-webkit-animation-name` and the `-webkit-animation-duration` properties as follows:

```
#spin {
    margin-top:2em;
    -webkit-animation-name: imageRotate;
    -webkit-animation-duration: 2s;
}
```

For this example, the `-webkit-animation-name` is the name of the animation you are specifying; the name is arbitrary, but you should use names that are logical. The property `-webkit-animation-duration` defines the length of the animation. These two properties are contained within this class; you now need to define the animation.

3   Add the following code below the `#spin` rule:

```
#spin {
    margin-top:2em;
    -webkit-animation-name: imageRotate;
    -webkit-animation-duration: 2s;
}

@-webkit-keyframes imageRotate {
    from {
    -webkit-transform:rotate(0deg);
    }
    to {
    -webkit-transform:rotate(360deg);
    }
}
```

The animation consists of a few lines of code: the code `@-webkit-keyframes` is a keyword followed by the name of the animation (`imageRotate`). Keyframes are a fundamental concept in virtually all animation, not just CSS. If you have used animation in other programs, such as Flash or After Effects, the concept should be familiar. Each keyframe has a value for a specific property. For this example, you are animating the `rotation` property; your first keyframe starts from a value of 0 degrees and goes to the second keyframe, which has a value of 360 degrees. The animation engine of the browser interpolates between these two keyframes, thus creating a smooth animation of 360 degrees.

Choose File > Save and preview in the browser.

Animating the rotation of an image using Webkit's animation properties

A Webkit-based browser should rotate the image once over a period of two seconds, and then stop. You can speed up and slow down the animation by adjusting the duration value; you will learn other properties first.

4   Add the following two declarations below the first two:

```
#spin {
    margin-top:2em;
    -webkit-animation-name: imageRotate;
    -webkit-animation-duration: .5s;
    -webkit-animation-iteration-count: 2;
    -webkit-animation-timing-function: ease-in-out;
}
```

The `-webkit-animation-iteration-count` property is one of the keys to understanding the difference between transitions and animation in CSS. In this example, you have instructed the animation to run twice, but you can specify any number of times or use the value infinite, which creates a never-ending loop. The `-webkit-animation-timing-function` lets you control the timing of the animation to create a smoother result.

Save your file and preview in the browser. The image should rotate twice and then stop. Additionally, you should notice the effect of the easing: when the image approaches the end of the rotation, it slows down.

You have finished this lesson. You learned about the different features of CSS3, including vendor-specific prefixes, CSS3 border-radius properties, CSS3 multiple backgrounds, CSS3 gradients and box-shadows, RGBA color values, and how to create animated effects with Webkit transforms, transitions, and animation.

Working with web fonts

As noted in Lesson 3, *Formatting Text with CSS*, currently there are a few cross-platform compatible fonts that designers can use with the certainty that users have them installed on their system. Over the years, several alternatives have appeared to let designers add specific fonts to their pages; for example, techniques such as sIFR and Cufón rely on methods that work well in certain situations. These techniques only represent a temporary solution.

CSS3 uses a technique called `@font-face` supported by designers and by the companies that make and license fonts. `@font-face` lets you embed fonts within a page by declaring the font you want and placing this font on your web server. When a user visits your site, the browser renders the page using this font where specified. This technique is an excellent solution to the problem of uninstalled fonts, but there are complications that require some work. The following sections explain the complications and their solutions.

Using `@font-face` to specify a web font

The initial CSS syntax for `@font-face` is straightforward. In this exercise, you will embed an OpenType font called Sigmar that is licensed for free commercial use. The exercise is followed by an explanation of the complexities involved with font licensing.

1   In your text editor, choose File > Open, navigate to your HTML5_11lessons folder, select the webfontbase.css file, and then click Open.

2   Choose File > Open again, navigate to your HTML05_11lessons folder, select the 11_webfonts.html page, and then click Open. Keep the documents from this and the previous step open.

3   Preview the page in your browser to see its default appearance. For this exercise, you will
style the heading 2 elements, *Top Rated Smoothies* and *Our Mission Statement*.

You will style the two heading 2 elements on this page.

These headings currently inherit the `font-family` property declared as follows in the
body rule within the base.css external stylesheet:

`font-family: "Trebuchet MS", Tahoma, Arial, sans-serif;`

Additionally, the H2 rule has other style properties set: `font-weight`, `text-transform`,
and `letter-spacing`. Lesson 3, "Formatting Text with CSS," explains how to create
these styles.

4   Return to your text editor; scroll to the bottom of the webfont_base.css stylesheet and
add the following code:

```
@font-face {
    font-family: Sigmar;
    src: url('SigmarOne.otf');
}
```

The `font-family` property creates a reference you can use in your CSS when you
want Sigmar. The src property declares the location of the font; in this case, within your
HTML5_11lessons folder on the same level as your HTML document.

Now, you need to specify where to use Sigmar. For this exercise, you will use it for the
heading 2 element.

5   Scroll your stylesheet to locate the style rules for H2, and then add the new font-family as follows:

```
h2 {
    font-size:1.125em;
    letter-spacing:0.2em;
    font-weight:lighter;
    text-transform:uppercase;
    font-family: Sigmar, Georgia, Palatino, Times New Roman, serif;
}
```

Sigmar is first in the list, but you need to provide alternative fonts in case the user's browser cannot render Sigmar. For this exercise, Georgia is the first alternative.

6   Save your HTML and CSS files, and then preview your page in the browser. If your browser supports @font-face and can render OpenType fonts, your two headings should use the Sigmar font, as shown by the following figure.

The two headings styled with the Sigmar web font.

If you are using a recent version of Mozilla or Webkit-based browsers, such as Firefox, Safari, or Chrome, your headings should appear as illustrated in the figure above. Most versions of Internet Explorer will display the heading as Georgia, as shown by the following figure.

The two headings rendered in Georgia for browsers that don't support OpenType font rendering (.otf).

All versions of Internet Explorer starting from IE 5.0 support @font-face, but only versions 5.0-8.0 support the Embedded OpenType font type (EOT). Internet Explorer 9.0 supports OpenType with a few qualifications. Mobile devices, such as iPod and iPad, do not support OpenType at all, but a format named SVG. If you want to display the Sigma font on as many browsers as possible, you need another method to display the font.

Browser font support

The following table lists the various levels of support for the different font-types:

BROWSER	OTF & TTF	SVG	WOFF	EOT
IE	IE9	—	IE9	IE5+
Firefox	FF3.5	FF3.5	FF3.6	—
Chrome	Chrome 4	Chrome 0.3	Chrome 5	—
Safari	3.1	3.1	—	—
Opera	Opera 10.00	Opera 9	—	—
iOS	—	iOS 1	—	—
Android	2.2	—	—	—

OpenType (OTF): a widespread font format heavily supported by the industry and developed as collaboration between Adobe and Microsoft; one of its primary advantages is cross-platform support. Other typesetting features, such as glyph support, make OpenType fonts the primary font choice for professional font designers.

TrueType (TTF): originally developed by Apple computer and later adopted by Microsoft, TrueType fonts are widely used because they are cross-platform compatible and offer sophisticated typesetting controls, such as hinting, a technique that improves the quality of the font in low resolution screens.

SVG: a vector-based format currently supported only by Apple's iOS for iPod and iPod devices. SVG fonts are text documents that define the font outlines as vector objects within the Scalable Vector Graphic language (SVG).

Web Open Font Format (WOFF): the latest addition to web fonts that can potentially become a standard since it is in the final stages of approval by the World Wide Web Consortium (W3C). WOFF includes the ability to heavily compress font files and optimize them for distribution over an Internet connection.

Embedded OpenType (EOT): a variation on OpenType created by Microsoft and largely supported by Internet Explorer. EOT has several copy protection features built in to prevent copying of fonts.

Using a web service to generate multiple fonts

The `@font-face` technique used in the last exercise requires you to declare multiple font alternatives for maximum compatibility; for example, you need to declare OpenType fonts, Embedded Open Type for Internet Explorer, and SVG for the iOS. There are web services you can use for this purpose, such as Font Squirrel. This site offers the following options:

- All the fonts on Font Squirrel are Commercial Free and can be used with the `@font-face` property.

- Font Squirrel provides several kits that include different font types you can add to your site, as well as generated CSS you can copy and paste into your own CSS.

- If necessary, you can generate your own kits using the site's `@font-face` generator.

The following exercise illustrates how to generate a font kit for the Sigmar font.

The files are included in the lesson folder. If you do not have access to the Internet, you can jump to step 6.

1   Using your web browser, navigate to *www.fontsquirrel.com*. In the navigation bar, click the link for `@font-face` kits. This section lists the available kits on the site. A standard kit includes multiple versions of a font, such as TrueType, EOT, WOFF, SVG, and Cufón. (Cufón is not explained in this lesson.)

The Sigmar font is NOT included in the current kits, so you need to generate the fonts manually.

2   Click the `@font-face` Generator link to open this page. Click the Add Fonts button. A file browser window appears. Navigate to your HTML5_11lessons folder and locate the SigmarOne.otf file. Select it and click Open.

3   Select the Agreement check box to indicate that the font you are uploading is legally eligible for web embedding. The Download Your Kit button is made available.

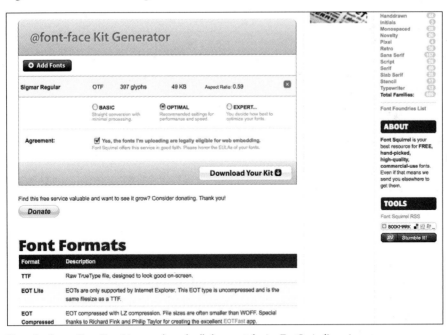

SigmarOne has an Open Font License and may legally be converted using FontSquirrel's service.

You can obtain the Sigmar font used for this exercise on the Font Squirrel site. The font has an Open Font License that lets you use it, study it, modify it, and freely redistribute it; but not sell it on its own.

4   Normally, you would click the Download Your Kit button to download the file, but the Sigmar font has already been added to your HTML5_11lessons folder; do NOT download this file to prevent increasing the Font Squirrel bandwidth.

5   Close your browser and return to your text editor. Choose File > Open, navigate to the fonts folder located in your HTML5_11lessons folder, select the stylesheet.css file from the Fonts folder, and then click Open.

This file is the CSS created by Font Squirrel for the Sigmar styles. Select the entire `@font-face` rule, choose Edit > Copy, switch to your webfont_base.css file, and locate the original `@font-face` code you added in the last exercise. Delete this code and replace it with the new code generated from Font Squirrel:

```
@font-face {
    font-family: 'SigmarRegular';
    src: url('fonts/sigmarone-webfont.eot');
    src: url('fonts/sigmarone-webfont.eot?#iefix') format('embedded-
opentype'),
    url('fonts/sigmarone-webfont.woff') format('woff'),
    url('fonts/sigmarone-webfont.ttf') format('truetype'),
    url('fonts/sigmarone-webfont.svg#SigmarRegular') format('svg');
    font-weight: normal;
    font-style: normal;
}
```

The web fonts generated by Font Squirrel have already been placed in the fonts folder. You can repeat these steps with a different font; if you do, move the web fonts from your download folder to your site folder.

The font-family property generated by Font Squirrel for Sigmar is different than the one you added in the last exercise, so you need to modify it.

6   In your webfont_base.css file, scroll to locate the H2 rule, and then change the value for Sigmar as follows:

```
font-family: 'SigmarRegular', Georgia, Palatino, Times New Roman,
serif;
```

This step provides a font-family value compatible with all the different web fonts.

7   Save your HTML and CSS files and preview in the browser. If your browser rendered Sigmar in the last exercise, you should not notice a change. If you are using any version of Internet Explorer from 5.0 and above, you should see Sigmar rendered on the page.

8   Return to your text-editor.

The basics of using custom fonts with `@font-face` are well supported; ome font-styling properties in CSS have different support based on the browser. For example, your headings are still using `letter-spacing`, `font-weight`, and `text-transform`. These properties are not always reliable with `@font-face` and are not always needed, so you must evaluate these properties' usability on a case-by-case basis. To illustrate with an example, you will modify the values of these properties.

9   In the rule for H2, change the `letter-spacing` value from 0.2em to 0em as follows:

```
h2 {
    font-size:1.125em;
    letter-spacing:0em;
    font-weight:lighter;
    text-transform:uppercase;
    font-family: 'SigmarRegular', Georgia, Palatino, Times New Roman, serif;
}
```

10   Save your files and preview in the browser. With `letter-spacing` set to 0, which is equivalent to removing the property, the width of the headings contract slightly. In the case of the first heading, *Top Rated Smoothies*, this has the added benefit of bringing the heading onto a single line.

With `letter-spacing` set to 0, the headings are reduced in width.

Changing the `font-weight` and `text-transform` values also alters the appearance of the headings. We strongly recommend that you test your pages on different browsers and platforms and make small changes as needed.

Alternative methods for adding web fonts

Font Squirrel is not the only option available for web fonts; there are several more. This website allows you the option of generating font-kits, but there are legal restrictions you should consider. Font foundries regard the licenses for web fonts separately from the license to use them on your desktop in programs such as Photoshop. The font Sigmar used in these exercises is licensed under the Open Font License, so there are no restrictions for converting it. Most well-known fonts do have restrictions and you might be prevented by copy-protection laws.

There are other ways in which you can use other fonts legally on your pages, such as the two examples listed below.

Typekit (*http://www.typekit.com*)

The Typekit web service has several licensed web fonts available for use from well-known type manufacturers, such as Adobe, Bitstream, Chank, FontFont, and others. Typekit has a monthly fee for the use of these fonts, but it also offers a free service that requires a badge on pages that use it. Typekit has a slightly different technical model than the one explained in the previous exercises: all fonts are hosted on Typekit servers, so you need to add references to these fonts in your stylesheets.

Google Font API (*http://code.google.com/apis/webfonts/*)

Google has a similar system to Typekit called the Google Font API. Like Typekit, all the fonts are hosted on the Google servers. Add references to these in your stylesheet, and then use them as needed. Unlike Typekit, these fonts are currently free to use and there are several options in different styles.

Self study

1   Set different border-radius numbers for the vertical and horizontal properties, such as `border-radius: 96px / 24px`.

2   Reverse the values and add larger values to see different effects.

3   Create a transition that uses the gradient property following the instructions in the CSS gradients and CSS transitions exercises.

Review

Questions

1   When using the CSS3 `border-image` property, how many segments are created automatically when applying a graphic to a border?

2   Is a color stop used for a CSS3 border, a CSS3 background image, or a CSS3 gradient? What is the role of a color stop?

3   What is a keyframe and where is it used in CSS3?

Answers

1   Graphics are automatically segmented into 9 parts; each segment can be applied to corresponding regions of a CSS container.

2   A color stop is used for a CSS3 gradient. A color stop is used to define a specific color value within a gradient. Two or more color stops with different color values create the smooth gradation of color associated with a gradient.

3   A keyframe is used in CSS3 animation and defines a specific value of a property, such as the degree of rotation. You can animate an element by setting at least two keyframes with different values.

What you'll learn in this lesson:

- How to use CSS3 Media Queries
- Using the CSS3 Grid property
- Understanding CSS3 Multi-columns and Flexboxes

CSS3 Media Queries and the Future of CSS3

In this lesson, you will learn to use CSS3 Media Queries to deliver a variety of page layouts depending on the device or screen width used. Additionally, you'll gain an understanding of evolving CSS3 techniques that may change the way web pages are designed.

Starting up

You will work with several files from the HTML5_12lessons folder in this lesson. Make sure you have loaded the HTML5lessons folder onto your hard drive from the supplied DVD. See "Loading lesson files" in the Starting Up section of this book.

See Lesson 12 in action!

Use the accompanying video to gain a better understanding of how to use some of the capabilities shown in this lesson. The video tutorial for this lesson can be found on the included DVD.

The role of CSS3 media queries

All web browsers, whether on desktops or mobile devices, communicate with the servers that host the websites you visit and identify themselves with a *user agent String*. In most cases, this information is never used by the website, but you can add user agent detectors to your web pages. Typically, these detectors are JavaScript code that identify the user agent, for example, Internet Explorer 9, and then change the default behavior of the page based on this information. This lesson does not focus on JavaScript detectors, but on a more recent form of detectors, called *CSS3 media queries*.

A CSS3 media query examines the capability of the user agent visiting the site and lets you send it styles based on certain values. Media queries can also detect the capabilities of a user's screen and serve styles suited for that screen, which makes media queries useful for different monitor resolutions on the desktop and for mobile devices. Examples of user agent capabilities include the ability to detect the width and height of the browser window, the device width and height, the device orientation (landscape or portrait), and the resolution.

Here is a more concrete example: suppose a user has a Smartphone with a screen resolution of 320 pixels wide by 480 high, and the phone is in portrait mode (vertical). This user visits a website with media queries in the stylesheet. When the user enters the site address into the web browser or clicks a link, the site's media queries detect the device capabilities of the phone. If the site's stylesheet includes specific styles for devices with this screen resolution, those are used to deliver a custom layout for the phone. Such a custom layout could be a single-column layout instead of the three-column layout used for larger desktop screens. The stylesheet designer could have also decided to include a layout for a phone screen in landscape mode; for example, add a second column. This way, when the user rotates the phone into landscape mode, a second column appears on the expanded horizontal space (480 pixels).

Using CSS3 media queries to deliver a mobile-optimized layout

In this exercise, you will add a media query to deliver a single-column layout to screens with a width less than 480 pixels. This is a mobile-optimized layout, but it should work with any browser window that has a width less than 480 pixels. The technique used in this exercise converts an existing two-column layout to a single-column layout by removing the floated elements.

By the end of this exercise, you will have a good foundation for a mobile-optimized web page, but you can expand it into a more robust and sophisticated mobile layout. The details for creating different layouts using media queries goes beyond the scope of this book, but useful resources are mentioned at the end of the exercise.

1 In your text editor, choose File > Open and navigate to the HTML5_12lessons folder. Locate the 12_home.html file and click Open. Preview this page in the browser.

The two-column design you will optimize for mobile devices.

Close your browser and return to your text editor. You will now add a media query to your base.css stylesheet.

2 In your text editor, choose File > Open and open the base.css stylesheet. Scroll to the bottom and add the following code:

```
@media only screen and (max-width: 480px) {

}
```

A media query is a new category added to the CSS3 specification. Many browsers still use the CSS2.0 or 2.1 specification, so they will not recognize this code. In the case of mobile devices, you are targeting browsers such as the Safari web browser on the iPhone that do support CSS3 media queries; consequently, you can use the code.

The keyword `only` that appears in this first line of code has a specific meaning related to the selected media type: screen. In this case, the keyword `only` hides this stylesheet from older user agents. The actual media query in this line of code is [max-width:480px]. You can interpret the `max-width` query as "less than or equal to." In other words, you are creating a media query that will deliver styles for screens that are 480 pixels wide or less.

3 Now you will add a new rule that will set a style for the width of the wrapper. Add the following code. Take careful note of the fact that you are placing this code *within* the brackets of the @media code, this is how media queries work. The rules for the body and the #wrap ID are nested inside the @media section.

```
@media only screen and (max-width: 480px) {
    body {
        padding: 5px;
        background-color:#FFF;
        background-image:url(images/smoothieworld_logo_mobile.jpg);
        background-repeat:no-repeat;
    }
#wrap {
        width: auto;
        margin-top:80px;
    }
}
```

This code accomplishes the following:

- Five pixels of padding are applied to all sides of the body to add space for any element you place within your page.

- The background image is a new image optimized for the mobile format.

- The rule for the wrap ID style redefines the main container of the page to an automatic width instead of the 960 pixels used for the current stylesheet.

- The top margin property adds 80 pixels of space between the wrap div and the top of the page to make your site logo visible.

4   Choose File > Save. Use a browser that supports CSS3 media queries to preview the page. Reduce the width of your browser; when the window becomes narrow enough, the small background image and the other changes you added in this step appear.

Your page layout changes when the width of the browser window is 480 pixels or less.

5   Return to your text editor.

If you wanted to, you could create a layout that only displays when the screen was between 480 pixels and some other number (say 800 pixels). To do that, you would have to use the `min-width` media query. This media query can be interpreted as "greater than or equal to."

Although you will not be doing this right now, the code would look like this: `(@media only screen and (min-width: 800px)`. Here, the styles you add would only be used if the screen were larger than 800 pixels. By using a combination of `min-width` and `max-width` media queries, a designer could create a number of different layouts depending on the width of the user's screen.

This technique is gaining traction within the world of web design and web development and goes by the name "responsive design." Although it is a concept well worth exploring, we do not cover it here and instead you will focus on a much more specific media query for a smartphone device, such as the iPhone.

The emerging discipline of responsive or adaptive design

The technique of adding multiple media queries that deliver different styles based on the user's screen capabilities is a recent advancement in the field of web design known as responsive or adaptive design. Here are a few resources to help you explore this new discipline in web design:

Responsive Design

An article by Ethan Marcotte that explores techniques to build sites based on proportion and better suited for desktop and mobile sites you create from the start.
http://www.alistapart.com/articles/responsive-web-design/

The Less Framework

This website provides HTML and CSS files under the MIT license (free to use and modify under certain conditions) that provide a series of CSS layouts targeted for different screen resolutions, including mobile.
http://lessframework.com/

6 Locate your media query and make the following change:

```
@media only screen and (max-device-width: 480px) {
```

Choose File > Save All, and then preview your page in the browser. Reduce the width of your browser window and it will no longer change. This is because the `max-device-width` media query is more specific than the `max-width` query: your style rules now apply only to devices with a screen width of 480 pixels or less.

At this point, the only way to preview your changes would be to use an emulator or place these pages on the Web and test from your phone. Neither of these options will be convenient for you, so for now, you will remove the `device` requirement and then add it back in at the very end of the lesson.

Testing your designs on mobile devices

The best way to test your web pages is to use the mobile device for which you are designing. There are software programs called emulators that let you test your designs in software versions of the phone. The most reliable source for emulators is the device manufacturer. For example, Apple provides an iPhone emulator as part of its iPhone development tools; Android and Windows Phone 7 also have emulators included with their development tools. You can use these emulators to obtain an accurate preview of your designs without placing your sample files online. Emulators are not often cross-platform compatible. For example, and as of the time of this writing, the iPhone emulator is only available on a Mac. Additionally, these emulators are installed with the assumption they will be used for application design, not web page design; as such, the installation process can seem overwhelming and unnecessary.

There are also online web services that claim to emulate your designs in the mobile format. These services are not always reliable and often require a hyperlink to your page online, rather than running locally on your desktop. In this case, we highly recommend using the phone itself.

7   In your text editor, locate the first line of your media query and delete the `device` code so your code is the same as it was in step 2:

```
@media only screen and (max-width: 480px) {
```

Again, this is just a temporary measure to help you preview the changes in your web browser.

Although you are previewing these changes in the browser, we will be using screenshots from the iPhone to help you get a sense of how your page would look on this device.

Your page layout as displayed in portrait mode on the iPhone.

You currently have two logos displaying on your page; the second one, in the masthead, is redundant and you will soon remove it. A common strategy to optimize a layout for mobile is to create a single column for your content. This is commonly done by adding code within the media query that removes floated elements and sets pixel widths from fixed values to auto values. In addition, you can also remove elements that do not work within the mobile layout. In this case, you will remove the masthead that contains the large SmoothieWorld logo.

8   Add the following code after the `#wrap` rule within your media query:

```
#masthead {
    display:none;
}
```

The `display:none` property prevents the masthead element from appearing. This property is useful because it "turns off" elements from the original stylesheet. Now you'll configure your navigation.

9   Add the following two style rules after the `#masthead` rule within your media query section. Both of these rules target the main navigation bar.

```
#mainnav {
    height: auto;
}

    #mainnav li {
        float: none;
        width: auto;
        text-align: left;
        border-top: 1px grey solid;
        border-bottom: 1px grey solid;
    }
```

Setting the `height` value for the mainnav to `auto` ensures that this container will expand and display the navigation items inside. Choose File > Save, and then preview your page in the browser. (Again, remember that our screenshot is for the iPhone and you will need to reduce the width of your browser window to see a similar effect.)

Your navigation reaches the edge of it's containing element after removing the float *and setting the* width *to* auto.

Setting the float property to none and the width to auto turns your navigation into a vertical list. The text-align left property places the navigation on the left side of the menu. The auto width value will work after you convert the rest of your page to a single column. You will continue to do that in the following steps.

Mobile navigation tips

This is a list of guidelines we recommend to make navigation easy on websites for mobile devices, especially touchscreen mobile devices.

- Navigation should be at, or near, the top of the screen to be easily accessible. Repeat navigation at the bottom of all your pages so the user does not have to scroll up after reading a page.

- For touchscreen devices, use a large target size for navigation links to prevent accidental clicking.

- Touchscreen devices do not always have a hover capability as triggered by the mouse cursor on desktops. Plan your styles accordingly and avoid rollover styles.

- Avoid image-based navigation; use list-based navigation styled with CSS.

10 You will now add more styles in your media query for the sidebar and the main content. First, locate the rule for the masthead ID, and then add the following selector:

```
#masthead, #sidebar {
    display:none;
}
```

This code also removes the sidebar from the page. By removing the sidebar, you remove the floated column on the left and can begin to reorganize your layout. Using floats for columns in a desktop layout is very useful, but not in mobile layouts. You will now remove the floated properties of your maincontent div.

When designing sites for mobile devices, keep in mind that simpler is often better, and what works for the desktop might not work for the mobile site.

11 To style the maincontent div, add the following code within your media query below your #mainnav li rule:

```
#maincontent {
    float: none;
    width: auto;
    background-color:white;
}
```

Again, by setting the float property to none and the width to auto, you are getting closer to a single column layout.

Choose File > Save, and then preview your page in the browser.

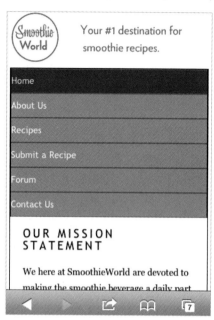

Your maincontent section fills a single column after removing the float *and setting the* width *to* auto.

Your content flows into a single column; if you scroll down, you will notice your footer is still floated. In the next step, you will style the footer.

12 Add the following rule set within your media query below your #maincontent rule:

```
#footer, #footer p {
    clear: none;
    width: auto;
    height: auto;
    background-image: none;
    padding-top: 20px;
    margin-top: 0px;
}
```

This code sets the styles for the footer and the paragraph inside the footer:

- The `clear:none` rule overrides the `clear:both` rule from the main stylesheet.
- The `width` and `height` are set to `auto`.
- The `background-image` is set to `none` to simplify the page design.
- Additional padding is given and the top margin is set to zero.

Choose File > Save, and then preview your page in the browser. Scroll to the bottom to see the footer change.

13 In order to make this page design work for the iPhone, you need to add the `max-device-width` media query, as seen earlier. Locate the first line of your media query and make the following change:

```
@media only screen and (max-device-width: 480px) {
```

Choose File > Save. If you have access to a server, upload your HTML and CSS files to a server and point your phone's browser to the address. Test your page in portrait and landscape mode by rotating the phone. You now have the foundation of a layout optimized for the iPhone!

This exercise gives you a preview of what media queries can do, however, it's just a small taste of what they are capable of delivering. In the future, media queries will become increasingly more important and widespread, especially as the range of different screen sizes and devices continues to expand.

Diving deeper into CSS3 media queries

This lesson only gives a preview of CSS3 media queries to target and style mobile devices. Here are some resources of tools and options you can use to create unique websites optimized for mobile devices.

Mozilla Developer Network

Mozilla offers extensive documentation and code examples for media queries on their developer network website. This site provides a good reference for media queries targeted for desktops.

https://developer.mozilla.org/En/CSS/Media_queries

Safari Reference Library

Apple provides free and useful documentation to optimize your site for WebKit-based browsers, which are primarily used for the iPhone, but can be used for other Smartphone browsers. The organization of the website might have changed since this lesson was written; we recommend you perform a search for Optimizing Web Content when you access the link. This documentation explores the various ways to use media queries.

http://developer.apple.com/library/safari/navigation/

Upcoming developments in CSS3

HTML5 and CSS3 include new developments and features that can let you create interesting designs and functionality for your websites and web applications. Some new features are still not fully implemented, and some are available only for certain browsers.

The following sections describe some of the new CSS3 features.

The CSS3 multi-column layout

Current implementations of CSS lack solid and reliable options for page layout. To create columns on a page using CSS, designers and developers have had to rely on a system of float and clear properties. CSS3 introduces multi-column layout, which lets you separate a column and change its appearance in notable ways. Some of the properties relating to multi-column layout are column-count, column-width, column-gap, and column-rule. Webkit and Gecko-based browsers provide support for these properties; the lack of support in Internet Explorer versions 7, 8, and 9 limit the use of these properties.

Microsoft has planned to adopt these properties for Internet Explorer 10, which should increase the use of multi-column layouts in the future.

For a chart displaying past, current, and future support for the multi-column, layout visit http://caniuse.com/#feat=multicolumn.

The following exercise demonstrates the use of multi-column layouts.

1 In your text editor, choose File > Open and navigate to the HTML_12lessons folder. Locate the 12_css3multicolumn.html file and click OK. In the style section of the page, locate the rule for #introduction-content; this rule currently sets the width of the column that contains all the content to 600 pixels wide.

```
#introduction-content {
    width: 600px;
}
```

Preview the page in your browser to see the current state of the page.

OUR MISSION STATEMENT

We here at SmoothieWorld are devoted to making the smoothie beverage a daily part of your life. Whether it be for breakfast, lunch or even dinner, smoothies are great way to get the nutrition you need and have fun while doing it.

The recipes on our site have all been tested in our lab of smoothie experts. Other smoothie sites might have more recipes or feature more exotic fruits than you'll find here, but we feel that quality beats out quantity and novelty any day. We also believe the best recipes come from you the reader, that's why we encourage you to join our smoothie community.

Learn more

A REVIEW OF THE BLEND-O-MATIC 3000

By Cheri White, posted December 21, 2012

THE LATEST ENTRY IN THE BLENDER WARS LIVES UP TO ITS HYPE

All blenders are created equal right? Start with a base unit and a motor, blades to spin and chop, and a jar for your ingredients. Well not so fast. The Blend-O-Matic 3000 gives you features that you never knew you wanted and in the increasingly competitive world of smoothie blenders the competition just recieved a new shot across their bow.

To be victorious in the Blender wars, a Blender must do two things extremely well: Turn chunks of fruit into pulp and crush ice. In our tests the Blend-O-Matic not only did this better than all the other competitors in its price range, but it did so 25% faster. The secret to this competition-craushingh prowess is in the mind-boggling 1400 Watt engine. That's two horsepower for those of you keeping track at home.

The default, single-column style of your page.

You'll now separate this column into three by adding the CSS3 `column-count` property for Gecko and Webkit browsers and the official syntax with no vendor prefix.

2   Add the following two properties to the ID rule:

```
#introduction-content {
    width: 600px;
    -moz-column-count: 3;
    -webkit-column-count: 3;
    column-count: 3;
}
```

Save your file and preview it in your browser. If your browser supports the multi-column layout, you should see the content separated into three equal columns.

OUR MISSION STATEMENT

We here at SmoothieWorld are devoted to making the smoothie beverage a daily part of your life. Whether it be for breakfast, lunch or even dinner, smoothies are great way to get the nutrition you need and have fun while doing it.

The recipes on our site have all been tested in our lab of smoothie experts. Other smoothie sites might have more recipes or feature more exotic fruits than you'll find here, but we feel that quality beats out quantity and novelty any day. We also believe that you never knew you wanted and in the increasingly competitive world of smoothie blenders the competition just recieved a new shot across their bow.

To be victorious in the Blender wars, a Blender must do two things extremely well: Turn chunks of fruit into pulp and crush ice. In our tests the Blend-O-Matic not only did this better than all the other competitors in its price range, but it did so 25% faster. The secret to this competition-craushingh prowess is in the mind-boggling 1400 settings. Instead of blending at one consistent speed, you have a number of customized blending options: the "frozen drink" setting, for example, will automatically reverse the direction of the blades for the first 30 seconds of the program, thereby mixing ice and liquids together. Then, the speed phase of the program kicks in and crushes everything to a consistent degree. End result: no more stray fruit and ice chunks!

There is one major flaw with this blender. Never, ever start the blender without the

Separating your column into three columns with the `column-count` *property*

You can modify the space between the three columns using the `column-gap` property. Notice that there is a default gap in your layout when no `column-gap` is defined. You can also use the `column-width` property to create columns instead of the `column-count` property.

3 Replace the `column-count` properties you added in the last step with the following code for `column-width`:

```
#introduction-content {
    width: 600px;
    -moz-column-width: 150px;
    -webkit-column-width: 150px;
    column-width: 150px;
}
```

Save your file and preview it in your browser. You will see three columns of 150 pixel width each. These columns are still constrained within a width of 600 pixels, so there is no change in appearance. You will now remove the overall pixel width style. Notice the change in effect.

4　Return to your text editor and remove the entire `width` property and value.

Save your file and preview the page in your browser. Notice the multiple columns across the page that repeat until the content runs out. Reduce and expand the width of your browser window to see how the content responds.

OUR MISSION STATEMENT

We here at SmoothieWorld are devoted to making the smoothie beverage a daily part of your life. Whether it be for breakfast, lunch or even dinner, smoothies are great way to get the nutrition you need and have fun while doing it.

The recipes on our site have all been tested in our lab of smoothie experts. Other smoothie sites might have more recipes or feature more exotic fruits than you'll find

join our smoothie community. Learn more

A REVIEW OF THE BLEND-O-MATIC 3000

By Cheri White, posted December 21, 2012

THE LATEST ENTRY IN THE BLENDER WARS LIVES UP TO ITS HYPE

All blenders are created equal right? Start with a base unit and a motor, blades to spin and chop, and a jar for your ingredients. Well not so fast. The Blend-O-Matic 3000 gives you features that you

To be victorious in the Blender wars, a Blender must do two things extremely well: Turn chunks of fruit into pulp and crush ice. In our tests the Blend-O-Matic not only did this better than all the other competitors in its price range, but it did so 25% faster. The secret to this competition-craushingh prowess is in the mind-boggling 1400 Watt engine. That's two horsepower for those of you keeping track at home.

But a fast motor does you no good without

easy to clean.

The Blend-O-Matic 3000 also comes with a number of bells and whistles that make smoothie recipes a breeze. The ice crusher and pulse function are exceptional and I especially loved the pre-programmed settings. Instead of blending at one consistent speed, you have a number of customized blending options: the "frozen drink" setting, for example, will automatically reverse the direction of the blades for the first 30 seconds of the

stray fruit and ice chunks!

There is one major flaw with this blender. Never, ever start the blender without the cover on! In our tests we started the blender without the cover and the speed of the motor sent a shard of ice rocketing into our ceiling. We hate to think what would have happened if we had been standing over it. I suppose here has to be a price to pay for a two horsepower engine. This small flaw not considering, you will likely be using this blender so much that it will find a

Without a defined width for the container, the `column-width` *property generates as many columns as needed.*

There are other properties related to the multi-column layout module that are currently under development and have limited support in current browsers, such as the `column-rule` and `column-span` properties. The `column-rule` property lets you specify a vertical rule between columns and functions much as a border with possible values for `color`, `style`, and `width`.

The `column-span` property lets you force an element to span across columns. Typical uses include creating a header that spans across one or more columns.

To learn more about the specification for the CSS3 multi-column layout module, visit the W3 site for up-to-date information at http://www.w3.org/TR/css3-multicol/.

The CSS3 Flexible Box layout module

Flexible Box, or flexbox, is another new layout feature in CSS3, and it represents a new model for layout in addition to the four models currently supported in CSS 2.1 (block layout, inline layout, table layout, and positioned layout). The flexbox model was added to CSS3 to help designers and developers create more sophisticated and responsive web applications and web pages. It also addresses a fundamental flaw in the current model that relies on floating and clearing elements, a technique that was never intended for true page layout. As the name implies, the flexbox is designed to provide flexible layout containers that shift and respond to other elements on a page or to content within the flexbox.

The following exercise illustrates the use of this new feature.

1. In your text editor, choose File > Open, navigate to the HTML5_12lessons folder, and open the file 12_flexbox.html. This is a simple HTML file that contains a div container with three paragraphs. The style for this div container defines rules for the `width`, `height`, and `border`. There is also a second rule set that defines a background color of gray for the paragraphs. Preview the page in your browser to see the style as it currently appears.

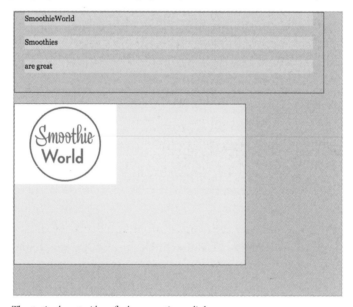

The starting layout with no flexbox properties applied.

2   Return to your text editor, and in the `introduction-content` ID styles, add the
    following rules:

```
#introduction-content {
    width: 600px;
    height: 150px;
    border: 1px solid #821738;
    display: -webkit-box;
    -webkit-box-orient: horizontal;
    display: -moz-box;
    -moz-box-orient: horizontal;
}
```

You need to add one set of rules for Webkit browsers and another set for Gecko-based
browsers. Past and current browsers provide good support for flexible box properties,
except for Internet Explorer 7, 8, and 9.

3   Choose File > Save and then preview the page in your browser. The three paragraphs
    are now aligned horizontally within the parent container. Notice the width of the
    paragraphs is only as long as the content.

The `display:box` property and value instructs the div to use the flexbox model. The
property `box-orient` has a value of `horizontal` to align the three child paragraphs.
There is also a `vertical` value that you can use.

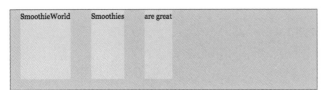

Your three paragraphs are aligned horizontally with the addition of the `display:box`
and `box-orient:horizontal` *rules.*

4   Return to your text editor. Using the flexbox module, you can also target any of the
    children elements. For example, you can add a rule to stretch the third paragraph until it
    fills the container. To illustrate, add this rule after the rule set for the paragraphs:

```
#introduction-content p {
    background-color:#CCC;
}

#introduction-content > p:nth-child(3) {
    -moz-box-flex: 1;
    -webkit-box-flex: 1;
}
```

This rule targets the third child paragraph within the div and uses the `box-flex` property with a value set to 1. The `box-flex` property represents a flexibility ratio for child elements. Since no `box-flex` property value has been specifically set for the first two child paragraphs, they are considered inflexible (the `box-flex` value is 0 by default). Given that the third paragraph has a `box-flex` value of 1 and the other paragraphs are inflexible, the third paragraph expands as far as it can.

You can make the second paragraph twice as wide as the third paragraph by adding a rule defining the `box-flex` value of the second paragraph to 2.

5   Add the following rules for the second paragraph:

```
#introduction-content > p:nth-child(3) {
    -moz-box-flex: 1;
    -webkit-box-flex: 1;
}

#introduction-content > p:nth-child(2) {
    -moz-box-flex: 2;
    -webkit-box-flex: 2;
}
```

The `box-flex` ratio of the second paragraph to the first is two to one, making the second paragraph twice as wide as the third.

Save your file and preview your page in the browser.

By adding rules targeting specific paragraphs, you can make the second paragraph twice as wide as the third.

One advantage to this method is that you can change the overall width of the parent element and the flexible ratios will allow the children elements to adapt. When you do not define a box value for a child element, the default is 0, the element is inflexible, and the width is defined by the amount of content.

For this exercise, the second and third child elements have flexboxes with widths defined by ratios, but the first child element has a width defined by the text *Smoothieworld*.

6   Return to your text editor; within the HTML, locate the div element on your page that has the class name `centered` (second div element). This box currently has an image within it placed at the default position of top left. Using the flexbox properties `box-orient`, `box-pack`, and `box-align`, you will automatically align this image vertically and horizontally inside the box, a task difficult to accomplish if you were not using CSS3 syntax..

You can horizontally align an object in the center of a box by setting the left and right margins to `auto` *in CSS 2.0 and 2.1. You cannot easily vertically align an object in the center of a box.*

7   Add the following properties and values to the `.centered` class:

```
.centered {
    width: 450px;
    height: 300px;
    border: 1px solid #555;
    background : #CFC;
    display: -moz-box;
    -moz-box-orient: horizontal;
    -moz-box-pack: center;
    -moz-box-align: center;
    display: -webkit-box;
    -webkit-box-orient: horizontal;
    -webkit-box-pack: center;
    -webkit-box-align: center;
}
```

The `box-orient` property is used here as it was in the first exercise: to align an element horizontally; in this case, the image. For this exercise, you have also added a `box-pack` property set to `center`: this sets the alignment based on the `box-orient` value. You need the `box-align` property to align the image vertically; the value is also set to `center`.

8   Choose File > Save and then preview the page in your browser. You will now have an image centered horizontally and vertically within your box.

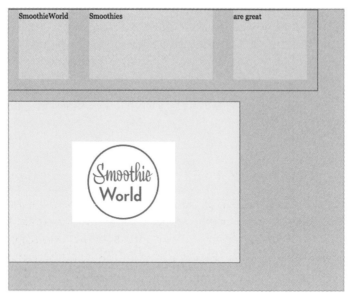

Horizontally and vertically centering an image using the flexbox properties.

To better understand how these properties work, set the `box-align` property to `stretch` and view the results.

9   Return to your text editor and change the values for the moz and webkit `box-align` properties as follows:

```
display: -moz-box;
-moz-box-orient: horizontal;
-moz-box-pack: center;
-moz-box-align: stretch;

display: -webkit-box;
webkit-box-orient: horizontal;
-webkit-box-pack: center;
-webkit-box-align: stretch;
```

10   Choose File > Save and then preview in your browser. The image is now stretched vertically down the box. Note that the stretch value is not a good option for this exercise because it distorts the image, but there are other cases where this value is useful; for example, to create flexible columns. (If your box does not stretch, check your code, but also realize it may be your browser. Google Chrome, for example, does not appear to render the stretch value accurately.)

11 Return to your text editor and change the `-moz` and `-webkit box-align` values back to `center`.

The vendor prefixes for Gecko and Webkit will eventually become redundant as the flexbox properties are fully adopted by web browsers. Microsoft has announced support for the flexible box module in Internet Explorer 10, thus increasing the probability of using flexbox for layout purposes in the future.

For a chart displaying past, current, and future support for the flexible layout module, visit http://caniuse.com/#feat=flexbox.

The CSS3 template layout module

Grid systems have been an important component of print design for years. For example, a typical newspaper has a complex column structure that integrates multi-column layouts with advertisements, images, and other elements. To make the process of designing a newspaper more manageable, editors rely on grid templates that can be reused daily; the front page of a newspaper has a different grid layout than the editorial page, which in turn has a different grid layout than the classifieds, and so on.

Different variables are used to design web pages; for example, screens are used instead of paper, but the concept of grid structure is just as important. Since there are no grid components in CSS2.0 and 2.1, designers and developers have implemented grid layouts using custom CSS solutions that provide a framework for basic layout solutions. In CSS3, there is a proposed Template Layout Module that attempts to incorporate grids directly into the language.

The Template Layout Module is still in the developmental stage, so few browsers natively support the CSS3 properties. This section gives you a preview of the future of CSS web layout.

Adding template-based position to CSS

To help you understand the new template layout module, compare it to the existing layout policy of absolute positioning in CSS. For example, consider the simple list in CSS:

```
<ul>
    <li>Blueberry Smoothies</li>
    <li> Mango Smoothies </li>
    <li> Banana Smoothies </li>
</ul>
```

The default layout policy for an unordered list is to treat each item as a block element and position it within its own line. The following figure shows the unordered list with a single `background-color` property added to help you visualize the style.

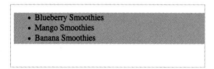

The standard block-level formatting appearance of an unordered list.

You can change the default block-level formatting of a list to inline using a simple rule. This technique is the foundation of many CSS horizontal navigation bars. The code you would add in your CSS would be:

```
li {
    display:inline;
}
```

This code places each list item on a single line. To separate each item in the list, you would need to add margins or padding between each item.

An unordered list that has a new style converting the list items to inline.

You can currently position elements absolutely in CSS, which removes the targeted element from the flow of the page and lets you position it horizontally and vertically on the page by setting offset values for the element. For example, to move your unordered list 100 pixels from the top of the page and 40 pixels from the left, you would add the following style:

```
ul {
    background-color:#B28A9C;
    position: absolute;
    left: 40px;
    top: 100px;
}
```

Absolute positioning is useful in many circumstances, but it is limiting because it relies on horizontal and vertical coordinates. Having multiple absolutely positioned elements on the page can work well until you need to change the size of one or more of these elements, need to reposition the elements, or the amount of content changes; in such cases, the layout often breaks and you need to update it. Absolutely positioned layout is very inflexible.

In contrast, template-based positioning is extremely flexible because it uses rows and columns to provide adaptable slots for content. The relative size and alignment of elements is governed implicitly by the rows and columns of the template. For example, consider the layout illustrated in the following figure:

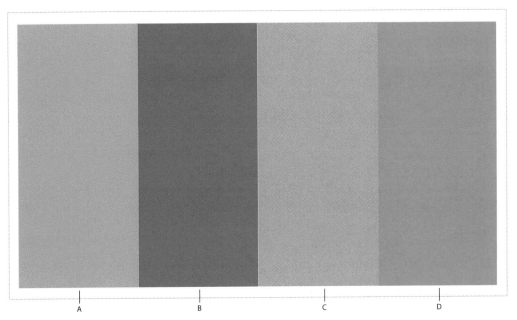

A four-column layout with sections A, B, C, and D

The four regions of the page (A, B, C, and D) receive different content. The HTML for this layout might appear as follows:

```
<div id="grid">
    <div id="a"></div>
    <div id="b"></div>
    <div id="c"></div>
    <div id="d"></div>
</div>
```

The style for this layout could start as follows:

```
#grid {
    width:800px;
    margin:auto;
}

#a {
    position: a;
}

#b {
    position: b;
}

#c {
    position: c;
}

#d {
    position: d;
}
```

The first rule for the parent div, called `grid`, defines a width of 800 pixels and sets the margins to `auto` to center the container. The four IDs use the `position` property and use a letter value instead of a number value.

Within the style for the parent div, you could arrange the order of the 4 child divs using the `display` property, as shown below:

```
#grid {
    width:800px;
    margin:auto;
    display: "abcd";
}
```

To style each row, you could link the letter values to a new CSS3 property called `slot`. A CSS3 slot has this unique syntax `::slot()`. The following code shows the position value connected to the slot:

```
#grid::slot(a) {
    background: orange;
}

#grid::slot(b) {
    background: blue;
}

#grid::slot(c) {
    background: gray;
}

#grid::slot(d) {
    background: pink;
}
```

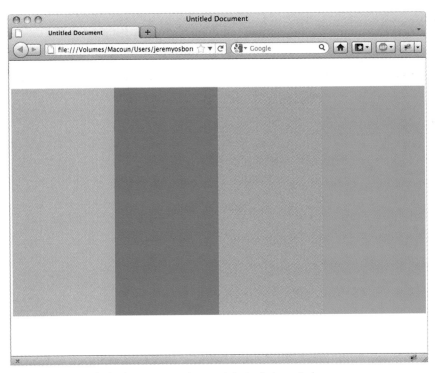

The CSS3 slot *pseudo-class lets you target each row and give it a background color.*

You can create more complex grid structures. For example, to create a header for slot a, you could add the following code to the grid ID style:

```
#grid {
    display: "aaa"
              "bcd";
}
```

This style repeats the three divs with the ID a across the page, and then places the next three divs below it. You might add additional styles to improve the aesthetic appearance.

An example of how you could create a header with three columns using template-based positioning.

Web developer Alexis Deveria has created a jQuery plug-in that lets you use his syntax in your pages so you can experiment with template-based positioning with help from JavaScript. You can locate this code here: http://code.google.com/p/css-template-layout/.

Self study

1 Create additional styles for the final 12_home.html file you had at the end of the Media Query exercise. To experiment with a second media query, add the following code below your last rule in the style sheet:

```
@media screen and (orientation:landscape) {
    #mainnav {
        width:350px;
        }
}
```

2 The previous step will change the width of the navigation menu when the phone is in landscape mode. What other styles could you use in landscape mode?

Review

Questions

1 Jason wants to convert his pre-existing website to mobile and uses CSS3 media query to do so. Jason would also like to convert his multi-column layout to a single column to maximize the screen space on the mobile browser. What are the two CSS properties relating to layout Jason should modify first?

2 What is the difference between multi-column layout and the flexible box layout in CSS3?

3 To center a div container in the middle of another div container, which of the following CSS3 techniques would be better to use: Media Queries, Multi-Column layout, Flexible Box Layout, or Template Layout?

Answers

1 To convert a multi-column layout to a single column, the first steps will often be to set a float property of none and a width property of auto to most or all elements using floats or that have fixed width values.

2 The multi-column layout properties can be used to divide a pre-existing element into a specified number of columns. The flexible box layout properties can be used to build a page layout by defining the properties of child elements, such as div containers, in a flexible manner.

3 Flexible Box Layout.

What you'll learn in this lesson:

- About the Application Cache API and how to cache files with HTML5

- About the manifest file and how web pages are stored for offline use

- To create your first offline web application

- To manage offline files using HTML5 storage

Offline Storage in HTML5

In this lesson, you will learn how offline storage works in HTML5, and how you can use it to store information gathered from the Internet onto your desktop or mobile device.

Starting up

You will work with several files from the HTML5_13lessons folder in this lesson. Make sure you have loaded the HTML5lessons folder onto your hard drive from the supplied DVD. See "Loading lesson files" in the Starting Up section of this book.

See Lesson 13 in action!

Use the accompanying video to gain a better understanding of how to use some of the capabilities shown in this lesson. The video tutorial for this lesson can be found on the included DVD.

On the road, again

Certain jobs require people to travel to locations out of reach of the Internet. For individuals who rely on the Internet to keep track of information gathered (such as clients, purchase orders, comments regarding the trip, and so on), being out of reach of the Internet can result in a cumbersome process that requires the individual to somehow annotate all the information gathered, and later manually post it onto the company's website. HTML5 offers offline storage capabilities, thus turning the out-of-reach website into a mobile application that stores data on the individual's computer or mobile device when access to the Internet is not possible, and later transmits that data when access is possible again.

Offline storage in HTML5

There are primarily two offline capabilities in HTML5: application caching and offline storage. Application caching saves an application's core logic and user-interface. Offline storage (or client-side storage) captures data generated by the user and specific resources the user is interested in. This lesson explains offline storage first. Application caching is explained later in the lesson.

HTML5 storage comprises several techniques to store data locally, from simple key/value pair caching, to file storage and SQL database stores. The technique you choose depends on the objective of the application and type of data stored.

In all cases, the data stored is directly connected to the origin of the site that creates it. In other words, data stored by one domain cannot be accessed from another domain. For example, AGI Training might have a number of web applications that store data. You can share data between these applications because they all originate from *agitraining.com*, but no outside application or website can read them.

HTML5 storage types

HTML5 storage saves data in named key/value pairs, much as browser cookies. Data is never transmitted back to a server, and HTML5 storage can accumulate a large amount of data (5Mb in FireFox, Chrome, Safari, and Opera, and up to 10Mb in IE 9).

There are two kinds of global storage objects: `sessionStorage` and `localStorage`.

sessionStorage

Data stored with `sessionStorage` only lasts for the duration of the current browser session. Once you close the browser window or navigate away from the website, the local data is cleared.

localStorage

`localStorage` is a persistent version of `sessionStorage`: you can store data on the computer until it is explicitly removed by the application or the user.

Use the `localStorage` object on the global `window` object to access HTML5 storage. To detect whether a browser supports this feature, you need to create a web page and add the following JavaScript function:

```
function supports_html5_storage() {
    try {
        return 'localStorage' in window && window['localStorage'] !=
null;
    } catch (e) {
        return false;
    }
}
```

This function returns a Boolean value of true if your browser supports HTML5 storage. Use the `in` modifier to easily determine whether an object contains another object.

`localStorage` methods

`setItem(key, value)`	Saves a value under a new key name or updates a value for an existing key.
`getItem(key)`	Retrieves the value for a given key name.
`removeItem(key)`	Deletes an entry in the data store for the given key name.
`clear()`	Deletes all key/value pairs in the data store for the current application.
`length`	Read-only property that returns the number of keys in a data store.

`localStorage` example

In this exercise, you will create a live application that saves to a local storage object data that the user enters. Source code is available in notepad_example.html in the HTML5_13lessons folder; the full listing is presented after this exercise.

1   In your text editor, open a new file and enter the markup to define a simple HTML5 page:

```
<!DOCTYPE html>
<html>
    <head>
    </head>
    <body>
        <section>
        </section>
    </body>
</html>
```

2   Insert a `<style>` section in the `<head>` section you created in step 1. You will make the text input area appear as a yellow sticky-note with a dashed border:

```
<head>
    <style type="text/css">
        #note{
            width: 320px;
            height: 200px;
            background: LightYellow;
            border: 1px dashed gray;
            overflow-y: scroll;
            padding: 4px;
            font: normal gray 13px Arial;
            }
    </style>
</head>
```

3   Change the `<body>` tag to include an `onload` event that calls an initialize function. This function will set up the local storage object when the page finishes loading:

```
<body onload="initialize()">
```

4   The page will consist of an input area for the notepad and a reset button within the `<section>` element. Add a `<div>` tag and an `<a href>` tag to the `<section>` element:

```
<section>
    <div id="note" contenteditable="true">
        (Enter some text, close your browser and reload this page.)
    </div>
    <a href="#" onclick="reset_note();return false">Reset Note</a>
</section>
```

For this exercise, use the contenteditable property of a `<div>` for the input area, instead of creating a `<textarea>` form tag.

Due to the page size of this book, some code will appear on a second line. All code in single quotes should be entered on one line in an editor.

5   Add a `<script>` area at the top of the `<section>` element for the `initialize()` function and several global variables:

```
<section>
    <script type="text/javascript">
        var noteref, mystorage;
        var defaulthtml = '<div id="note" contenteditable="false">(Enter
some text, close your browser and then open this page again.)</div>\n';
        function initialize() {
    <div id="note" contenteditable="true">
```

6   Within the initialize function, enter the code to call the function that checks whether your browser supports HTML5 storage:

```
function initialize {
    if (supports_html5_storage()) {
    // save a reference to the note area
```

7   Add the following line of code so when the value of the previous `If` statement is true, you obtain a reference to the `<div>` element using `getElementById`:

```
if (supports_html5_storage()) {
// save a reference to the note area
    noteref = document.getElementById("note");
```

8   You need to get an instance of the browser's local storage object. Depending on your browser, local storage might be defined as `localStorage` or `globalStorage`. The following code covers either variation and should be written on one line in your editor:

```
noteref = document.getElementById("note");
mystorage = window.localStorage ||
    (window.globalStorage ? globalStorage[location.hostname] : null);
```

The code shown above obtains the storage object from `window.localStorage` *or from* `window.globalStorage` *("or" is symbolized by the two pipes* `||`*). The second line is an immediate if clause. This statement determines whether the* `window.globalStorage` *object exists, and if so (symbolized by the question mark* `?`*), returns the* `globalStorage` *object for your web host. The* `null` *value is used to represent the absence of the* `globalStorage` *object (symbolized by the colon* `:`*). So, if* `globalStorage` *is the default storage object, then retrieve the object from the current browser instance,* `location.hostname`*; otherwise, return* `null`*.*

9 Now that you have a storage object, check whether there is a note stored from a previous session; if so, load its value into the text area from the name/value key pair:

```
if (supports_html5_storage()) {
// save a reference to the note area
        noteref = document.getElementById("note");

        mystorage = window.localStorage || (window.
globalStorage ? globalStorage[location.hostname] : null);

    if (mystorage) {
    // if there is a note already stored
        if (mystorage.notedata) {
        // re-load it
            noteref.innerHTML = mystorage.notedata;
        }
```

To save the data, the user types into the local storage object. Use the KeyUp event and write a closure function to automatically save text to the storage object at the same time the user types a note:

```
noteref.innerHTML = mystorage.notedata;
    }
// capture keystrokes and save to local data store
    noteref.onkeyup = function (e) {
    mystorage.notedata = this.innerHTML;
    }
```

Notice you are not using setItem("notedata", this.innerHTML). This is because you can assign and retrieve variables as associative arrays, just as with any other JavaScript object.

Putting it all together

Here is the complete source code for the simple notepad example found in the HTML5_13lesson folder named notepad_example.html.

```html
<!DOCTYPE html>
<html lang="en">
<head>
    <style type="text/css">
        #note{
            width: 320px;
            height: 200px;
            background: LightYellow;
            border: 1px dashed gray;
            overflow-y: scroll;
            padding: 4px;
            font: normal gray 13px Arial;
            }
    </style>
</head>

<body onload="initialize()">
    <section>
        <script type="text/javascript">
            var noteref, mystorage;
            var defaulthtml = '<div id="note" contenteditable="false">
(Enter some text, close your browser and then open this page again.)
</div>\n';
            function initialize() {
                if (supports_html5_storage()) {
                    noteref = document.getElementById("note");

                    mystorage = window.localStorage ||
                    (window.globalStorage ? globalStorage[location.
hostname] : null);
                    if (mystorage) {
                        // if there is a note already stored
                        if (mystorage.notedata) {
                            // re-load it
                            noteref.innerHTML = mystorage.notedata;
                        }
                        // capture keystrokes and save to local data store
                        noteref.onkeyup = function (e) {
                            mystorage.notedata = this.innerHTML;
                        }
```

It is important to enter all of the closing braces '}' to match the opening braces '{' for each function and if statement.

10 Add an `else` condition to the `if` statement to notify the user if local storage is not available. Also, add the function to check whether local storage is available. We'll also add a label above the editor using a `<div>` tag. Add the following code and be sure the quoted string in the `alert()` function appears on one line in your editor:

```
mystorage.notedata = this.innerHTML;
    }

            }
        } else {
        alert('local storage not available with your
browser.');
            }
        }

        function supports_html5_storage() {
            try {
                return 'localStorage' in window &&
window['localStorage'] != null;
            } catch (e) {
                return false;
            }
        }
    </script>

    <div>Note to self:</div>
    <div id="note" contenteditable="true">
    (Enter some text, close your browser and reload this page.)
    </div>

    </section>
</body>
</html>
```

Test your code in a browser that supports HTML5 storage; anything you type in the text area should be automatically saved in the local storage area. Please note that some browsers require the file to be uploaded to a web server before `localStorage` will function properly. Close your browser and reload the page; your note is retrieved from the data store and displayed in the text area instead of the default directions.

Note to self:

(Enter some text, close your browser and reload
this page.)

Notepad form at start-up.

Note to self:

Monday:
- Mail that sales letter!
- Technical support calls: 2 hrs.
- Don't forget to pick up milk.

Tuesday:
- 8:00 AM meeting with client.
- Lunch with the boss.

Data entry saved after page reloaded.

Advanced data storage

Current browsers support the basic key/value pair methods of the localStorage API. There
is also an advanced specification called the Web SQL Database that permanently stores large
amounts of data in a SQL database. This specification is no longer in active maintenance and the
Web Applications Working Group does not intend to maintain it further.

You can find this disclaimer at http://dev.w3.org/html5/webdatabase/.

To replace Web SQL Database, the W3C is developing an Indexed Database API called
IndexedDB. The Indexed Database API exposes what's called an object store, which shares
many concepts with a SQL database. For example, object stores have databases with records.
Each record has a set number of fields, and each field has a specific datatype, defined when the
database is created. You can select a subset of records, and then enumerate them with a cursor.
Changes to the object store are handled within transactions.

Status update!

Web SQL Database is no longer actively maintained by W3C. Use IndexedDB, instead.

The primary difference between IndexedDB and Web SQL Database is that the IndexedDB object store has no structured query language; for example, you don't construct a statement such as `SELECT * from CUSTOMER`. Instead, you use programming methods to open a cursor, enumerate and filter records, and use accessor methods to obtain field values.

IndexedDB is a new technology for which the W3C Working Group has laid out a foundation; IndexedDB has only been implemented in a beta version of Firefox 4. Mozilla has stated that they will never implement Web SQL Database. Google has stated that they are considering IndexedDB support for Chromium and Google Chrome. Microsoft has said that IndexedDB "is a great solution for the Web." We strongly recommend that you research the current state of each browser's support for advanced data storage before you develop an application with this technology.

Application caching

In the previous section of this lesson, you learned about HTML5 storage using named key/value pairs and briefly looked at IndexedDB to save data. You will likely use these techniques for the majority of online storage tasks. You can also take an application offline by saving its stylesheets, scripts, and graphic elements with application caching.

The cache manifest file

The cache manifest is a simple text file specified in the <HTML> tag of a web page that lists the resources that should be cached for offline use. Resource files can include HTML, CSS, JavaScript files, and other resources, such as images and video. The following line of code is an example.

```
<html manifest="http://www.example.com/cache.manifest">
```

You need to include the manifest attribute on every page of your web application you want cached for offline storage. The browser will not cache a page for offline use without this attribute, unless the page is explicitly listed in the manifest file. In other words, any page the user navigates to that includes a manifest attribute will be implicitly added to the application cache, thus avoiding the need to list every page in your manifest.

The manifest attribute can point to an absolute URL (as in the example above), or to a relative path; keep in mind that an absolute URL must be stored in the same server as the web application. A manifest file can have any file extension, but it needs to be served with the correct MIME-Type.

MIME-Type required

The MIME-Type of the manifest file must be text/cache-manifest. You will need to add a custom file type to your web server, or .htaccess configuration file, to recognize manifest files. A .htaccess file has been included with this lesson, demonstrating how a MIME-type would be configured.

Cache manifest structure

Here is an example of a simple manifest file:

```
CACHE MANIFEST
stylesheet.css
logo.png
main.js
index.html
```

Here is an example of a complete manifest file:

```
CACHE MANIFEST
# 2011-06-18:v2
# Explicitly cached 'master entries'.
CACHE:
/favicon.ico
index.php
stylesheet.css
fonts/MoolBoran.ttf
images/logo.png
scripts/main.js

# Resources that require the user to be online.
NETWORK:
login.php
/api
http://api.twitter.com

# files to serve if not accessible
FALLBACK:
/index.php /index.html
images/large/ images/offline.jpg
*.html /offline.html
```

There are three sections in a manifest file:

1   CACHE—the default section; lists files to be stored offline.

2   NETWORK—identifies files to always retrieve from the network. You can use wildcards (*).

3   FALLBACK—optional section that defines files when a resource is inaccessible. You can use wildcards (*).

Every page pointing to the manifest is automatically added to the cache as a MASTER entry and behaves as though it were listed in the CACHE section.

Updating the cache

An offline application remains cached until one of the following happens:

- The user clears their browser's data storage for your site.
- The manifest file is modified.
- The app cache is programmatically updated.

Lines starting with the pound symbol (#) are comment lines, but they can also serve another purpose. An application's cache is updated only when its manifest file changes. For example, if you edit an image resource or change a JavaScript function, those changes will not be re-cached. Creating a comment line with a generated version number or timestamp is one way to ensure the cache is updated and users have the latest version of your application. You can also programmatically update the cache once a new version is ready as discussed in The Application Cache Object section.

Updating a file listed in the manifest does not re-cache that resource. You must change the manifest file before the application re-caches all files.

The `applicationCache` object

The `window.applicationCache` object is your programmatic access to the browser's cache. You can use this object's status property to check the current state of the cache:

```
var appCache = window.applicationCache;

switch (appCache.status) {
    case appCache.UNCACHED:              // UNCACHED = 0
        return 'UNCACHED';
        break;
    case appCache.IDLE:                  // IDLE = 1
        return 'IDLE';
        break;
    case appCache.CHECKING:              // CHECKING = 2
        return 'CHECKING';
        break;
    case appCache.DOWNLOADING:           // DOWNLOADING = 3
        return 'DOWNLOADING';
        break;
    case appCache.UPDATEREADY:           // UPDATEREADY = 5
        return 'UPDATEREADY';
        break;
    case appCache.OBSOLETE:              // OBSOLETE = 5
        return 'OBSOLETE';
        break;
    default:
        return 'CACHE STATUS UNKNOWN';
        break;
};
```

To programmatically update the cache, first call the `applicationCache.update` function, which updates the user's cache when the manifest file changes. The next step is to call the `applicationCache.swapCache` function when the `applicationCache.status` is in UPDATEREADY state to swap the old cache for the new one. The most efficient way to update users to the newest version of your application is to set a listener on page load to monitor the UPDATEREADY event:

```
// Check if a new cache is available on page load.
var appCache = window.applicationCache;

window.addEventListener('load', function(e) {
    appCache.addEventListener('updateready', function(e) {
        if (appCache.status == appCache.UPDATEREADY) {
            // Browser has downloaded a new app cache.
            // Swap it in and reload the page to get the new files.
            appCache.swapCache();
            window.location.reload();
        } else {
            // Manifest hasn't changed.
        }
    }, false);
}, false);
```

If the manifest file or a resource specified in it fails to download, the entire update fails and the browser continues to use the current application cache.

Bringing it all together

The source files that accompany this lesson contain an offline application, its manifest file, and its resource files. The notepad_example_offline.html page located in the Offline folder inside the HTML5_13lessons folder contains a URL placeholder for your actual domain name. The following line of code shows the manifest file declaration.

```
<html manifest="http://www.[your_website].com/offline/cache.manifest">
```

1   Change the text [your_website] in the html element's manifest attribute to your actual domain name.

2   Copy the offline folder onto your web server.

Contact your web service provider before you run the application to ensure text/cache-manifest is added to your MIME types or .htaccess configuration file.

The first time you run the application, it will download all files listed in the manifest. When you run the application again, it will check whether the manifest has changed; if so, the application will update all downloaded files.

Self study

The advanced data storage in HTML5 is still being implemented by the browser vendors. See *http://www.w3.org/TR/IndexedDB/* for information about IndexedDB Storage and *http://www.w3.org/TR/webstorage/* for the latest web storage specifications.

Review

Questions

1   True or False: The `manifest` attribute only needs to be added to the home page of an application.

2   Can data stored by one domain be accessed from another domain?

3   How are cached files updated?

Answers

1   False. Every page of your web application needs a manifest attribute that points to the cache manifest file unless that page is explicitly listed in the manifest file.

2   No. Data is accessible only from the originating domain. It is possible to share data between applications from the same domain, but no outside application or website can access them.

3   The manifest file must be changed before the application will re-cache all files. Changing a comment line with a generated version number or timestamp is one way to ensure the cache gets updated. You can also programmatically update the cache.

What you'll learn in this lesson:

- Understanding Geolocation API and its limitations
- Detecting the user's geographic location
- Displaying the user's location on a map
- Utilizing fallbacks for varying devices
- Understanding JavaScript callbacks and how to use them
- Creating a "mash-up" geolocation application

HTML5 Geolocation

In this lesson, you will learn to detect and display the location of your site's users with the Geolocation API from HTML5. You can use this information to pinpoint a user's location for a variety of reasons, such as displaying the user's location on a map.

Starting up

You will work with several files from the HTML5_14lessons folder in this lesson. Make sure you have loaded the HTML5lessons folder onto your hard drive from the supplied DVD. See "Loading lesson files" in the Starting Up section of this book.

See Lesson 14 in action!

Use the accompanying video to gain a better understanding of how to use some of the capabilities shown in this lesson. The video tutorial for this lesson can be found on the included DVD.

To accurately preview the HTML5 content you will create in this lesson, you need a browser that supports HTML5 tags. See "Using web browsers that support HTML5 tags" in the Starting Up section of this book to determine whether you are using such a browser, or for instructions on downloading one.

Understanding Geolocation

Geolocation lets you determine a user's position anywhere on Earth using a geographic coordinate system (latitude and longitude). To detect the user's location, browsers and devices rely on GPS hardware, wireless infrastructure, or a user's IP address.

HTML5 has expanded JavaScript's capabilities to include this ability in its Geolocation API, which consists of functions you can use to find or track a user's movement.

Not everyone wants to share their location, so the user must give their express permission before any browser can divulge this level of personal information. The Geolocation API clearly states, "User agents must not send location information to Web sites without the express permission of the user." All major browsers prompt the user for permission before sharing their location.

Prompts are used to get the user's permission; this figure shows an example from Firefox.

Getting the user's location

The HTML5 Geolocation API lets JavaScript request permission to obtain a user's geographic location through one of the methods listed above. The majority of this functionality relies on the `navigator.geolocation` object, specifically the `getCurrentPosition` function.

The following exercise illustrates the use of this API.

1   Using your text editor, open the location.html file within the HTML5_14lessons folder. Save a copy of the file as location_work.html. Notice that a span and a single function have been defined in this file. The function is called from the body's `onload` event.

```
function setup()
{
    output = document.getElementById( 'output' );
    if( navigator.geolocation )
    {
    }
}
```

2   The setup function from the previous step determines whether the HTML5 Geolocation API is supported. Within the if statement, insert the following call to the navigator.geolocation object's getCurrentPosition function:

```
if( navigator.geolocation )
{
    navigator.geolocation.getCurrentPosition();
}
```

Calls to getCurrentPosition usually result in a prompt to the user requesting permission for your application to access the user's location; the specific method to obtain this permission varies, but all browsers have it.

The getCurrentPosition function receives a maximum of three arguments. The first is a function to call when the user's location has been determined. The second is a function used for any errors in the location process. The third argument is optional, and it is an PositionOptions object used to configure several properties of the getCurrentPosition function.

The PositionOptions object

The PositionOptions object used to configure the getCurrentPosition function is not required for this activity, but you might need it for applications that require precise timing. This object contains a maximum of three properties. The enableHighAccuracy property is a Boolean property that causes the getCurrentPosition results to be more accurate by increasing the time and/or power consumed by a device when detecting the user's location. More accurate results may be necessary for applications such as a GPS navigator where all instructions need to be as exact as possible. The timeout property specifies how long your application should wait for results (in milliseconds) before issuing a failed attempt message. The maximumAge property allows devices to use dated information to improve performance, but precision is lost.

The following table describes the properties of the PositionOptions object, in addition to the properties' type, default value, and comments to note.

PositionOptions Properties

PROPERTY	TYPE	DEFAULT	NOTES
enableHighAccuracy	Boolean	false	true (might be slow)
timeout	long	(no default)	milliseconds
maximumAge	long	0	milliseconds

3   After the setup function's curly braces, create a function called showLocation with a single argument: a position object. The function is called when the position of the user has been determined, and the position object contains the information regarding the user's position.

```
function showLocation( position )
{
}
```

The position object has two properties: a coords object and a timestamp. The timestamp indicates when the user's position was calculated. The coords object has a number of properties, which are the many values that might have been obtained from the device, including the coords.latitude and coords.longitude properties.

4   Within the showLocation function, the user's location is displayed using the position object's coords properties. The output.innerHTML property controls the text that appears within a span that has been included with this activity for demonstration purposes only.

Add the following lines of code.

```
function showLocation( position )
{
    output.innerHTML = 'Your location is '
    + position.coords.latitude + ' lat '
    + position.coords.longitude + ' lon';
}
```

5   Return to the setup function and add the showLocation function as the first argument for the call to getCurrentPosition. When the user grants permission, the showLocation function will be called as a result:

```
navigator.geolocation.getCurrentPosition( showLocation );
```

6   This code is enough to get the user's location, but it does not allow for any errors that might occur. Create a function called locationError to call in the event of an error, and to notify the user of said error.

```
function locationError( error )
{
    output.innerHTML = 'Location could not be determined';
}
```

The error object passed into this function contains two properties: a numeric code and a message representing that error code in text. You can use the code property to determine the cause of the error:

- Error code 0: unknown error.
- Error code 1: the user denies permission to the network.
- Error code 2: caused by a network failure. You can try to read the user's position again.
- Error code 3: caused by a timeout. You can try to read the user's position again.

Unfortunately, the message property does not always provide enough information.

7   Use the `locationError` function as the second argument for the `getCurrentLocation` function:

```
navigator.geolocation.getCurrentPosition( showLocation,
locationError );
```

8   Add an `else` case to the conditional `if` in the setup function to notify users that Geolocation is not supported:

```
if( navigator.geolocation )
{
    navigator.geolocation.getCurrentPosition( showLocation,
locationError );
}
else
    locationError();
```

9   Save your file and open it in the browser. Grant permission to share your location when prompted; you should see your geographic coordinates displayed in your browser, similar to what is shown in the following figure:

| Your location is 42.5630734 lat -71.2633941 lon |

Your location will be shown only after granting permission to share your location.

If you simply see 'Location can not be determined', your browser does not support Geolocation.

The `getCurrentPosition` function determines the user's location at the current moment, but you can watch the user's location as it changes using the Geolocation API's `watchPosition` function. This function has the same arguments as `getCurrentPosition`, and it also invokes the callback function as the user's location changes. You could use the `watchPosition` function for a mobile application that needs to provide directions to the user.

Displaying the user's location with Google Maps

Now that you have used the Geolocation API to determine the user's geographic location, your next goal is to show where the user is on a map. Normally, this task would be long and expensive to develop; Google has provided an open-source API for Google Maps. The Google Maps API uses geographic coordinates to create an interactive map of an area, thus opening a large number of opportunities for JavaScript developers.

Google Maps uses a div within an HTML document to render the map. It does not need to be used in conjunction with Geolocation, but together they show enormous potential.

The following exercise illustrates how this feature works. The file map.html contains the necessary HTML markup required to make Google Maps work.

1 Use your text editor to open the map.html file within the HTML5_14lessons folder. Save a copy of the file as **map_work.html**. In this file, you will notice that an external JavaScript file is referenced. This file contains all the functionality for the Google Maps API.

```
<script type="text/javascript"
    src="http://maps.google.com/maps/api/js?sensor=false">
</script>
```

Unlike many JavaScript libraries, you do not need to copy the file containing Google Maps onto your file server. The absolute link works wherever there is an internet connection.

The `meta` tag defined at the top of map_work.html prevents mobile device users from resizing the Google Maps application. Google Maps includes a zoom in and out button, preventing the need for the device's native zoom feature.

```
<meta name="viewport" content="initial-scale=1.0, user-scalable=no" />
```

2 Within the `showLocation` function, add the following line of code to initialize a set of Google Maps coordinates:

```
function showLocation( position )
{
    var latlng = new google.maps.LatLng( position.coords.latitude,
    position.coords.longitude );
}
```

3 After the code you added in step 2, add the following line of code to create a `mapOptions` object containing the parameters for the map itself:

```
function showLocation( position )
{
    var latlng = new google.maps.LatLng( position.coords.latitude,
    position.coords.longitude );
    var mapOptions = {
        zoom: 8,
        center: latlng,
    mapTypeId: google.maps.MapTypeId.ROADMAP
    };
}
```

The `mapOptions` object contains the following properties:

- The starting zoom setting.
- The center coordinates for the map.
- One of many possible map types implemented in the Google Maps API and set for the `mapTypeID` property.

For more information about the Google Maps API, visit the developer's guide at *code.google.com/apis/maps*.

4   Finally, create the map with the following line of code.

```
function showLocation( position )
{
    var latlng = new google.maps.LatLng( position.coords.latitude,
    position.coords.longitude );
    var mapOptions = {
        zoom: 8,
        center: latlng,
        mapTypeId: google.maps.MapTypeId.ROADMAP
    };
    var map = new google.maps.Map( map_canvas, mapOptions );
}
```

5   Save your file and test it in the browser. You will be prompted for your location; share your location so the map displays properly. You should see your location displayed on the map similar to what is shown in the following figure:

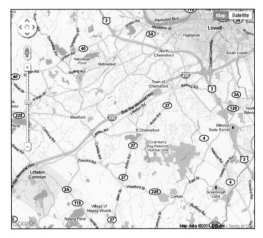

Google Maps displays the location of any user visiting this page.

Browsers lacking HTML5 Geolocation

You should note that many mobile devices and browsers have their own Geolocation capabilities, some requiring a plug-in, such as Gears. Since many of the native APIs are different from the HTML5 Geolocation, it would be difficult to support all the different user agents. Fortunately, MIT offers an open-source JavaScript library with a simple API known as geo.js to add support for these cases.

What is Gears?

Gears is an open source plug-in that Google makes available on all operating systems, thus allowing older browsers to use newer features, such as Geolocation. Gears uses an alternate syntax, so you need additional JavaScript to use this fallback.

The watchPosition *function is not supported by geo.js at the time of this writing.*

Before you can use Gears, you must include references in your code to the script for Gears support. You must also make changes to the setup function.

The following exercise shows the changes you must make to use geo.js.

1 Inside map_work.html, locate the head of the document. Insert a reference to Google's Gears API with the following script tag:

```
<script type="text/javascript"
    src="http://code.google.com/apis/gears/gears_init.js">
</script>
```

2 You must reference the geo.js file to use it. Add the following script tag directly after the previous step:

```
<script type="text/javascript" src="geo.js">
</script>
```

3 Locate the setup function in the body of the document. Change the conditional checking for Geolocation support to use the geo.js init function instead:

```
function setup()
{
    map_canvas = document.getElementById( 'map_canvas' );
    if( geo_position_js.init() )
```

The init function determines the ideal configuration for the user and returns true if Geolocation is supported; false if it is not.

4   In the same function, use the geo.js getCurrentPosition function instead of HTML5's standard API:

```
if( geo_position_js.init() )
{
    geo_position_js.getCurrentPosition( showLocation, locationError
);
}
```

5   Save your file and preview in the browser. You might not notice any difference, but your map application is now available to a much broader audience.

Creating a HTML5 Geolocation and Google Maps mashup

To further illustrate the use of the geolocation feature, you will create a functional application to plot the location of MegaBooks, a fictional bookstore chain, on a map relative to a user's location. Using the HTML5 Geolocation API and Google Maps API, you will create a "mashup" application that finds the user's position, places a marker on a map to indicate the user's current location, and shows all the MegaBooks stores nearby. The term mashup is used to describe the process of combining APIs from at least two different sources in order to create a new creation you could not otherwise achieve.

This tutorial is not intended to delve into all the features of Google maps, but it reviews some of the key points necessary to complete the exercise. For more information about writing map applications using Google's API, see the online documentation at *http://code.google.com/apis/maps/documentation/javascript/basics.html*.

In the following exercise, you will first get the current location of the user, and then create and center the map based on the user's coordinates much as you did in the last exercise. Then you will plot the bookstores within a certain distance of the user's location and display them using markers on the map. For this exercise, you will randomly generate a maximum of 10 longitude and latitude coordinates to simulate the company's store locations, which would normally be defined and stored in a database.

Adding Google Map markers to your geolocation page

In this exercise, there is a significant amount of code and we have attempted to minimize the amount you will have to type in by providing most of the code in the lesson file and allowing you to fill in the rest. If you are not as comfortable or familiar with working with JavaScript syntax, you may choose to open the 14_geolocation_mashup_finished.html file, located in the HTML5_14lessons folder, and view the completed working version there.

1   Choose File > Open and browse to the HTML5_14lessons folder to 14_geolocation_mashup.html. You will need to initialize the Geolocation API by adding an onload event to the `<body>` tag and a function above the existing code in the script tag:

```
<body onload="initialize()" onunload="GUnload()">
    <section id="wrapper">
    <script type="text/javascript" src="http://maps.google.com/maps/
api/js?sensor=false"></script>
        <article>
            <p>Finding your location: <span id="status">checking...</span></p>
        </article>

<script>
    function initialize() {
        if (navigator.geolocation) {
            navigator.geolocation.getCurrentPosition(show_
location,error_handler);
        } else {
            alert('Geolocation not supported in this browser.');
        }
    }...
</script>
```

There is additional script in the code above, as represented by the ellipse (...). You do not need to add any code after the closing bracket.

Using the `onload` event of the `<body>` tag, you specify an initialize function to call when the page content has completely loaded in the browser. You then define two callback functions in the parameters: `show_location`, to process the location object returned; and `error_handler`, to manage errors that might occur while attempting to retrieve the location object. Obtaining geolocation information can be slow sometimes, so you should use a wait message to give the user feedback while her location is found.

2   The next step is to obtain the user's coordinates. Add the following variables to the `show_location` function, the `Position` object and the Google Maps coordinates:

```
function show_location (position) {
    var s = document.querySelector('#status');s.innerHTML = "found you!";
    // Get the user's latitude and longitude
    var latlng = new google.maps.LatLng(
    position.coords.latitude,
    position.coords.longitude);
```

If the Geolocation API is available in the browsers' navigator object, the function `getCurrentPosition` is called. A `Position` object is then returned by `getCurrentPosition` and contains the `position.coords.latitude` and `position.coords.longitude` properties. Using these properties, you then initialize a Google maps Point object and place it in a variable called `latlng`.

3   Create the map within the `show_location` function:

```
// Create a container for the map
var mapcanvas = document.createElement('div');
mapcanvas.id = 'mapcanvas';
mapcanvas.style.height = '400px';
mapcanvas.style.width = '560px';
document.querySelector('article').appendChild(mapcanvas);
```

In this step, you create a new `<div>` element with an ID called `mapcanvas`. You set the map's dimensions to 560 pixels wide and 400 pixels tall, and then dynamically add it to the HTML5 `<article>` element of the web page, which serves as the map's viewport.

4   Once the map is created, center the map display on the user's marker with the following options array:

```
var myOptions = {
    center: latlng,
    zoom: 15,
    mapTypeId: google.maps.MapTypeId.ROADMAP
};
```

In this step, you create an array of options for the map and call it `myOptions`. You then define three attributes: `center`, `zoom`, and `mapTypeID`.

You set the `center` attribute to the `latlng` variable. Recall that `latlng` contains the user's coordinates returned in the geolocation `Position` object, which was in turn created by the call to the HTML5 `navigator.getCurrentPosition` function. By setting the user's actual coordinates in Google Maps from the Geolocation API, you created a "mashup" between the two APIs, thus feeding data from one service into another.

Feeding the user's geolocation coordinates into a Google Maps object creates a mash-up application.

The `zoom` attribute sets a zoom factor, so the map displays a fairly close-in view of the city. Finally, the `mapTypeID` attribute specifies the style of map to draw.

5   Next, create a new map container using the `mapcanvas` div directly after the code added in the previous step:

```
var map = new google.maps.Map(document.getElementById("mapcanvas"),
myOptions);
```

This line of code centers the map on the longitude and latitude coordinates by passing the `myOptions` array to the `maps.Map` object.

6 Create a marker to show the user's location:

```
var marker = new google.maps.Marker({
    position: latlng,
    map: map,
    title:"You are here!"
});
```

Within the `marker` object, you set the `position` property to `latlng`, the coordinate object created earlier; as a result, the marker appears on the map at the same `latlng` position the map is centered on. The `title` attribute displays a tooltip message when the user places the mouse cursor over the marker.

7 Calculate and draw all the bookstore markers. Fill in the following code inside the `show_location` function and enter a right brace '}' to close the function:

```
// Create a blue marker for the stores
var iconFile = 'http://maps.google.com/mapfiles/ms/icons/blue-dot.png';
// Add some store markers to the map (random locations for our example)
var southWest = new google.maps.LatLng(latlng.lat() - .10,
latlng.lng() - .10);
var northEast = new google.maps.LatLng(latlng.lat() + .10,
latlng.lng() + .10);
var bounds = new google.maps.LatLngBounds(southWest, northEast);
var lngSpan = northEast.lng() - southWest.lng();
var latSpan = northEast.lat() - southWest.lat();
map.fitBounds(bounds);
for (var i = 0; i < 10; i++) {
    var point = new google.maps.LatLng(
        southWest.lat() + latSpan * Math.random(),
        southWest.lng() + lngSpan * Math.random());
    var storeMarker = new google.maps.Marker({
        position: point,
        map: map,
        title: "store #" + i
});

storeMarker.setIcon(iconFile)
}
}
```

For this exercise, you are using the built-in JavaScript random number generator to create longitude and latitude values and plot them within the boundaries of the map's container. In a real application, you would query a database to obtain the longitude and latitude coordinates of each store, along with other details such as name, address, and store hours.

The `google.maps.LatLng` *boundary ranges are based on the* `latlng` *variable.*

8 The last step is to implement an error handler for the `getCurrentPosition` function, which has already been defined at the bottom of the script tag:

```
function error_handler(msg) {
    var s = document.querySelector('#status');
    s.innerHTML = msg + " failed.";
}
```

Just like the `show_location` function, `error_handler` is a callback function to receive instructions if the call to the geolocation API fails.

As you would in a fully functional application, you plot only those stores that fall within the visual boundaries, or viewport, of the map. As such, you use the map object's `LatLng` method to set a minimum and maximum range for the markers to plot, based on the coordinates in the original `latlng` variable.

There are additional callback events incorporated into Google Maps that determine when the viewable region changes; unfortunately a complete review of those callback functions is beyond the scope of this tutorial. For more information about working with the map's viewport and boundary events, see the Google Maps documentation available online at *http://code.google.com/apis/maps/documentation/javascript/events.html*.

You can now save and test your application. Accept the browser's prompt to share your location; a map with the location of 10 bookstores within driving distance should appear.

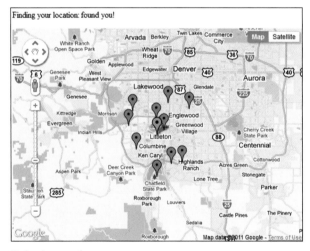

Geolocation example.

The new capabilities in HTML5 offer great opportunities to create exciting new applications; the Geolocation API promises to be one of the most powerful features leveraged by social networking, e-commerce, mobile, and web-based applications.

Self study

Experiment with some of the other map types available for Google Maps. The `mapTypeId` for the `mapOptions` object supports the following: ROADMAP, SATELLITE, HYBRID, and TERRAIN.

Review

Questions

1   Can a browser share the user's location without permission?

2   What is the difference between the Geolocation API's `getCurrentPosition` and `watchPosition` functions?

3   What role does geo.js play in determining the user's location?

Answers

1   Browsers cannot share the user's location without permission. Technically, browsers and mobile devices have the ability to share this information without consent, but all major browsers prompt the user for permission.

2   The `getCurrentLocation` function finds the user at a single point in time; the `watchPosition` function attempts to follow users as they move.

3   You can use geo.js to determine a user's location for browsers that do not support HTML5 Geolocation API, thus offering the maximum number of possibilities to capture the largest possible audience.

Lesson 15

What you'll learn
in this lesson:

* Working with the drag-and-drop interface

* The differences in browser APIs and how to account for them

* Showing visual indicators for drag-and-drop operations

* Transfering data with a drag-and-drop operation

HTML5 Drag and Drop

In this lesson, you will learn to incorporate the HTML5 drag-and-drop feature into your website to let your users actively interact with your site.

Starting up

You will work with several files from the HTML5_15lessons folder in this lesson. Make sure you have loaded the HTML5lessons folder onto your hard drive from the supplied DVD. See "Loading lesson files" in the Starting Up section of this book.

See Lesson 15 in action!

Use the accompanying video to gain a better understanding of how to use some of the capabilities shown in this lesson. The video tutorial for this lesson can be found on the included DVD.

To accurately preview the HTML5 content you will create in this lesson, you need a browser that supports HTML5 tags. See "Using web browsers that support HTML5 tags" in the Starting Up section of this book to determine whether you are using such a browser, or for instructions on downloading one.

Drag and drop on the Web

Drag-and-drop operations let users visually position elements on the screen instead of positioning elements by clicking a button. This ability has made certain applications, such as Dreamweaver and Photoshop, easy to use.

The HTML5 Drag and Drop API is based on the original Internet Explorer implementation. Some details have changed and certain browsers have an alternate syntax, but a standardized API is close to being finalized. At the time of this writing, support for certain drag-and-drop features are not shared between browsers. For example, some browsers allow selections or files from other windows or applications to be dropped into the browser; others do not.

Note that in most browsers, you can drag images, links, and text selections by default. This functionality was included to allow selections from the browser to be dragged into other applications. You can also drag file and text selections from the operating system into some browsers.

Cross-browser drag and drop

This lesson focuses on the drag-and-drop features that are supported across multiple browsers. Several differences exist in the visual indicators of a drag-and-drop operation; the functionality of the operation remains fairly consistent with only a small number of fallbacks.

The following exercise illustrates the use of drag and drop.

1   Using your text editor, open the file shopping.html found within the HTML5_15lessons

folder. Save a copy of this file as **shopping_work.html**. Open the file in your browser; notice that a shopping cart exists on the page. The goal of this activity is to create a drag-and-drop interface for purchasing items. We have added the initial JavaScript code for you, but you will be adding the remaining code to make the page fully functional.

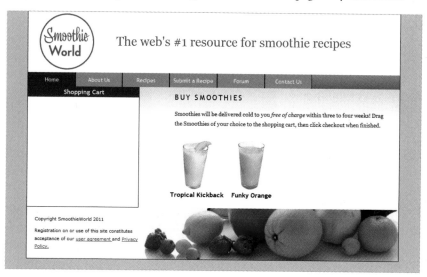

The initial appearance of your page.

Move the mouse cursor over the products on the page. The cursor pointer as well as the outline of the images change. This will let users know that they will be able to drag the image. These rules are set in the base.css style sheet. You will learn about other visual indicators throughout this lesson.

2   The variable `shoppingcart` found within the setup function has been assigned a reference to the shopping cart div. Your code will use this reference to register the div as a drop zone.

Add the following line of code to prevent the default behavior of the `dragenter` event:

```
function setup(){
    shoppingcart = document.getElementById('shoppingcart');
    shoppingcart.ondragenter = preventDefault;
}
```

By default on some browsers, the `dragenter` event displays an icon indicating that an area is not a drop zone. You need to assign this event, the `preventDefault` function, to maintain consistency between browsers. The code below has already been added to your script section and defines the `preventDefault` function, which requires three specific tasks to occur to prevent the default action of some browsers:

```
function preventDefault( event ){
    event.stopPropagation();
    event.preventDefault();
    return false;
}
```

- The `stopPropagation` function prevents other containers from responding to this event.

- The `preventDefault` function prevents the default behavior of the event on some browsers.

- Since `preventDefault` is an event callback function, returning `false` prevents the default behavior in some browsers.

3   In some browsers, the `dragover` event displays an icon similar to the `dragenter` event, indicating that this container is not a valid drop zone. To prevent the default behavior of the `dragover` event, add the code highlighted in red after the line of code from the previous step.

```
function setup(){
    shoppingcart = document.getElementById('shoppingcart');
    shoppingcart.ondragenter = preventDefault;
    shoppingcart.ondragover = preventDefault;
}
```

4   Scroll down to the bottom half of your HTML code. To allow dragging from within the list containing each image, add an `ondragstart` attribute to the div that has a CSS class called `tile_list`, and assign to the attribute the value shown below:

```
<div class="tile_list" ondragstart="dragStarted(event);">
```

At the time of this writing, the Drag and Drop API was not designed to perform drag-and-drop operations; the Drag and Drop API allows developers to respond to the events, not actually move elements. The following implementation provides the drag-and-drop capabilities you need for a basic shopping cart.

5   Within the `dragStarted` function, already defined for this activity, add the following line of code to save a reference to the element dragged by the user into the predefined dragging variable:

```
function dragStarted( event ){
    dragging = event.target;
}
```

6   To implement the drop behavior for the shopping cart, use the `dragDrop` function to respond to the shopping cart's drop event:

```
function setup(){
    shoppingcart = document.getElementById('shoppingcart');
    shoppingcart.ondragenter = preventDefault;
    shoppingcart.ondragover = preventDefault;
    shoppingcart.ondrop = dragDrop;
}
```

7   Within the predefined `dragDrop` function, enter the following line of code to add to the shopping cart the object currently being dragged:

```
function dragDrop(event){
    addToCart( dragging, 1 );
}
```

Making any object draggable in HTML5

Note that on some browsers you can, by default, drag images, links, and text selections and save their inability to be dropped, all without a JavaScript callback. To let users drag objects to other elements, add the `draggable` attribute with a value of `true`, as shown below:

```
<li draggable="true">List Item 1</li>
```

8   Choose File > Save and preview this page in the browser. Depending on the browser you are using, you will have dramatically different results if you drag one of the images onto the shopping cart. In Webkit browsers, such as Safari 5 or Chrome 11, you will get the desired effect and the image will appear in the cart. In other browsers, such as Firefox 4, the default behavior of an image dropped into a drop zone is to open that image in the same window in which the drop zone exists. To ensure this behavior does not occur, return to your text editor and add the following line of code:

```
function dragDrop(event){
    addToCart( dragging, 1 );
    return preventDefault(event);
}
```

9   Save and test this file in your browser. Dragging smoothies into the shopping cart adds

them to the shopping cart for purchase.

The shopping cart keeps track of the items dropped within it, displays those items, and displays a checkout link.

You can choose to display an alternate image when a drag-and-drop operation starts and use any element as a visual indicator, including a canvas. The canvas provides several options, such as images or the ability to display dynamic text; for example, item names and prices.

10 Within the `dragStarted` function, add the following lines of code to create a canvas containing the source image and the price:

```
function dragStarted( event ){
    dragging = event.target;
    var dragImage = document.createElement( 'canvas' );
    var ctx = dragImage.getContext( '2d' );
    ctx.drawImage(dragging, 0, 0);
    ctx.font = 'bold 1.8em sans-serif';
    ctx.fillText( '$5',  30,  100);
}
```

The only visual difference from this change is text added below the image. The code you added in this step is specific to the canvas element. For more information about the capabilities of the canvas element, see "Working with Canvas" in Lesson 10 of this book.

11 To use the newly created canvas as the drag image for the event target, you must call the `setDragImage` function in the event's `dataTransfer` object. Add following line of code directly after the code from the previous step:

```
function dragStarted( event ){
    var dragImage = document.createElement( 'canvas' );
    ...
    event.dataTransfer.setDragImage( dragImage, 0, 0);
}
```

The `setDragImage` function receives three arguments. The first argument is a reference to an element used as the drag image. The other two arguments are the x and y offset for the image. At the time of this writing, full support for the `setDragImage` function was not available in all browsers.

The canvas element is essential for this application, because the `setDragImage` function only allows a single element to be used as the drag image. With a canvas element, you can combine text, images, and vector graphics as a visual indicator.

12 Save all changes and preview the result in your browser. Images on the right may be dragged into the shopping cart on the left.

Transferring data with a drag-and-drop operation

In the previous activity, you learned about using the image's source to determine the item added to the shopping cart. You can transfer a wide range of values with a drag-and-drop operation, thus granting you access to several options.

You can transfer data with the drag event's `dataTransfer` object. The `dataTransfer` object contains several functions for storing data in one or more formats. The normal flow of events is to store data in the `dataTransfer` object during the `dragstart` phase, and then access the same data during the `drop` phase.

The following exercise illustrates how to use this feature.

1 Use your text editor to open the file checkers.html located within the HTML5_15lessons folder. Save a copy of this file as **checkers_work.html**. Open this file in your browser; you will notice that a checkerboard has been created using a series of divs and some CSS positioning. The goal of this activity is to let the user move the pieces on the checkerboard.

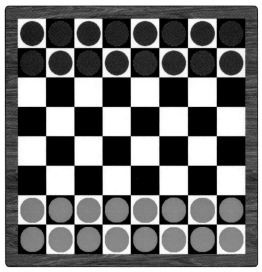

The initial preview of the checkers file.

2 Locate the setup function; the three lines of code listed below enable drag-and-drop on the squares. Note that the callback functions have not been implemented, except for the

preventDefault function.

```
function setup(){
    . . .
    for(var i = 0, square; square = squares[i]; i++){
        // Enable drag and drop on squares
        square.ondragenter = preventDefault;
        square.ondragover = preventDefault;
        square.ondrop = dragDrop;
```

This code uses a loop to access each square as the variable square. The square variable has individual callbacks assigned to it that will be used for the drag-and-drop functionality. In addition, the squares are organized into rows in this loop for easy access.

3   Within the dragStarted function, add the following line of code to store the HTML from the container of the dragged checker piece:

```
function dragStarted( event ){
    dragging = event.target;
    event.dataTransfer.setData( 'text/html',
dragging.parentNode.innerHTML );
}
```

Data stored in the dataTransfer object's setData function is defined by the two arguments passed to the setData function: the first argument specifies the data type ('text/html' in the example above); the second argument specifies the actual data (in the example above, the HTML code that represents a checker piece). Data saved in this fashion is always stored as a String value.

At the time of this writing, the dataTransfer object is not supported by all browsers that have drag and drop support. Despite this fact, the dataTransfer object could play a critical part in future interactions between the browser and outside applications.

4   Within the dragDrop function, add the following condition to ensure the square where a checker piece will be dropped is empty:

```
function dragDrop(event){
    if(this.innerHTML == ' '){

    }
}
```

In the example above, the word this refers to where the function is running, and it's called the scope of a function. The scope of a function could refer to a different object, depending on how the function is used. Since the dragDrop function is attached to individual squares through their dragdrop event callback, this refers to the square itself. If the same function were called elsewhere, the scope of the function might be the root of the document, where the function was originally defined.

5   Enter the following line of code to clear the contents of the square that currently contains the dragged checker piece:

```
function dragDrop(event){
    if(this.innerHTML == ' '){
        dragging.parentNode.innerHTML = ' ';
    }
}
```

6   Enter the following line of code to copy the checker piece being dragged from the dataTransfer object's getData function to the target square's innerHTML property:

```
function dragDrop(event){
    if(this.innerHTML == ' '){
        dragging.parentNode.innerHTML = ' ';
        this.innerHTML = event.dataTransfer.getData( 'text/html' );
    }
}
```

7   The default behavior for a dragdrop event on some browsers is to open the dragged image in the current window or tab. Add the following line of code to prevent the default behavior of the dragdrop event.

```
function dragDrop(event){
    if(this.innerHTML == ' '){
        dragging.parentNode.innerHTML = ' ';
        this.innerHTML = event.dataTransfer.getData( 'text/html' );
    }
    return preventDefault( event );
}
```

8   To include a visual indicator of illegal moves, the dragover event must use an alternative callback. The current setting prevents the default behavior from taking place. Create a new function called dragOver, which determines whether another piece is already on a given square.

```
function dragOver( event ){

}
```

9   Within the function you created in the previous step, add the following condition to check whether a target square (the square on which a piece might be dragged to) is empty:

```
function dragOver( event ){
    if( this.innerHTML == ' ' )
}
```

10   Remember that the default behavior of a `dragover` event is to visually indicate that a container is not a drop zone. If the square is empty, prevent the default behavior of the `dragover` event by adding the following code:

```
function dragOver( event ){
    if( this.innerHTML == ' ' )
        return preventDefault(event);
}
```

11   If the condition in the previous step returns a value of `false`, it means the target square already has a checker piece on it. Add the following line of code to use the default behavior of the `dragover` event to indicate that this square is an invalid move:

```
function dragOver( event ){
    if( this.innerHTML == ' ' )
        return preventDefault(event);
    return true;
}
```

12   Finally, return to the `setup` function and change the callback function used for the `dragover` event to the newly created `dragOver` function:

```
function setup(){
    ...
    for(var i = 0, square; square = squares[i]; i++){
        square.ondragenter = preventDefault;
        square.ondragover = dragOver;
        square.ondrop = dragDrop;
```

13 Save and test your work in the browser. You should be able to move the pieces freely onto any empty square. Creating an application that follows the rules of the game is beyond the scope of this lesson, but you have just created the foundation for a fully interactive drag-and-drop game.

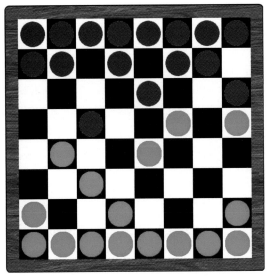

You can move pieces on the checkerboard to any empty square.

Keyboard accessibility

Applications such as the one you created in this lesson let users visually move elements to perform certain tasks; people with disabilities might not be able to fully utilize the capabilities of such applications. For this reason, the W3C organization has created a road map, known as WAI-ARIA, designed to encompass the key requirements for full accessibility on the Web. Opera developers have outlined the steps for accessibility implementation with JavaScript and HTML5 drag-and-drop applications at *dev.opera.com/articles/view/accessible-drag-and-drop*.

 You can find the WAI-ARIA outline at www.w3.org/WAI/intro/aria.

Self study

Create turns for each player using JavaScript in checkers_work.html. Prevent pieces from being dragged when it is not their turn. You can find a complete solution in the checkers_game.html file.

Review

Questions

1 Why is it necessary to prevent the default behavior and return false for many of the drag-and-drop callback functions?

2 What kind of data can be transferred during a drag-and-drop operation? When would this data be used?

3 How many images can be used with the `setDragImage` function as visual indicators?

Answers

1 The default behavior on many browsers is to prevent drag-and-drop and display a visual indicator to the user that not all containers are drop targets. Preventing the default behavior shows a separate visual indicator and enables drag-and-drop functionality on certain browsers.

2 You can transfer any type of data during a drag-and-drop operation as a String value. The `setData` function allows data to be stored under a specific type, and a single value is associated with that type. You can use data stored in this manner at later stages of the drag-and-drop operation, such as the `drop` or `dragover` events.

3 The `setDragImage` function allows only a single element to be used as a visual indicator. You can use the canvas element to show text, vector graphics, and multiple images together as a visual indicator.

HTML5 Elements and Attributes

These tables provide a reference to some of the most commonly used HTML5 elements, the category of content they belong to as well as their attributes. Although there are new elements in HTML5, some elements from HTML 4.0.1 (such as b and i) have been revised.

This table is not a complete list, for complete references please visit *http://www.w3.org/TR/html5/index.html*.

For an overview of HTML5 syntax, be sure to read Lesson 2 "Using HTML5 markup".

In the Attributes column, "globals" refers to common attributes that may be specified on all HTML elements. These attributes are accesskey, class, contenteditable, contextmenu, dir, draggable, dropzone, hidden, id, lang, spellcheck, style, tabindex, title, *and are described in further detail below.*

Table 1 List of current HTML5 elements

ELEMENT	DESCRIPTION	ATTRIBUTES
a	Hyperlink	globals; href; target; rel; media; hreflang; type
abbr	Abbreviation	globals
address	Contact information for a page or section	globals
area	Hyperlink or dead area on an image map	globals; alt; coords; shape; href; target; rel; media; hreflang; type
article	Self-contained syndicatable or reusable composition	globals
aside	Sidebar for tangentially related content	globals
audio	Audio player	globals; src; preload; autoplay; mediagroup; loop; controls
b	Represents a span of text to which attention is being drawn for utilitarian purposes without conveying any extra importance and with no implication of an alternate voice or mood.	globals

ELEMENT	DESCRIPTION	ATTRIBUTES
base	Base URL and default target browsing context for hyperlinks and forms	globals; href; target
block quote	A section quoted from another source	globals; cite
body	Document body	globals; onafterprint; onbeforeprint; onbeforeunload; onblur; onerror; onfocus; onhashchange; onload; onmessage; onoffline; ononline; onpagehide; onpageshow; onpopstate; onredo; onresize; onscroll; onstorage; onundo; onunload
br	Line break, e.g. in poem or postal address	globals
button	Button control	globals; autofocus; disabled; form; formaction; formenctype; formmethod; formnovalidate; formtarget; name; type; value
canvas	Scriptable bitmap canvas	globals; width; height
caption	Table caption	globals
cite	Title of a work	globals
code	Computer code	globals
col	Table column	globals; span
colgroup	Group of columns in a table	globals; span
command	Menu command	globals; type; label; icon; disabled; checked; radiogroup
datalist	Container for options for combo box control	globals
dd	Content for corresponding dt element(s)	globals
del	A removal from the document	globals; cite; datetime
div	Generic flow container	globals
dl	Association list consisting of zero or more name-value groups	globals
dt	Legend for corresponding dd element(s)	globals

ELEMENT	DESCRIPTION	ATTRIBUTES
em	Stress emphasis	globals
embed	Plugin	globals; src; type; width; height; any*
fieldset	Group of form controls	globals; disabled; form; name
figcaption	Caption for figure	globals
figure	Figure with optional caption	globals
footer	Footer for a page or section	globals
form	User-submittable form	globals; accept-charset; action; autocomplete; enctype; method; name; novalidate; target
h1, h2, h3, h4, h5, h6	Section heading	globals
head	Container for document metadata	globals
header	Introductory or navigational aids for a page or section	globals
hgroup	heading group	globals
hr	Thematic break	globals
html	Root element	globals; manifest
i	Alternate voice	globals
iframe	Nested browsing context	globals; src; srcdoc; name; sandbox; seamless; width; height
img	Image	globals; alt; src; usemap; ismap; width; height
input	Form control	globals; accept; alt; autocomplete; autofocus; checked; dirname; disabled; form; formaction; formenctype; formmethod; formnovalidate; formtarget; height; list; max; maxlength; min; multiple; name; pattern; placeholder; readonly; required; size; src; step; type; value; width
ins	An addition to the document	globals; cite; datetime

ELEMENT	DESCRIPTION	ATTRIBUTES
label	Caption for a form control	globals; form; for
legend	Caption for fieldset	globals
li	List item	globals; value*
link	Link metadata	globals; href; rel; media; hreflang; type; sizes
map	Image map	globals; name
mark	Highlight	globals
menu	Menu of commands	globals; type; label
meta	Text metadata	globals; name; http-equiv; content; charset
meter	Gauge	globals; value; min; max; low; high; optimum; form
nav	Section with navigational links	globals
noscript	Fallback content for script	globals
object	Image, nested browsing context, or plugin	globals; data; type; name; usemap; form; width; height
ol	Ordered list	globals; reversed; start
optgroup	Group of options in a list box	globals; disabled; label
option	Option in a list box or combo box control	globals; disabled; label; selected; value
output	Calculated output value	globals; for; form; name
p	Paragraph	globals
param	Parameter for object	globals; name; value
pre	Block of preformatted text	globals
progress	Progress bar	globals; value; max; form
q	Quotation	globals; cite
script	Embedded script	globals; src; async; defer; type; charset
section	Generic document or application section	globals
select	List box control	globals; autofocus; disabled; form; multiple; name; required; size

ELEMENT	DESCRIPTION	ATTRIBUTES
small	Side comment	globals
source	Media source for video or audio	globals; src; type; media
span	Generic phrasing container	globals
strong	Importance	globals
style	Embedded styling information	globals; media; type; scoped
sub	Subscript	globals
summary	Caption for details	globals
sup	Superscript	globals
table	Table	globals; border
tbody	Group of rows in a table	globals
td	Table cell	globals; colspan; rowspan; headers
textarea	Multiline text field	globals; autofocus; cols; disabled; form; maxlength; name; placeholder; readonly; required; rows; wrap
tfoot	Group of footer rows in a table	globals
th	Table header cell	globals; colspan; rowspan; headers; scope
thead	Group of heading rows in a table	globals
time	Date and/or time	globals; datetime; pubdate
title	Document title	globals
tr	Table row	globals
track	Timed text track	globals; default; kind; label; src; srclang
u	Keywords	globals
ul	List	globals
var	Variable	globals
video	Video player	globals; src; poster; preload; autoplay; mediagroup; loop; controls; width; height
wbr	Line breaking opportunity	globals

Table 2 List of element content categories

For an overview of content categories be sure to read Lesson 6 "Using HTML5 markup".

CATEGORY	ELEMENTS
Metadata content	base; command; link; meta; noscript; script; style; title
Flow content	a; abbr; address; article; aside; audio; b; bdi; bdo; blockquote; br; button; canvas; cite; code; command; datalist; del; details; dfn; div; dl; em; embed; fieldset; figure; footer; form; h1; h2; h3; h4; h5; h6; header; hgroup; hr; i; iframe; img; input; ins; kbd; keygen; label; map; mark; math; menu; meter; nav; noscript; object; ol; output; p; pre; progress; q; ruby; s; samp; script; section; select; small; span; strong; sub; sup; svg; table; textarea; time; u; ul; var; video; wbr; Text
Sectioning content	article; aside; nav; section
Heading content	h1; h2; h3; h4; h5; h6; hgroup
Phrasing content	abbr; audio; b; bdi; bdo; br; button; canvas; cite; code; command; datalist; dfn; em; embed; i; iframe; img; input; kbd; keygen; label; mark; math; meter; noscript; object; output; progress; q; ruby; s; samp; script; select; small; span; strong; sub; sup; svg; textarea; time; u; var; video; wbr; Text
Embedded content	audio canvas embed iframe img math object svg video
Interactive content	a; button; details; embed; iframe; keygen; label; select; textarea;
Sectioning roots	blockquote; body; details; fieldset; figure; td
Form-associated elements	button; fieldset; input; keygen; label; meter; object; output; progress; select; textarea
Listed elements	button; fieldset; input; keygen; object; output; select; textarea
Labelable elements	button; input; keygen; meter; output; progress; select; textarea
Submittable elements	button; input; keygen; object; select; textarea
Resettable elements	input; keygen; output; select; textarea
formatBlock candidates	section; nav; article; aside; h1; h2; h3; h4; h5; h6; hgroup; header; footer; address; p; pre; blockquote; div

Table 3 List of attributes

ATTRIBUTE	ELEMENT(S)	DESCRIPTION	VALUE
accept	input	Hint for expected file type in file upload controls	Set of comma-separated tokens* consisting of valid MIME types with no parameters or audio/*, video/*, or image/*
accept-charset	form	Character encodings to use for form submission	Ordered set of unique space-separated tokens, ASCII case-insensitive, consisting of preferred MIME names of ASCII-compatible character encodings*
accesskey	HTML elements	Keyboard shortcut to activate or focus element	Ordered set of unique space-separated tokens, case-sensitive, consisting of one Unicode code point in length
action	form	URL to use for form submission	Valid URL potentially surrounded by spaces
alt	area; img; input	Replacement text for use when images are not available	Text*
async	script	Execute script asynchronously	Boolean attribute
autocomplete	form; input	Prevent the user agent from providing autocompletions for the form control(s)	"on"; "off"
autofocus	button; input; keygen; select; textarea	Automatically focus the form control when the page is loaded	Boolean attribute
autoplay	audio; video	Hint that the media resource can be started automatically when the page is loaded	Boolean attribute
border	border	Explicit indication that the table element is not being used for layout purposes	The empty string, or "1"

ATTRIBUTE	ELEMENT(S)	DESCRIPTION	VALUE
challenge	keygen	String to package with the generated and signed public key	Text
charset	meta	Character encoding declaration	Preferred MIME name of an encoding*
charset	script	Character encoding of the external script resource	Preferred MIME name of an encoding*
checked	command; input	Whether the command or control is checked	Boolean attribute
cite	blockquote; del; ins; q	Link to the source of the quotation or more information about the edit	Valid URL potentially surrounded by spaces
class	HTML elements	Classes to which the element belongs	Set of space-separated tokens
cols	textarea	Maximum number of characters per line	Valid non-negative integer greater than zero
colspan	td; th	Number of columns that the cell is to span	Valid non-negative integer greater than zero
content	meta	Value of the element	Text*
contenteditable	HTML elements	Whether the element is editable	"true"; "false"
contextmenu	HTML elements	The element's context menu	ID*
controls	audio; video	Show user agent controls	Boolean attribute
coords	area	Coordinates for the shape to be created in an image map	Valid list of integers*
data	object	Address of the resource	Valid non-empty URL potentially surrounded by spaces
datetime	del; ins	Date and (optionally) time of the change	Valid date string with optional time
datetime	time	Value of the element	Valid date or time string*
default	track	Enable the track if no other text track is more suitable.	Boolean attribute
defer	script	Defer script execution	Boolean attribute
dir	HTML elements	The text directionality of the element	"ltr"; "rtl"

ATTRIBUTE	ELEMENT(S)	DESCRIPTION	VALUE
dirname	input; textarea	Name of form field to use for sending the element's directionality in form submission	Text*
disabled	button; command; fieldset; input; keygen; optgroup; option; select; textarea	Whether the form control is disabled	Boolean attribute
draggable	HTML elements	Whether the element is draggable	"true"; "false"
dropzone	HTML elements	Accepted item types for drag-and-drop	Unordered set of unique space-separated tokens, ASCII case-insensitive, consisting of accepted types and drag feedback*
enctype	form	Form data set encoding type to use for form submission	"application/x-www-form-urlencoded"; "multipart/form-data"; "text/plain"
for	label	Associate the label with form control	ID*
for	output	Specifies controls from which the output was calculated	Unordered set of unique space-separated tokens, case-sensitive, consisting of IDs*
form	button; fieldset; input; keygen; label; meter; object; output; progress; select; textarea	Associates the control with a form element	ID*
formaction	button; input	URL to use for form submission	Valid URL potentially surrounded by spaces

ATTRIBUTE	ELEMENT(S)	DESCRIPTION	VALUE
`formenctype`	`button;` `input`	Form data set encoding type to use for form submission	`"application/x-www-form-urlencoded";` `"multipart/form-data";"text/plain"`
`formmethod`	`button;` `input`	HTTP method to use for form submission	`"GET";"POST"`
`formnovali date`	`button;` `input`	Bypass form control validation for form submission	Boolean attribute
`formtarget`	`button;` `input`	Browsing context for form submission	Valid browsing context name or keyword
`headers`	`td; th`	The header cells for this cell	Unordered set of unique space-separated tokens, case-sensitive, consisting of IDs*
`height`	`canvas;` `embed;` `iframe;` `img; input;` `object;` `video`	Vertical dimension	Valid non-negative integer
`hidden`	HTML elements	Whether the element is relevant	Boolean attribute
`high`	`meter`	Low limit of high range	Valid floating point number*
`href`	`a; area`	Address of the hyperlink	Valid URL potentially surrounded by spaces
`href`	`link`	Address of the hyperlink	Valid non-empty URL potentially surrounded by spaces
`href`	`base`	Document base URL	Valid URL potentially surrounded by spaces
`hreflang`	`a; area; link`	Language of the linked resource	Valid BCP 47 language tag
`http-equiv`	`meta`	Pragma directive	Text*
`icon`	`command`	Icon for the command	Valid non-empty URL potentially surrounded by spaces
`id`	HTML elements	The element's ID	Text*

ATTRIBUTE	ELEMENT(S)	DESCRIPTION	VALUE
ismap	img	Whether the image is a server-side image map	Boolean attribute
keytype	keygen	The type of cryptographic key to generate	Text*
kind	track	The type of text track	"subtitles"; "captions"; "descriptions"; "chapters"; "metadata"
label	command; menu; optgroup; option; track	User-visible label	Text
lang	HTML elements	Language of the element	Valid BCP 47 language tag or the empty string
list	input	List of autocomplete options	ID*
loop	audio; video	Whether to loop the media resource	Boolean attribute
low	meter	High limit of low range	Valid floating point number*
manifest	html	Application cache manifest	Valid non-empty URL potentially surrounded by spaces
max	input	Maximum value	varies*
max	meter; progress	Upper bound of range	Valid floating point number*
maxlength	input; textarea	Maximum length of value	Valid non-negative integer
media	a; area; link; source; style	Applicable media	Valid media query
mediagroup	audio; video	Groups media elements together with an implicit MediaController	Text
method	form	HTTP method to use for form submission	"GET"; "POST"
min	input	Minimum value	varies*

ATTRIBUTE	ELEMENT(S)	DESCRIPTION	VALUE
min	meter	Lower bound of range	Valid floating point number*
multiple	input; select	Whether to allow multiple values	Boolean attribute
name	button; fieldset; input; keygen; output; select; textarea	Name of form control to use for form submission and in the form.elements API	Text*
name	form	Name of form to use in the document.forms API	Text*
name	iframe; object	Name of nested browsing context	Valid browsing context name or keyword
name	map	Name of image map to reference from the usemap attribute	Text*
name	meta	Metadata name	Text*
name	param	Name of parameter	Text
novalidate	form	Bypass form control validation for form submission	Boolean attribute
open	details	Whether the details are visible	Boolean attribute
optimum	meter	Optimum value in gauge	Valid floating point number*
pattern	input	Pattern to be matched by the form control's value	Regular expression matching the JavaScript *Pattern* production
placeholder	input; textarea	User-visible label to be placed within the form control	Text*
poster	video	Poster frame to show prior to video playback	Valid non-empty URL potentially surrounded by spaces
preload	audio; video	Hints how much buffering the media resource will likely need	"none"; "metadata"; "auto"

ATTRIBUTE	ELEMENT(S)	DESCRIPTION	VALUE
pubdate	`time`	Whether the element's value represents a publication time for the nearest `article` or `body`	Boolean attribute
radiogroup	`command`	Name of group of commands to treat as a radio button group	Text
readonly	`input;` `textarea`	Whether to allow the value to be edited by the user	Boolean attribute
rel	`a; area; link`	Relationship between the document containing the hyperlink and the destination resource	Set of space-separated tokens*
required	`input;` `select;` `textarea`	Whether the control is required for form submission	Boolean attribute
reversed	`ol`	Number the list backwards	Boolean attribute
rows	`textarea`	Number of lines to show	Valid non-negative integer greater than zero
rowspan	`td; th`	Number of rows that the cell is to span	Valid non-negative integer
sandbox	`iframe`	Security rules for nested content	Unordered set of unique space-separated tokens, ASCII case-insensitive, consisting of `"allow-same-origin"`, `"allow-forms"`, and `"allow-scripts"`
spellcheck	HTML elements	Whether the element is to have its spelling and grammar checked	`"true"; "false"`
scope	`th`	Specifies which cells the header cell applies to	`"row"; "col"; "rowgroup"; "colgroup"`
scoped	`style`	Whether the styles apply to the entire document or just the parent subtree	Boolean attribute
seamless	`iframe`	Whether to apply the document's styles to the nested content	Boolean attribute

ATTRIBUTE	ELEMENT(S)	DESCRIPTION	VALUE
selected	option	Whether the option is selected by default	Boolean attribute
shape	area	The kind of shape to be created in an image map	"circle"; "default"; "poly"; "rect"
size	input; select	Size of the control	Valid non-negative integer greater than zero
sizes	link	Sizes of the icons (for rel="icon")	Unordered set of unique space-separated tokens, ASCII case-insensitive, consisting of sizes*
span	col; colgroup	Number of columns spanned by the element	Valid non-negative integer greater than zero
src	audio; embed; iframe; img; input; script; source; track; video	Address of the resource	Valid non-empty URL potentially surrounded by spaces
srcdoc	iframe	A document to render in the iframe	The source of an iframe srcdoc document*
srclang	track	Language of the text track	Valid BCP 47 language tag
start	ol	Ordinal value of the first item	Valid integer
step	input	Granularity to be matched by the form control's value	Valid floating point number greater than zero, or "any"
style	HTML elements	Presentational and formatting instructions	CSS declarations*
tabindex	HTML elements	Whether the element is focusable, and the relative order of the element for the purposes of sequential focus navigation	Valid integer
target	a; area	Browsing context for hyperlink navigation	Valid browsing context name or keyword
target	base	Default browsing context for hyperlink navigation and form submission	Valid browsing context name or keyword
target	form	Browsing context for form submission	Valid browsing context name or keyword

ATTRIBUTE	ELEMENT(S)	DESCRIPTION	VALUE
title	HTML elements	Advisory information for the element	Text
title	abbr; dfn	Full term or expansion of abbreviation	Text
title	command	Hint describing the command	Text
title	link	Title of the link	Text
title	link; style	Alternative style sheet set name	Text
type	a; area; link	Hint for the type of the referenced resource	Valid MIME type
type	button	Type of button	"submit"; "reset"; "button"
type	button; input	Type of form control	input type keyword
type	command	Type of command	"command"; "checkbox"; "radio"
type	embed; object; script; source; style	Type of embedded resource	Valid MIME type
type	menu	Type of menu	"context"; "toolbar"
usemap	img; object	Name of image map to use	Valid hash-name reference*
value	button; option	Value to be used for form submission	Text
value	input	Value of the form control	varies*
value	li	Ordinal value of the list item	Valid integer
value	meter; progress	Current value of the element	Valid floating point number
value	param	Value of parameter	Text
width	canvas; embed; iframe; img; input; object; video	Horizontal dimension	Valid non-negative integer

ATTRIBUTE	ELEMENT(S)	DESCRIPTION	VALUE
wrap	textarea	How the value of the form control is to be wrapped for form submission	"soft"; "hard"

Table 4 List of event handler content attributes

ATTRIBUTE	ELEMENT(S)	DESCRIPTION	VALUE
onabort	HTML elements	abort event handler	Event handler content attribute
onafterprint	body	afterprint event handler for Window object	Event handler content attribute
onbeforeprint	body	beforeprint event handler for Window object	Event handler content attribute
onbeforeunload	body	beforeunload event handler for Window object	Event handler content attribute
onblur	body	blur event handler for Window object	Event handler content attribute
onblur	HTML elements	blur event handler	Event handler content attribute
oncanplay	HTML elements	canplay event handler	Event handler content attribute
oncanplaythrough	HTML elements	canplaythrough event handler	Event handler content attribute
onchange	HTML elements	change event handler	Event handler content attribute
onclick	HTML elements	click event handler	Event handler content attribute
oncontextmenu	HTML elements	contextmenu event handler	Event handler content attribute
oncuechange	HTML elements	cuechange event handler	Event handler content attribute
ondblclick	HTML elements	dblclick event handler	Event handler content attribute
ondrag	HTML elements	drag event handler	Event handler content attribute

ATTRIBUTE	ELEMENT(S)	DESCRIPTION	VALUE
ondragend	HTML elements	dragend event handler	Event handler content attribute
ondragenter	HTML elements	dragenter event handler	Event handler content attribute
ondragleave	HTML elements	dragleave event handler	Event handler content attribute
ondragover	HTML elements	dragover event handler	Event handler content attribute
ondragstart	HTML elements	dragstart event handler	Event handler content attribute
ondrop	HTML elements	drop event handler	Event handler content attribute
ondurationchange	HTML elements	durationchange event handler	Event handler content attribute
onemptied	HTML elements	emptied event handler	Event handler content attribute
onended	HTML elements	ended event handler	Event handler content attribute
onerror	body	error event handler for Window object, and handler for script error notifications	Event handler content attribute
onerror	HTML elements	error event handler	Event handler content attribute
onfocus	body	focus event handler for Window object	Event handler content attribute
onfocus	HTML elements	focus event handler	Event handler content attribute
onhashchange	body	hashchange event handler for Window object	Event handler content attribute
oninput	HTML elements	input event handler	Event handler content attribute
oninvalid	HTML elements	invalid event handler	Event handler content attribute
onkeydown	HTML elements	keydown event handler	Event handler content attribute

ATTRIBUTE	ELEMENT(S)	DESCRIPTION	VALUE
onkeypress	HTML elements	keypress event handler	Event handler content attribute
onkeyup	HTML elements	keyup event handler	Event handler content attribute
onload	body	load event handler for Window object	Event handler content attribute
onload	HTML elements	load event handler	Event handler content attribute
onloadeddata	HTML elements	loadeddata event handler	Event handler content attribute
onloadedmetadata	HTML elements	loadedmetadata event handler	Event handler content attribute
onloadstart	HTML elements	loadstart event handler	Event handler content attribute
onmessage	body	message event handler for Window object	Event handler content attribute
onmousedown	HTML elements	mousedown event handler	Event handler content attribute
onmousemove	HTML elements	mousemove event handler	Event handler content attribute
onmouseout	HTML elements	mouseout event handler	Event handler content attribute
onmouseover	HTML elements	mouseover event handler	Event handler content attribute
onmouseup	HTML elements	mouseup event handler	Event handler content attribute
onmousewheel	HTML elements	mousewheel event handler	Event handler content attribute
onoffline	body	offline event handler for Window object	Event handler content attribute
ononline	body	online event handler for Window object	Event handler content attribute
onpagehide	body	pagehide event handler for Window object	Event handler content attribute
onpageshow	body	pageshow event handler for Window object	Event handler content attribute

ATTRIBUTE	ELEMENT(S)	DESCRIPTION	VALUE
onpause	HTML elements	pause event handler	Event handler content attribute
onplay	HTML elements	play event handler	Event handler content attribute
onplaying	HTML elements	playing event handler	Event handler content attribute
onpopstate	body	popstate event handler for Window object	Event handler content attribute
onprogress	HTML elements	progress event handler	Event handler content attribute
onratechange	HTML elements	ratechange event handler	Event handler content attribute
onreadystatechange	HTML elements	readystatechange event handler	Event handler content attribute
onredo	body	redo event handler for Window object	Event handler content attribute
onreset	HTML elements	reset event handler	Event handler content attribute
onresize	body	resize event handler for Window object	Event handler content attribute
onscroll	body	scroll event handler for Window object	Event handler content attribute
onscroll	HTML elements	scroll event handler	Event handler content attribute
onseeked	HTML elements	seeked event handler	Event handler content attribute
onseeking	HTML elements	seeking event handler	Event handler content attribute
onselect	HTML elements	select event handler	Event handler content attribute
onshow	HTML elements	show event handler	Event handler content attribute
onstalled	HTML elements	stalled event handler	Event handler content attribute
onstorage	body	storage event handler for Window object	Event handler content attribute

ATTRIBUTE	ELEMENT(S)	DESCRIPTION	VALUE
`onsubmit`	HTML elements	`submit` event handler	Event handler content attribute
`onsuspend`	HTML elements	`suspend` event handler	Event handler content attribute
`ontimeupdate`	HTML elements	`timeupdate` event handler	Event handler content attribute
`onundo`	`body`	`undo` event handler for `Window` object	Event handler content attribute
`onunload`	`body`	`unload` event handler for `Window` object	Event handler content attribute
`onvolumechange`	HTML elements	`volumechange` event handler	Event handler content attribute
`onwaiting`	HTML elements	`waiting` event handler	Event handler content attribute

Table 5 List of events

EVENT	INTERFACE	DESCRIPTION
`DOMContentLoaded`	`Event`	Fired at the `Document` once it and its scripts have loaded, without waiting for other subresources
`abort`	`Event`	Fired at the `Window` when the download was aborted by the user
`afterprint`	`Event`	Fired at the `Window` after printing
`beforeprint`	`Event`	Fired at the `Window` before printing
`beforeunload`	`BeforeUnloadEvent`	Fired at the `Window` when the page is about to be unloaded, in case the page would like to show a warning prompt
`blur`	`Event`	Fired at nodes losing focus
`change`	`Event`	Fired at controls when the user commits a value change
`click`	`Event`	Fired at an element before its activation behavior is run

EVENT	INTERFACE	DESCRIPTION
contextmenu	Event	Fired at elements when the user requests their context menu
error	Event	Fired at elements when network and script errors occur
focus	Event	Fired at nodes gaining focus
hashchange	HashChangeEvent	Fired at the Window when the fragment identifier part of the document's current address changes
input	Event	Fired at controls when the user changes the value
invalid	Event	Fired at controls during form validation if they do not satisfy their constraints
load	Event	Fired at the Window when the document has finished loading; fired at an element containing a resource (e.g. img, embed) when its resource has finished loading
message	MessageEvent	Fired at an object when the object receives a message
offline	Event	Fired at the Window when the network connections fails
online	Event	Fired at the Window when the network connections returns
pagehide	PageTransitionEvent	Fired at the Window when the page's entry in the session history stops being the current entry
pageshow	PageTransitionEvent	Fired at the Window when the page's entry in the session history becomes the current entry
popstate	PopStateEvent	Fired at the Window when the user navigates the session history

EVENT	INTERFACE	DESCRIPTION
readystatechange	Event	Fired at the Document when it finishes parsing and again when all its subresources have finished loading
reset	Event	Fired at a form element when it is reset
show	Event	Fired at a menu element when it is shown as a context menu
submit	Event	Fired at a form element when it is submitted
unload	Event	Fired at the Window object when the page is going away

Table 6 Media element events

EVENT NAME	INTERFACE	DISPATCHED WHEN...	PRECONDITIONS
loadstart	Event	The user agent begins looking for media data, as part of the resource selection algorithm.	networkState equals NETWORK_LOADING
progress	Event	The user agent is fetching media data.	networkState equals NETWORK_LOADING
suspend	Event	The user agent is intentionally not currently fetching media data, but does not have the entire media resource downloaded.	networkState equals NETWORK_IDLE
abort	Event	The user agent stops fetching the media data before it is completely downloaded, but not due to an error.	error is an object with the code MEDIA_ERR_ABORTED. networkState equals either NETWORK_EMPTY or NETWORK_IDLE, depending on when the download was aborted.

EVENT NAME	INTERFACE	DISPATCHED WHEN...	PRECONDITIONS
error	Event	An error occurs while fetching the media data.	`error` is an object with the code `MEDIA_ERR_NETWORK` or higher. `networkState` equals either `NETWORK_EMPTY` or `NETWORK_IDLE`, depending on when the download was aborted.
emptied	Event	A media element whose `networkState` was previously not in the `NETWORK_EMPTY` state has just switched to that state (either because of a fatal error during load that's about to be reported, or because the `load()` method was invoked while the resource selection algorithm was already running).	`networkState` is `NETWORK_EMPTY`; all the IDL attributes are in their initial states.
stalled	Event	The user agent is trying to fetch media data, but data is unexpectedly not forthcoming.	`networkState` is `NETWORK_LOADING`.
loadedmetadata	Event	The user agent has just determined the duration and dimensions of the media resource and the text tracks are ready.	`readyState` is newly equal to `HAVE_METADATA` or greater for the first time.
loadeddata	Event	The user agent can render the media data at the current playback position for the first time.	`readyState` newly increased to `HAVE_CURRENT_DATA` or greater for the first time.

EVENT NAME	INTERFACE	DISPATCHED WHEN...	PRECONDITIONS
canplay	Event	The user agent can resume playback of the media data, but estimates that if playback were to be started now, the media resource could not be rendered at the current playback rate up to its end without having to stop for further buffering of content.	`readyState` newly increased to `HAVE_FUTURE_DATA` or greater.
canplaythrough	Event	The user agent estimates that if playback were to be started now, the media resource could be rendered at the current playback rate all the way to its end without having to stop for further buffering.	`readyState` is newly equal to `HAVE_ENOUGH_DATA`.
playing	Event	Playback is ready to start after having been paused or delayed due to lack of media data.	`readyState` is newly equal to or greater than `HAVE_FU-TURE_DATA` and `paused` is false, or `paused` is newly false and `readyState` is equal to or greater than `HAVE_FU-TURE_DATA`. Even if this event fires, the element might still not be potentially playing, e.g. if the element is blocked on its media controller (e.g. because the current media controller is paused, or another slaved media element is stalled somehow, or because the media resource has no data corresponding to the media controller position), or the element is paused for user interaction.

EVENT NAME	INTERFACE	DISPATCHED WHEN...	PRECONDITIONS
waiting	Event	Playback has stopped because the next frame is not available, but the user agent expects that frame to become available in due course.	`readyState` is equal to or less than `HAVE_CURRENT_DATA`, and `paused` is false. Either `seeking` is true, or the current playback position is not contained in any of the ranges in `buffered`. It is possible for playback to stop for other reasons without `paused` being false, but those reasons do not fire this event (and when those situations resolve, a separate `playing` event is not fired either): e.g. the element is newly blocked on its media controller, or playback ended, or playback stopped due to errors, or the element has paused for user interaction.
seeking	Event	The `seeking` IDL attribute changed to true and the seek operation is taking long enough that the user agent has time to fire the event.	
seeked	Event	The `seeking` IDL attribute changed to false.	
ended	Event	Playback has stopped because the end of the media resource was reached.	`currentTime` equals the end of the media resource; `ended` is true.
durationchange	Event	The `duration` attribute has just been updated.	
timeupdate	Event	The current playback position changed as part of normal playback or in an especially interesting way, for example discontinuously.	

EVENT NAME	INTERFACE	DISPATCHED WHEN...	PRECONDITIONS
play	Event	The element is no longer paused. Fired after the `play()` method has returned, or when the `autoplay` attribute has caused playback to begin.	`paused` is newly false.
pause	Event	The element has been paused. Fired after the `pause()` method has returned.	`paused` is newly true.
ratechange	Event	Either the `defaultPlaybackRate` or the `playbackRate` attribute has just been updated.	
volumechange	Event	Either the `volume` attribute or the `muted` attribute has changed. Fired after the relevant attribute's setter has returned.	

Index

A

a, 369
a:active, 122
abbr, 369
abort, 388, 390
absolute positioning, 128–131, 319–320
absolute-size, 56
accept attribute, 375
accept-charset attribute, 375
Accessible Rich Internet Applications
  Suite, 153
accesskey attribute, 375
action attribute, 170, 375
active page, creating style for, 125–127
active pseudoclass, 284
adaptive design, 304
adjacent selectors, 256
Adobe Dreamweaver, 3, 37
Adobe Flash, 194
Adobe Flash Player, 5, 15, 218
:after, 119
afterprint, 388
a:hover, 122
Ai-)Canvas, 253
a:link, 122
alt attribute, 375
angles, 277
Apple Safari, 19, 27, 178, 199, 219, 259,
  276, 309
application caching
  ApplicationCache object, 339–340
  cache manifest file, 336–338

description of, 328, 336
application programming interfaces
  definition of, 19
  geolocation, 18–20, 344
  web storage, 21
  Web Workers, 20
ApplicationCache object, 339–340
arc function, 232, 254
area, 369
article element, 155–159, 369
articleaside class style, 159
aside element, 155–159
async attribute, 375
a.transition, 282, 284
attributes. *see also specific attribute*
  adding, 177–187
  list of, 375–384
  name, 171
audio, adding, 223
audio attribute, 215
<audio> element, 14–15, 369
autocomplete attribute, 182, 375
autofocus attribute, 181, 375
autoplay attribute, 375
a:visited, 122

B

b, 162, 369
background color
  of HTML lists, 72

removing of, 112–115
background images
    CSS3, 263–268
    footer styled with, 105–108
    multiple, 263–268
    working with, 115–131
background-color, 72
background-image property, 274
background-position, 117–118
base, 370
beforeprint, 388
beforeunload, 388
best practices, 39
bezierCurveTo function, 235
block elements, 144
block quote, 370
block-level elements, 85
block-level formatting, 320
blur, 388
body, 370
<body> element, 35–36
Boolean property, 345
border attribute, 375
<border> property, 63
border-image, 257–263
border-radius, 24, 174, 257–263
borders, 63
box-align property, 318
boxes
    border-image, 257–263
    border-radius, 257–263
box-flex property, 316
box-orient property, 317
br, 370
braces, 333
break element, 220

browsers
    adding support for, 215–216
    CSS layout support by, 82
    Doctype use, 32
    fallbacks, 188–191, 216–219
    font support, 292
    geolocation lacking in, 350–355
    HTML code as rendered in, 31
    HTML5 support, 3, 144–146, 179
    multiple background images
      supported by, 268
    placeholder attribute supported
      by, 190
    text resize option in, 57
    updating of, 212
button, 370

C

cache
    ApplicationCache object, 339–340
    manifest file, 336–338
    updating, 338
caching, 328
callback function, 190
canplay, 392
canplaythrough, 392
Canvas element
    adding text, 237–239
    benefits of, 227
    <canvas>, 14, 16–17, 227
    circles, drawing, 230–233
    colors, 239–243
    curves, drawing, 234–237
    description of, 226, 370
    drawing loop, creating, 250–253

jQuery
  definition of, 204
  description of, 209
  hiding elements with, 204–207
  plug-in, 324

K

kerning, 67
keyframes, 286
`keytype` attribute, 379
keyword, 58
`kind` attribute, 379

L

`label` attribute, 372, 379
`<label>` element, 171–172, 175
`lang` attribute, 379
leading, 65
`legend`, 372
`<legend>` element, 171, 183
lesson files, 3–4
`letter-spacing`, 67
`li`, 372
linear gradient, 242
`linear-gradient`, 274
`line-height`, 65–66
lines, drawing, 230–233
`link`, 372
list(s)
  background color of, 72
  definition lists, 68, 71
  indentation of, 71

ordered lists, 68, 70, 73
  spacing of, 71, 73–74
  styling of, 71–75
  unordered lists, 68, 73
  working with, 68–71
`list` attribute, 182, 379
list-based navigation, 93–96
`load`, 389
`loadeddata`, 391
`loadedmetadata`, 221, 391
`loadstart`, 390
`localStorage`, 328–335
`locationError`, 346
`loop` attribute, 215, 379
`low` attribute, 379
Lucidchart, 253

M

Mac OS
  text editors, 3
  unlocking files, 4
`main`, 92
`maincontent` div, 128, 130
`mainnav` div, 94
`manifest` attribute, 379
manifest file, 336–338
`map`, 372
`<margin>` property, 62–65
`<margin-bottom>` property, 63
margins
  fixed-width layout affected by, 98–104
  review of, 105
  setting to zero, 78

ondrag attribute, 384

ondragend attribute, 385

ondragenter attribute, 385

ondragleave attribute, 385

ondragover attribute, 385

ondragstart attribute, 385

ondrop attribute, 385

ondurationchange attribute, 385

onemptied attribute, 385

onended attribute, 385

onerror attribute, 385

onfocus attribute, 385

onhashchange attribute, 385

oninput attribute, 385

oninvalid attribute, 385

onkeydown attribute, 385

onkeypress attribute, 386

onkeyup attribute, 386

online event, 389

onload attribute, 386

onloadeddata attribute, 386

onloadedmetadata attribute, 386

onloadstart attribute, 386

onmessage attribute, 386

onmousedown attribute, 386

onmouseout attribute, 200, 386

onmouseover attribute, 200–201, 386

onmouseup attribute, 386

onmousewheel attribute, 386

onoffline attribute, 386

ononline attribute, 386

onpagehide attribute, 386

onpageshow attribute, 386

onpause attribute, 387

onplay attribute, 387

onplaying attribute, 387

onpopstate attribute, 387

onprogress attribute, 387

onratechange attribute, 387

onreadystatechange attribute, 387

onredo attribute, 387

onreset attribute, 387

onresize attribute, 387

onscroll attribute, 387

onseeked attribute, 387

onseeking attribute, 387

onselect attribute, 387

onshow attribute, 387

onstalled attribute, 387

onstorage attribute, 387

onsubmit attribute, 388

onsuspend attribute, 388

ontimeupdate attribute, 388

onundo attribute, 388

onunload attribute, 388

onvolumechange attribute, 388

onwaiting attribute, 388

opacity, 241, 269–274

open attribute, 380

opening paragraph tags, 69–70

OpenType, 291–292

Opera, 25, 182

operating systems, 3

operators, JavaScript, 197

optgroup, 372

optimum attribute, 380

option, 372

order form, 182–187

ordered lists, 68, 70, 73

output, 372

P

p, 372

padding
 description of, 73–74
 fixed-width layout affected by, 98–104
 review of, 105

page layout
 building of, 112–115
 fixed-width, 83, 85–88
 flexible, 83–84
 options for, 83–84

page preview, 69, 139

pagehide, 389

pageshow, 389

paragraph, 65–66

paragraph tags
 closing, 69–70
 opening, 69–70

param, 372

paths, drawing, 227–236

pattern attribute, 380

pause, 394

percent, 57–61

phrasing content, 141, 374

pixels, 56–57, 117

placeholder attribute, 188, 190, 380

play, 394

playing, 392

.png file, 230

points, 56–57

polyfill, 189

popstate, 389

PositionOptions Object, 345

poster attribute, 213, 380

poster file, 224

pound symbol, 338

pre, 372

prefixes, 259

preload attribute, 215, 380

preventDefault function, 360

previewing of page, 69, 139

progress, 372, 390

pseudoclass, 122, 282, 284, 323

pubdate attribute, 381

Q

q, 372

R

radial gradients, 242, 277

radial-gradient, 274

radiogroup attribute, 381

ratechange, 394

readonly attribute, 381

ready function, 206

readystatechange, 390

rectangles, drawing, 227–230

regressive enhancement, 189

rel attribute, 381

relative positioning, 131

relative-size, 56

repeating gradients, 278

required attribute, 381

reset, 390

reset file, 78–80

reset style sheets, 80

resettable elements, 374

resizing text, 57, 60

transforms
    Canvas element, 246–250
    CSS3, 279–285
transition point, 275
transitions
    CSS3, 279–285
    description of, 23
translating, 246
transparency, 269–274
TrueType, 292
two-column fixed-width layout, 85–88, 139
`type` attribute, 383
type selector, 43
typeface, 52
Typekit web service, 296
typography, 52

U

`u`, 373
`ul`, 373
`unload`, 390
unordered lists, 68
URL, 180
`usemap` attribute, 383
user agent String, 300

V

validation of web pages, 33–34, 138
`value` attribute, 383
`var`, 373
vendor-specific prefixes, 259
video
    adding, 212–215

    embedded, 15
    fallbacks in, 216–219, 224
    JavaScript control of, 219–223
    playback of, 222
`video`, 373
`video` element
    description of, 14, 219
    media files embedded with, 15
video tutorials, 5–6
`volumechange`, 394

W

WAI-ARIA, 153, 367
`waiting`, 393
`wbr`, 373
web applications 1.0, 11
web browsers. *See* browsers
web fonts. *see also* font(s)
    alternative methods for adding, 296
    description of, 53, 55
    `@font-face`, 25, 288–290, 292
    working with, 288
web forms, 17
web interactivity, 194
web languages, 30
web layout
    history of, 80–83
    table-based, 81–82
Web Open Font Format, 292
web page
    validation of, 33–35
    World Wide Web Consortium
        validation of, 33–34, 138
Web SQL Database, 335–336

Web storage, 21
Web Workers, 20
Webkit, 259, 272, 279
webkit-animation-iteration-
  count, 287
webkit-transition-property, 282
WebM video codec, 219
WHATWG, 11, 144, 168
width attribute, 383
Windows OS, 3
World Wide Web Consortium
    description of, 27, 32, 256

IndexedDB, 336
  page validation and, 33–34, 138
wrap attribute, 384

X

XHTML
  history of, 11
  HTML and, 30, 32
  HTML4 versus, 11
  syntax, 32
  tags, 32

John Wiley & Sons, Inc.
End-User License Agreement

Important: Read carefully before opening software package. This is a legal agreement between you, the end user, and John Wiley & Sons, Inc. ("Wiley").

The enclosed Wiley software program and accompanying data (the "Software") is licensed by Wiley for use only on the terms set forth herein. Please read this license agreement. Registering the product indicates that you accept these terms. If you do not agree to these terms, return the full product (including documentation) with proof of purchase within 30 days for a full refund. In addition, if you are not satisfied with this product for any other reason, you may return the entire product (including documentation) with proof of purchase within 15 days for a full refund.

1. License: Wiley hereby grants you, and you accept, a non- exclusive and non-transferable license, to use the Software on the following terms and conditions only:

(a) The Software is for your personal use only.

(b) You may use the Software on a single terminal connected to a single computer (i.e., single CPU) and a laptop or other secondary machine for personal use.

(c) A backup copy or copies of the Software may be made solely for your personal use. Except for such back up copy or copies, you may not copy, modify, distribute, transmit or otherwise reproduce the Software or related documentation, in whole or in part, or systematically store such material in any form or media in a retrieval system; or store such material in electronic format in electronic reading rooms; or transmit such material, directly or indirectly, for use in any service such as document delivery or list serve, or for use by any information brokerage or for systematic distribution of material, whether for a fee or free of charge. You agree to protect the Software and documenation from unauthorized use, reproduction, or distribution.

(d) You agree not to remove or modify any copyright or proprietary notices, author attribution or disclaimer contained in the Software or documentation or on any screen display, and not to integrate material from therefrom with other material or otherwise create derivative works in any medium based on or including materials from the Software or documentation.

(e) You agree not to translate, decompile, disassemble or otherwise reverse engineer the Software.

2. Limited Warranty:

(a) Wiley warrants that this product is free of defects in materials and workmanship under normal use for a period of 60 days from the date of purchase as evidenced by a copy of your receipt. If during the 60-day period a defect occurs, you may return the product. Your sole and exclusive remedy in the event of a defect is expressly limited to the replacement of the defective product at no additional charge.

(b) The limited warranty set forth above is in lieu of any and all other warranties, both express and implied, including but not limited to the implied warranties of merchantability or fitness for a particular purpose. The liability of Wiley pursuant to this limited warranty will be limited to replacement of the defective copies of the Software. Some states do not allow the exclusion of implied warranties, so the preceding exclusion may not apply to you.

(c) Because software is inherently complex and may not be completely free of errors, you are advised to verify your work and to make backup copies. In no event will Wiley, nor anyone else involved in creating, producing or delivering the Software, documentation or the materials contained therein, be liable to you for any direct, indirect, incidental, special, consequential or punitive damages arising out of the use or inability to use the Software, documentation or materials contained therein even if advised of the possibility of such damages, or for any claim by any other party. In no case will Wiley's liability exceed the amount paid by you for the Software. Some states do not allow the exclusion or limitation of liability for incidental or consequential damages, so the above limitation or exclusion may not apply to you.

(d) Wiley reserves the right to make changes, additions, and improvements to the Software at any time without notice to any person or organization. No guarantee is made that future versions of the Software will be compatible with any other version.

3. Term: Your license to use the Software and documentation will automatically terminate if you fail to comply with the terms of this Agreement. If this license is terminated you agree to destroy all copies of the Software and documentation.

4. Ownership: You acknowledge that all rights (including without limitation, copyrights, patents and trade secrets) in the Software and documentation (including without limitation, the structure, sequence, organization, flow, logic, source code, object code and all means and forms of operation of the Software) are the sole and exclusive property of Wiley and/or its licensors, and are protected by the United Sates copyright laws, other applicable copyright laws, and international treaty provisions.

5. Restricted Rights: This Software and/or user documentation are provided with restricted and limited rights. Use, duplication, or disclosure by the Government is subject to restrictions as set forth in paragraph (b)(3)(B) of the Rights in Technical Data and Computer Software clause in DAR 7-104.9(a), FAR 52.2227-14 (June 1987) Alternate III(g)(3)(June 1987), FAR 52.227-19 (June 1987), or DFARS 52.227-701 (c) (1)(ii)(June 1988), or their successors, as applicable. Contractor/manufacturer is John Wiley & Sons, Inc., 111 River Street, Hoboken, NJ 07030.

6. Canadian Purchase: If you purchased this product in Canada, you agree to the following: the parties hereto confirm that it is their wish that this Agreement, as well as all other documents relating hereto, including Notices, have been and will be drawn up in the English language only.

7. Technical Support: Wiley will respond to all technical support inquiries within 48 hours.

8. General: This Agreement represents the entire agreement between us and supersedes any proposals or prior Agreements, oral or written, and any other communication between us relating to the subject matter of this Agreement. This Agreement will be construed and interpreted pursuant to the laws of the State of New York, without regard to such Stateís conflict of law rules. Any legal action, suit or proceeding arising out of or relating to this Agreement or the breach thereof will be instituted in a court of competent jurisdiction in New York County in the State of New York and each party hereby consents and submits to the personal jurisdiction of such court, waives any objection to venue in such court and consents to the service of process by registered or certified mail, return receipt requested, at the last known address of such party. Should you have any questions concerning this Agreement or if you desire to contact Wiley for any reason, please write to: John Wiley & Sons, Inc., Customer Sales and Service, 10475 Crosspoint Blvd, Indianapolis, IN 46256.

The on-line companion to your Digital Classroom book.

DigitalClassroomBooks.com

Visit DigitalClassroomBooks.com for...

 Updated lesson files

 Errata

 Contacting the authors

 Video Tutorial samples

 Book Samples

DIGITAL CLASSROOM

For information about the Digital Classroom series
visit www.DigitalClassroomBooks.com

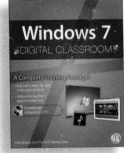

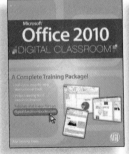
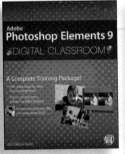